SLOW BOAT TO NASHVILLE

Sequel to *Stranger to Caution*

ISBN 978-1-7391967-1-4

Cover: **Capricorn under Sail**
©**2017** Painting by Peter Newby

moniquenewby.com
(Photos related to ***Slow Boat to Nashville*** can be viewed online, as well as samples of her music
m.newbybooks@yahoo.com

SLOW BOAT TO NASHVILLE

A MUSICAL ODYSSEY UNDER SAIL

Monique Newby

Before we set sail from Scarborough into the big blue, I asked Peter what he was looking for.

'Contentment, he replied.

'What does this look like?'

Peter shrugged his shoulders in response. So I gazed at the horizon for an answer.

CONTENTS

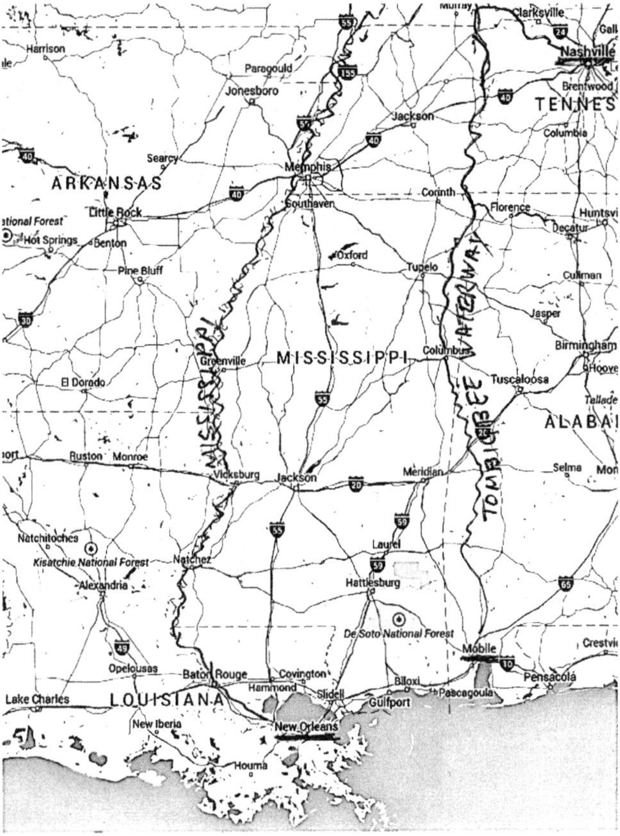

Mississippi and Tombigbee Waterway

I didn't choose the sea; the sea chose me. My initiation began when I was offered a job as a cordon bleu cook on a luxurious sailing vessel in Lanzarote. Little did I know I would spend more than twenty-four years living and sailing on boats.

My first book, *Stranger to Caution* (about Peter's intrepid exploits on his boat, *Ellis of Tamar*) and the sequel, *Slow Boat to Nashville,* recount a rollercoaster of adventures where danger and survival are never far apart.

The people we've met along the way, with their generosity, eccentricities, and humour, have made these voyages of a lifetime unique and unforgettable. I pay homage to them, but above all to my husband Peter, who has always believed in my talent as a songstress and my ambition to become a writer. His support has been invaluable.

We have unconditionally followed each other's dreams as far as they could be achieved. So, neither of us will ever need to say, 'IF ONLY…'

1. Breaststroke

Now wasn't the time to convalesce on the shores of the broken-hearted. I would be like a ship at sea, hove-to while waiting for the storm to abate.

Why did Peter have to leave? The question kept whirling through my mind like an unending tune on a scratchy old vinyl record. I wondered if sailing across an ocean to the Caribbean might lift the arm of the stylus out of the groove.

My legs were aching, trudging through the narrow streets of Los Cristianos with a backpack and a guitar that weighed more heavily with every step. Why make such awkward handles on cases? They must have been designed for roadies to carry them from limousines to concert halls.

Rounding a corner, I came across a deserted, shady terrace. By then, I was desperate for a sit-down and a drink. I found a table under a large blue parasol and collapsed into a chair. A waiter came to take my order. He was tall with a mahogany complexion, but what struck me most were his black shoes. They shone so brightly that had he been a Scotsman; I could have seen what he wore under his kilt.

El Camarero returned with my San Miguel - I watched him hold the glass at waist height, pouring the beer from just above his shoulders into a stream, forming a perfect frothy head. I said, *'Gracias'* appraisingly. He smiled and then walked away. I took the glass between my hands to soothe my blisters and sipped the yeasty brew, hoping the alcohol would dilute my angst.

Leaning back in my seat, I thought about the day I met Peter. I had arrived on the island of Tenerife aboard the large and luxurious schooner *Spirit of Labrador*, though not as a guest. I could only afford to hop between sun-soaked islands by working as a cook, purser, and linguist for German and English charter guests on unique two-week vacations. Toiling in the galley, I was forever amazed at how people on a boat could develop such large appetites. It wasn't as though we were becalmed in the horse latitudes where bygone sailors, unlucky enough to run out of food, were forced to eat their horses to survive. On my watch, the charterers on the *Good Ship Labrador* never starved.

Then there was the *mal de mer*. When the wind and sea got up, it was like sailing inside a cocktail shaker, and there was no need for ice with the cold Atlantic spray! But that wasn't all; dealing with Florence, the Irish skipper, was challenging, too. One morning, I found him slumped on the cabin floor like a trophy animal rug. The dark-haired man with a beard and deep blue eyes boasted he could drink for Ireland. He must have reached his target that night. I left him in his stupor and went to fetch some last-minute shopping before the arrival of our new charterers. I was still ashore when they arrived. The agency had given us the wrong timing. How did these people feel when they saw a man on the cabin floor and empty beer bottles lined up on the saloon table like props for the song 'Ten Green Bottles?' When I returned, laden with shopping, I had to shake Florence out of his drunken state under the charterers' steely stare. No one would know how close I came to jumping ship that day.

It was through Florence that I met Peter. Their paths crossed at La Paloma bar while having a beer. When Peter told Florence he had run out of drinking water on his boat and the harbour master had turned the quay tap off, Florence offered to fill up his jerrycans from *Spirit of Labrador's* tanks. I was cooking pizza in the galley when Peter walked into the wheelhouse saloon. I looked at his thick blond tousled hair hanging loosely over his striking blue eyes, then at his tight short-cut jeans and thought, *'What a shapely pair of legs on a man!'* I saw his eyes diving into my low-cut green dress; we glanced at each other, and something clicked. But time wasn't on our side. The charter season had ended, and *Spirit of Labrador* was scheduled to sail to Iceland with a film crew. So, we only shared a kiss on the cheek before I left the yacht to fly to Germany and try my luck in the music business.

I finished my beer, paid the waiter, and headed along the promenade. The place was bustling with tourists. Many were overweight and wearing skimpy clothes. Some looked grotesque. Terraces on the seafront were heaving with diners. The aroma of grilled seafood, lemon, and garlic made me hungry. The two bananas in my backpack were a poor substitute for the lavish food that caught my eye. I stopped beyond the touristy area and sat on a wall to eat a banana. I was glad of the cool breeze drying the pearling sweat on my face. As I watched the yachts bobbing over blue and turquoise wavelets in the bay, I pictured myself bound for the Caribbean on one of these floating chariots. They say every journey starts with a single step - mine would be a breaststroke across the Bay of Los Cristianos in search of a yacht that would whisk me over the Atlantic Ocean. Sadly, nobody was waiting for me on the other side of the pond, but that wouldn't stop me.

With renewed energy, I made for the outskirts of the resort, where I hoped to find somewhere to sleep for the night. A hotel room would have been the answer, but I needed to be frugal if I wanted this journey to happen.

As I reached some wasteland by a beach, I noticed a camp of ad hoc tents made of tarpaulins and branches. The smouldering embers of a campfire suggested people might be squatting there. At a glance, the area looked like the perfect setting for a spaghetti western movie. My breathing became shallow, and I could taste the fear in my mouth. Maybe I had been watching too many movies with shoot-outs, but this wasn't America; only the Guardia Civil Police carry guns in Spain. Then, when I saw a young man, tall and skinny, sauntering towards me, I wanted to flee, but my feet felt rooted to the ground.

'Hola, estas buscando a alguien?' 'Are you looking for someone?' the man asked, staring at me inquisitively. This kind of chat-up line was unsettling. To give him his due, he might have been surprised to see a newcomer on his patch.

'Me perdí,' 'I got lost,' I told the man before walking away swiftly. What if he followed me and hid behind some bushes, ready to pounce on me?

As I marched on, I noticed an old ruin tucked away amongst heavy undergrowth and thought this might be a spot to set camp for the night. With more than a twinge of apprehension, I trudged along the overgrown path to reach the derelict house. I pushed the door open, which creaked eerily. Inside, the ground was all rubble, hardly a place for a good night's sleep, but I was far too tired to start looking elsewhere. I shuffled a few stones aside with my feet to flatten the surface, laid my sleeping bag on the dry, uneven soil, and got inside, using my rucksack as a pillow. Seeing my guitar case, which I had placed on some stones beside me, felt strangely comforting. Yet, I wouldn't pick it up and sing: *I Was Born Under a Wanderin' Star.* I looked at the ceiling of the old ruin and saw millions of twinkling stars through the bare rafters. I thought of *The Little Prince* by *St Exupéry,* in the chapter where he stumbles across the planet of a businessman, who, pointing at the sky, says to him: 'Those small golden objects set lazy men to idle dreams.'

The businessman had counted five hundred and one million, six hundred and twenty-two thousand, seven hundred and thirty-one stars and felt he owned all these constellations. So, to induce sleep, I counted a few, settled down, and nodded off.

I woke up sensing an intense light shining straight into my face. My heart thudded. Was I about to be attacked and murdered amidst the loud, droning sound of the *cicadas* filling the air with their song? I readied myself to face the assailant, but nobody was there, just the moon glowing in its full glory. It took me a while to calm down.

My back was aching, but I adjusted my position, yawned a few times, and fell asleep despite the discomfort.

I woke up feeling tearful after a restless night. I thought of my father. He used to call me *le saule pleureur*- the weeping willow because I cry easily. Still, I felt overwhelmed by the 'little me' from a landlocked country about to embark on the most epic adventure of my life, hoping to sail across an ocean in a boat I had yet to find! Thumbing a lift while swimming might be harder than standing on Jungfrau Mountain, hailing a helicopter to fly me to the Matterhorn!

But now wasn't the time to give in to doubt. Delaying my plan of action could ruin my resolve. I was a young woman on my own, yet it had never worried me before because I always had a job to go to and a place to stay. And, like the character in *The Hitchhiker's Guide to the Galaxy*, I had no instructions on how to hitch a lift across an ocean. There was no solid tarmac at this aquatic crossroads upon which to stand and wait for someone to offer me a ride. The only way would be to breaststroke far across the bay and hope the mermaid in me might enchant the right skipper to whisk me to the Caribbean.

When I walked along the promenade in the morning, it was a shock and a surprise to see the broad-shouldered blonde with glasses *à la Nana Mouskouri* heading towards me. I didn't know anyone in Los Cristianos, or so I thought until then. I had met Arlette in Alicante a few months earlier with her stunning-looking Italian boyfriend, Alberto. I wondered at the time how Arlette had found such a stallion on a large yacht. But the woman had elbows like the spikes on Boudicca's chariot wheels that could part any crowd.

'What on earth are you doing here?' Arlette cried out as she saw me.

'Well, what a coincidence to meet here,' I said.

'Are you still with the Yorkshireman on that little red boat? What's his name?'

'You mean, Peter. Oh, no, he sailed back to England. I didn't go with him. I had the chance of a break in the music business in Germany.'

'You have such a beautiful voice,' she piped. Arlette and Alberto had heard me sing one night when they came to dinner on *Ellis of Tamar.*

'What happened in Germany?'

'The manager only wanted well-known singers like *Catherine Valente* on his books. Maybe my boobs weren't big enough?'

'Shame,' Arlette intoned. 'But where is Peter now?'

'He sailed back to England, but this is a long story. He was caught in a storm and dismasted.'

'Oh My God! Did he survive?'

'He managed to sail three hundred miles to Portugal under makeshift rigging.'

'Have you two split up?'

'Yes, and No! He is now back in England building a bigger yacht.'

'Are you waiting for him?'

'Not really.'

'What are you doing here?'

'I'm looking for a passage to the Caribbean. Are you still with your dishy Alberto?'

'No, he was a bit of a wimp and couldn't get his *shit* together. He was never going to leave Alicante.' Arlette opined. 'I'm on a German boat now with a five-man crew. We're sailing to Guadeloupe.'

'Any room for me?'

'We're full!'

No doubt Arlette was revelling in an all-male crew. When she met a man for the first time, she didn't just shake his hand; she also lifted his testicles. Arlette reckoned she could tell the man's character by hand-weighing his jewels. I had read somewhere that a handshake is just a hug for scaredy cats!

After exhausting all the gossip, Arlette and I said, 'Cheerio.'

'Maybe we'll meet again on the other side of the pond,' Arlette concluded.

'Who knows,' I replied, unsure whether we had more to say to each other.

I spent another uncomfortable night in the old ruin but had no reason to complain. Staying in a luxurious hotel room couldn't have offered me that many stars in the open sky. In the morning, I folded my sleeping bag tight enough to fit back in the cover, brushed my teeth, and hid my belongings behind a bush. There was no one I could ask to keep an eye on them, not even Arlette on the German yacht anchored off in the bay. If someone robbed me, I would be left destitute, with just a swimsuit and a green towel wrapped around as a sari. I couldn't call Papa or Maman if this happened. I had learned not to expect anything from them, and if I went missing, I felt their sorrow would only amount to a ripple in a puddle. After all, I was the unwanted child - the extra mouth my parents could have done without. It was hard to forget that.

As I strode along the promenade, I felt my legs shaking. Was I mad to hitch a lift across an ocean? I only told my parents I was heading for the Canary Islands and not to expect me back soon. They never questioned this. I think they were relieved - my mother, especially. She could talk to people about her daughter travelling the world, which made her proud. When I lived at home, my parents behaved as if they were staying at a hotel. They expected me to be their cook and housekeeper, which seemed so unfair.

It was late morning when I reached the area on the beach directly opposite the Caribbean-bound yachts. I had stolen a glance at somebody's watch on the way, leaving mine with my possessions at the old ruin. At a guess, from where I stood, it could be a twenty-minute swim to the flotilla. Seeing all the yachts lulling gently in the emerald bay felt encouraging. I thought, 'YES, I can do this.' I folded my old towel and left it well above the tideline. I prayed it would still be there on my return. I hadn't thought about the cold of the Atlantic Ocean until it lapped over my calves. A man approached the water's edge, his tummy preceding him. 'Surely, a pretty thing like you isn't about to commit suicide,' he said with a smirk.

Maybe I was missing something in his humour. I replied with a scowl, 'If I wanted to drown myself, would I be wearing a swimsuit?'

'It's a bit cold for a dip,' the man continued.

'I'm swimming to the yachts anchored off in the bay, hoping for an invitation to tea!' My answer didn't seem that unreasonable. Maybe someone might offer me a drink, seeing me that far away from the shore.

'You must be mad!' the fat man said. 'Who do you think you are, Gertrude Ederle?'

I laughed nervously and replied, 'You may think me eccentric, but it's not the freezing English Channel.' The man shook his head. Not wanting to hear more discouraging comments, I turned with a swirl and quickly waded into the water up to my waist. His mocking words prompted me to strike across the bay and thrust destiny forward.

After a powerful crawl, with the current hampering my progress, I eased into a gentle breaststroke. By then, I was cold. Still, I needed to keep my strength up, for I had seriously misjudged the distance from the beach to the yachts. Unwaveringly, I continued swimming with determination. When I stopped to look at how far I had swum, I was nearer to the vessels than the shore. At that point, there was no turning back.

As I closed in on the first yacht, I recognised Paul tidying up on deck. The day before, I had met him while having coffee at La Paloma Bar. He had tried to chat me up, and I had brushed him off. But I was getting tired and thought, 'What the heck. Any port in a storm.' So I shouted out, 'Hi Paul.' I saw his jaw drop.

'Didn't I see you at La Paloma Bar yesterday?' he cried.

'Yes,' I muttered through chattering teeth, amazed that Paul recognised me in the water.

'You sound as if you could do with a hot drink.

'Would you like to come aboard?' he said with a smile that implied he was my saviour.

'Yes, please.'

There was a rope ladder slung over the side of the boat. I climbed it and then sat in the cockpit, feeling lost for words. I couldn't very well say, 'Fancy meeting you here!'

Paul was tall with a bony frame and big brown eyes which seemed to be grieving for someone. Was he like me, trying to soothe a broken heart? He didn't strike me as the sort of man to be skippering a yacht to the Caribbean. Moreover, I felt he lacked confidence, although he had approached me at the bar and told me he was looking for crew to sail with him to Antigua.

'Is this something you do every day, swimming across the bay to keep fit?' Paul asked, sounding half-serious.

'I've just swum from the beach looking for a passage to the Caribbean, as one does,' I replied with a grin.

'I mentioned I was looking for a crew at the bar yesterday,' Paul remarked, 'but I concluded by how you reacted that you'd already found a boat. I'm leaving in three weeks or thereabouts if you are interested.'

I was flattered by his offer but wondered who would be the one to reach the Caribbean if we fell out midway across the ocean. *Fair Wind* was an old wooden gaff-rigged sailboat, which meant it would be heavy work pulling up the mainsail. The inside was sparse, with two single berths in the main cabin and one underneath the cockpit. It had no standing headroom, and there was only a curtain to allow some privacy when using the loo. The smell of bilge water and diesel seemed to linger. I thought the boat needed a good clean, including the skipper. But, most importantly, might the old vessel spring a plank and sink? I finished my coffee, and after warming up in the winter sun, I was ready to go and find my floating chariot.

'Come for lunch tomorrow if you're free,' Paul said as I prepared to leave. 'I'll be going ashore to shop and could pick you up by El Capitan Restaurant, maybe at 1 pm. You can ride with me in the dinghy to my boat, or you might prefer to swim across.'

'Maybe,' I answered evasively. I didn't want to tell Paul to 'sling his hook,' and dived over the side like a salmon, trying to avoid the clutches of a brown bear.

As I headed towards the main fleet, I noticed an elegant white ketch with two masts flying the French flag. I thought: 'This will do me very well.' As I closed in, I saw two men on deck, one reading, the other watching me and looking amused.

'*Bonjour,*' I said.

'*Est-ce que c'est un poisson, un dauphin ou une sirène?*' - 'Is it a fish, a dolphin, or a mermaid?' the bearded man called out, standing on the deck, smiling behind his whiskers. '*Vous venez de loin,*' - 'Have you come from afar?'

'The other side of the world,' I stated with a grin.

'You're a good swimmer,' the man remarked.

'Ah, thank you. Are you sailing to the Caribbean, and do you need extra crew?' I asked, surprising myself at such a casual approach. It must have seemed I was inquiring about the local bus timetable!

'We have five crew members already,' the bearded man answered. 'We don't need anyone else.'

'Oh,' I said, sounding disappointed.

'Are you French?' his clean-shaven companion asked.

'Swiss,' I replied with a hint of pride in my voice. The men exchanged a glance and giggled. I wasn't surprised. Parisians usually make fun of the Swiss because of our slow delivery and singing accent. I don't have the typical twang, but to them, it was as clear as a cowbell in the Alps.

'We're heading for Martinique,' the bearded man said. 'Let me think about it. By the way, this is Bernard, and I'm Marc, *Aubade's* owner.'

'I'm Monique,' I called out as I trod water.

'Can you cook?' Marc asked.

'You catch it, and I'll cook it!'

He laughed.

'Can you come back tomorrow? I'll talk to the skipper and crew. If we decide to take you, I'll be asking for a contribution to the food. I cannot give you a figure today, but I'll have something worked out by tomorrow.'

'I'll be back,' I shouted out enthusiastically. 'By the way, when do you intend to leave?'

'In the next few days!' Marc said. 'Can you be ready?

'I'll go anytime.'

'What about luggage?'

'All I have is a backpack and a guitar.'

'Do you sing as well?'

'As sweetly as *Neptune*'s daughter!'

He chuckled.

I bade the two men *'Au revoir.'* There was a splash in my tail when I headed back towards the beach. Was Marc impressed enough that I had ventured far into the bay to chase my dream? Tomorrow, I'd have more purpose in my stroke, swimming to the luxurious yacht *Aubade*, but would I get what I hoped for?

2. The Answer

I woke up early, feeling as if I had been sleeping on a bed of nails. I ate my last apple, finished my bottled water, and hid my backpack and guitar behind some bushes, as I had done the day before. If someone stole my passport and traveller's cheques, it would mark the end of my adventure and the beginning of an administrative nightmare.

Walking along the promenade, I felt a twinge in my stomach. Was I about to face disappointment, though Marc had seemed open to the idea of an extra crew member, and had he seen other women swimming across the Bay of Los Cristianos, hitching a lift to the Tropics?

The beach was deserted when I arrived. A fair breeze had picked up, stirring the water in the bay into wavelets. I quickly put my flip-flops on the sand, laid my towel on top, and waded myself into the ocean, breaking into a front crawl with attitude. I kept the pace until my brain felt numbed by the cold water splashing on my face. It was like being waterboarded without the hood. The thought of Marc saying 'yes' urged me on. I had seen a twinkle in his eye yesterday when I cried out to him, '*à demain,*' Till Tomorrow.

I was halfway across the bay when I needed to stop. I lay spreadeagled on my back, floating like driftwood while watching the fluffy trade wind clouds sailing across a celestial blue sky, the type sailors like to see when they set off across an ocean.

The short respite gave me renewed energy, and I sallied onwards. By the time I reached *Aubade,* I was wheezing like the bellows of a church organ, leaking air. I grasped the anchor chain and hung on until I recovered my breath. Then, as I drifted alongside the hull, I saw Marc sitting in the cockpit and hailed: '*Bonjour.*' He lifted his nose from his book and looked in my direction.

'Come aboard,' he called out. 'Swim to the stern and use the boarding ladder.' I climbed gingerly up the stainless steel rungs, which felt harsh on my bare feet, then headed for the cockpit, leaving wet footprints on the pristine teak deck. 'Sit down; you must be exhausted,' Marc hinted.

I hesitated, fearing I would leave a puddle on the seat.

'You might like to dry yourself first,' he suggested. He pulled a fresh towel from one of the lockers and handed it to me. I thanked him and smiled.

'We've just finished lunch, and I've made coffee. Would you like some?'

'It's just what I need.'

He brought the coffee pot and cups and asked, 'Black with sugar?'

'No sugar, thank you.'

Marc was tall and slim with greyish hair. He had a receding forehead and a bushy beard. Bernard, who joined us, looked fifty-something, bald with a face one could easily forget. He had a posh Parisian accent, which he exaggerated by elongating each vowel like the character *Tartuffe* in Molière's play. Marc explained he and Bernard had been at university together. The subject of food expenses came up. Marc quoted me six hundred French francs, which seemed a little steep. Could I be expecting caviar and champagne? Still, I agreed to the price and would pay him with Swiss travellers' cheques.

Another crew member popped up on deck. 'This is our new addition, Monique,' Marc announced with a grin. 'Christophe is our skipper.'

The young man shook my hand. It was a relief he didn't have an eye patch and a hook at the end of his arm! He was handsome with an immature goatee beard, which he kept stroking as if he was encouraging it to grow. Maybe he suffered from a nervous disposition.

'Have you done much sailing?' he asked.

'I've sailed on a sixty-five-foot schooner island-hopping in the Canary Islands, then a twenty-five-foot Bermuda sloop. I also worked on two large gin palaces in the South of France.'

'Tell us about the *sloop*,' Marc interjected. 'It's a big drop in boat size!'

'I fell in love with the skipper. It's a long story.'

'Where did you sail?'

'Down the Portuguese coast to Alicante.'

'Where is your skipper now?'

'He sailed back to England and is now building his dream boat.'

Marc must have noticed the sad look on my face. My breakup with Peter was hard to conceal.

A fourth crew member appeared soon after. He was a thirty-plus chap, short with tight, curly hair and had teeth one sees in a Colgate advertisement. He introduced himself as Jean-Marie. Marc mentioned the other crew member, Jeanne. He thought she might be asleep. Then, he showed me the quarters. I followed him down the companionway. With such steep steps, I would have to hang on tight to the handrail in a swell.

Below decks, on the starboard side, was the chart table with navigation instruments. Adjacent to it was a narrow passage serving as a galley, leading into a generous aft cabin. Beyond was a cabin the size of storage space with two small berths and no headroom. It had a large hatch above. Naturally, one would need the air in such a confined area. Marc and I retraced our steps to the saloon and made for the forward sleeping quarters where he occupied the en-suite double-berth on the port side. Amidships was Bernard's cabin directly opposite Jeanne's. The skipper slept in the forward V-shaped quarters with four berths, two of which were being used to store spare sails. To one side was a shower and toilet. It seemed I had the choice of two cabins, one in the forward bow to share with the handsome skipper, the other at the stern with Jean-Marie oozing with joie de vivre.

After the grand tour, Marc said: 'Okay, how about picking you up in the dinghy at 4 pm tomorrow? You could stand on the beach near the restaurant El Capitán. By the way, we plan to leave the following day. Is that all right with you?'

'*Absolument,*' I replied, beaming.

'Oh, there's one more thing. During the crossing, we'll all have to shower in seawater using a bucket and then rinse off with fresh water. The same applies to washing up. For cooking, we'll only use seawater. No need to add salt, of course!'

'I know about saving water on a small yacht,' I remarked. Mark offered to ferry me ashore, but I told him I needed the exercise and bade everyone *Au Revoir.*

'*À Demain,*' Marc chirped.

All eyes were on me when I dived over the side like a mermaid returning to the deep. I believed the Atlantic Ocean would be my rite of passage to another life.

I waited by El Capitan well before 4 pm the next day, feeling as flimsy as a sapling in a storm. Until then, I had been strong and defiant. Was I mad to embark on a voyage with a crew I'd only met briefly? There would be no getting off the boat halfway across the Atlantic.

I saw Marc motoring his rib towards the beach, and as the bow rumbled onto the shingle, I couldn't have been more excited than if the royal barge were picking me up to ferry me to the Queen's yacht.

Mark cheerfully greeted me. He glanced at my black case and asked hesitantly, 'Is there a guitar in there?'

'No, it's a machine gun,' I responded with a smile.

'We'll be able to defend ourselves against pirates,' he grinned. He took my case, secured it with my backpack in the bow of the rib, and then asked me to sit amidships while he resumed his position. He pressed the ignition button, and the motor fired immediately. How often had I watched Peter pull the cord on *Ellis*'s Seagull 2.5 hp outboard like a demented lumberjack trying to start his stubborn chainsaw? At the same time, I would beg silently, *'Please get this thing going, even if it means giving it mouth-to-mouth resuscitation!'*

Marc's 54-foot ketch was a luxurious yacht with immaculate teak decks and woodwork varnished to perfection. Its shining stainless steel stanchions would have outshone the royal silver cutlery at the Queen's banquet.

As we approached *Aubade*, I wondered if the crew would be piping me aboard while they raised the Swiss flag of courtesy from the yardarm. I could imagine *Cinderella's* thrill when her carriage whisked her to the ball. I only hoped mine wouldn't turn into a sea urchin halfway across the Big Pond!

Climbing into the cockpit, I saw Jeanne sunbathing on the foredeck. She came to meet me. At a guess, the woman was in her early thirties. She possessed all the attributes of a sex goddess - long, wavy black hair, legs up to her armpits, and curves in all the right places. How could four healthy men cope with this nautical *Sophia Loren* in such close quarters? Was Jeanne putting bromide in their muesli?

While pondering this unlikelihood, Mark suggested I take my belongings below deck. I never asked him which cabin I should use. Maybe he was giving me *carte blanche.*

I made my way to the forward quarters as it offered more living space, but who was I kidding! The skipper was better looking than Colgate-smile Jean-Marie. Besides, he didn't have a cubby hole of a cabin. I laid my guitar and backpack on the empty bottom bunk and returned to the cockpit. Marc served us coffee, which was strong enough to stimulate a sloth. He mentioned he owned a supermarket in Paris. (I had pictured him as a lecturer at the Sorbonne University.) He explained his girlfriend and her sister were due to fly to Martinique for a holiday aboard *Aubade.* I thought he had mentioned a wife *en passant* to me earlier!

Jean-Marie was one of Marc's employees in Paris, married with a young son. Bernard, Marc's university friend, said his wife didn't like sailing and would remain at home. Christophe, our skipper, had a girlfriend, too, and Jeanne lived in Toulouse with an eight-year-old son.

The conversation amongst the crew was lively, and I excused myself to get my camera. Now was the time to record the start of my voyage to the Caribbean.

I headed to the forward cabin and found my things had gone. Was there a poltergeist aboard? When I checked

Jean-Marie's cubby hole, I found my chattels flung atop one of the bunks. My first reaction was surprise, followed by disappointment. Nobody had allocated me a cabin. I had chosen the skipper's, unaware of the dynamics amongst the crew. I picked up my worldly goods, returned them to the skipper's quarters, and rejoined the deck party. Somehow, I felt embarrassed at this clash of wills and wondered if anybody noticed. Marc asked me for my passport for safekeeping.

I returned to the forward quarters only to discover my belongings had gone again. I made for Jean-Marie's cabin, and there they were. Was I in a game of 'musical cabins? I never heard the music stop! It was evident someone wanted me with Jean-Marie. His tiny quarters would be a challenge for both of us. I wondered if Jeanne and the skipper were having an affair. It was hard to imagine them together. Christophe looked more like a teenager, and Jeanne *une femme fatale.* Her cabin was near Christophe's, next to Marc's and Bernard's. There would be plenty of time at sea to unveil the intrigue. Martinique was three thousand miles away.

3. Strange Encounters

I watched the anchor chain break the surface, and as it dripped its way to the roller, my heartbeat quickened to the pace of the clinking over the winch gypsy. Next, I heard the clang of the anchor settle in its cradle and saw the first ripples of the bow wave. By then, I could hardly contain this whirlwind of emotions. With *Aubade* now set free, our voyage had begun.

Marc slowly steered the yacht across the bay, weaving through the anchored vessels, while I waved at the people on their decks like a Queen reviewing her fleet. The skipper hoisted the sails, Marc switched the engine off to steer 225° on the compass course, and we headed out to sea with a lively westerly wind. Our first port of call will be Sao Vicente, eight hundred miles away.

Bygone sailors adopted the same route across the Atlantic Ocean. From Cape Verde, they would steer a westerly course towards the Caribbean, keeping close to the Meridian Line, taking advantage of the most predominant trade wind, blowing between November and May. Those choosing a more northerly route could find themselves in the doldrums for weeks in great danger of starvation.

The first time I sailed on a yacht was on Lake Neuchâtel. They say it is a mill pond, but that day felt like the Bermuda Triangle in a storm, not that I knew much about sailing then. I could still picture the yacht heeling over and the mainsail dipping into the water like a wounded bird with its wings outstretched. Falling overboard and being caught underneath the keel had seemed inevitable until the skipper turned the yacht into the wind to spill the gust out of the sails. As she righted herself, the mast quivered, and the sails flogged like the cracking sound of a bullwhip. I thought the mast would land on us if it didn't stand the strain. Ropes became entangled around my feet like a nest of vipers. Was this the aquatic version of being hanged, drawn, and quartered?

Thankfully, the gale-force wind abated to a gentle breeze, the sails filled up, and we resumed our course as if nothing had happened. When the skipper noticed the torment on my face, he said with a grin, 'Now you know why we don't have women in the Swiss Navy! This phenomenon is called a *Katabatic* wind. It's not unusual.' The other crew looked at each other, and there were beads of sweat on their brows.

Marc interrupted my reminiscing when he called out from the wheelhouse, 'How about lunch?' Jeanne and I agreed that I would do the cooking and that she would make the desserts. '*Tarte aux Pommes*' was a favourite of hers.

It didn't take long for me to boil some potatoes, warm a tin of French cassoulets and serve the meal at the large table in the aft cabin. Marc and Bernard came off their watch while the auto-pilot kept our course. Now and then, Marc poked his head out of the hatchway to check our heading. Christophe and Jean-Marie joined us shortly after. Jeanne was last to arrive.

She had answered Marc's advertisement in a yachting magazine, offering a passage to the Caribbean that included a short stay in Martinique and a trip to the Grenadine Islands. She had embarked aboard *Aubade* in Sète, known as 'The Little Venice' of the South of France, leaving her son at his granny's until her return. Jeanne had paid handsomely for the trip, desperate for a change of scenery from the 'Pink City' of Toulouse. I hoped she had nothing to lose but everything to gain from this adventure!

Jeanne enjoyed exposing her naked body to God Horus, tucking herself behind the wheelhouse, away from the crew's prying eyes, or so she thought. Other times, she stood like a figurehead on the bowsprit, the sun casting her shadow on the rushing water beneath. She told me she enjoyed the challenge of taking pictures on a heaving deck, unafraid of the crashing waves or the danger of being washed overboard. *Turner* was known for tying himself to the mast to experience storms at sea so that he could convey the drama on canvas later. Jeanne craved the adrenaline rush, courting danger and sensuality in equal measure. Blessed with fine looks and a certain *je ne sais quoi*, I wondered why she wasn't aboard a gin palace in Monte-Carlo where she would have fitted in perfectly.

After we finished our lunch, we sat together on the foredeck. I asked Jeanne if she was on an extended vacation and what she did for a living.

'I work at the council office as an administrator,' she explained.

I couldn't imagine Jeanne in such a conventional establishment. It was like a top model having a full-time job at McDonald's. Covering my surprise, I said, 'It must be difficult bringing up a child on your own.'

'Actually, I've clients, too. One of them paid for my trip.'

'Are you a therapist?'

'You could say that. I provide sex for lonely hearts.'

I was dumbfounded.

'Some women marry for comfort and security,' Jeanne remarked curtly, noticing the expression on my face.

'At least I'm upfront with my partners. There is no love lost between them and me. It's a mutual arrangement which suits both parties.'

Her declaration hung in the air. Perhaps it was intended as a confession! Jeanne was a courtesan, and I admired her courage to speak out so openly. I had caught snippets of Bernard's invitations, 'If you're feeling lonely, Jeanne, my cabin is open to you.' She would dismiss it with a laugh, but had she ever taken him up on it? Bernard was known to brag about his mistresses, claiming it improved his marriage. But for whom, I pondered?

Marc admitted he also indulged in extramarital affairs. After all, he was the proud owner of an expensive yacht. Intrigued by Jeanne, Marc probed her about her son and seemed to disapprove of leaving him with his grandmother for an extended period. He must have thought she was running away from something.

Christophe enjoyed fishing, although he often lost his bait. He would say, 'The fish must have been too big.'

Other times, he retreated to his cabin just as Jeanne was taking a nap in hers. I wondered if she had moved my belongings from the skipper's quarters. As for Jean-Marie, he seemed to treat Jeanne like a sister, although I suspected he could have dropped the platonic shield if provoked. There were hidden innuendoes between Christophe and Jeanne, leaving everyone guessing whether she had succumbed to his candid charm.

Meanwhile, my cabin mate and I cohabited happily in the 'airing cupboard.' Being zipped up inside my sleeping bag (it can get cold at night on the ocean) seemed just as effective as wearing a chastity belt, not that I ever tried one. Luckily, Jean-Marie's testosterone seemed on good behaviour, at least for now. To me, he was the brother I would have loved to have had. He was one of five boys raised in a small village near Casablanca. After leaving school, he went to work in Paris, met a French girl, and married her. He talked a great deal about Mireille and their two-year-old son Michel and wrote to them each day, planning to post his letters in Cape Verde. He couldn't wait for us to get there.

He and I shared night watches, taking turns at the wheel. During the day, solar panels recharged the ship's batteries so we could use the autopilot. Keeping a straight course for long at the wheel, especially in the dark, proved challenging. The danger of the yacht turning sideways in the following sea was only half a wheel-turn away in these mountainous waves. I remembered being at the tiller in Peter's yacht *Ellis of Tamar,* sailing in such a massive swell through the Straits of Gibraltar that we had to stream long ropes from the stern to stop us from turning sideways. With just a storm sail, Peter and I surfed down the back of the waves as fast as a water chute at a theme park.

Five days on and feeling less queasy, I made pizza for lunch. I harnessed myself to the cooker to avoid being pushed about like a tennis ball in a washing machine. Juggling the dough above my head *Italian style* wasn't an option in such a cramped space. Once the pizza was cooked, I had to judge the boat's motion before opening the oven door to avoid an unwanted landing on my lap.

I astonished Marc and Bernard with my culinary prowess. They presumed Swiss people could only make soup. Their views were changing with the variety of food I served. They approved of my *gratin dauphinois,* pizza and *quiche Lorraine* and enjoyed everything I dished out. And it wasn't just because the food tended to taste better at sea. We were becoming lethargic with the Atlantic swell. Our watches were like slow revolving doors made up of two hours on and four off between preparing meals and sleeping.

When showering on deck, the only element missing from self-torture was a sack over my head. First, I had to dip the bucket overboard on the lee side (the opposite side to where the wind was blowing) and hang on tight to the rope around the handle, but I needed to choose my moment in the trough to scoop water up before lifting the pail aboard. Pouring the freezing sea over my head was equally challenging, and the crew always knew when I showered because of all the shrieks and giggles.

By then, we had been at sea for one hundred and sixty-eight hours without a sign of a possible mutiny aboard. Everyone inhabited their inner space while *Aubade* rose and fell on the ocean like a Rolls Royce on a never-ending undulating highway.

When Marc announced over lunch that there were one hundred and forty-four miles left to San Vicente, the land suddenly felt so near. His heart must have been bursting with excitement. Some people buy a yacht and park it in a marina like a prestigious car they keep in their garage, only using it on a sunny Sunday afternoon. Not Marc! He loved his big toy bobbing on the ocean.

We approached land two days later. Marc and Bernard shaved for the first time since leaving Los Cristianos. Christophe changed into a clean T-shirt, and Jean-Marie donned white cotton slacks. I wore yellow shorts and a khaki-coloured blouse, and Jeanne remained in her bikini. The crew, like me, must have been overwhelmed to reach *terra firma*. I wondered if I would see the world differently after this, though I promised myself never to waste a moment on pettiness or idle talk again. Was I setting the bar too high?

We dropped the sails as we entered the bay and motored up into the harbour of San Vicente. As we drew near the quayside, Christophe jumped ashore and tied the fore and aft lines to some bollards. Two customs officers waited for us to secure the yacht before boarding. They inspected all quarters, asked for our papers, and checked all passports. Marc gave them a generous tip, and the men left happy, taking our documents for safekeeping until departure.

After six long days at sea, it was a strange sensation to be walking on dirt roads. We passed some shacks and saw people squatting behind bushes. Stray dogs and cats roamed in the market, barely carrying their skeletal frames. On a stall, we found tiny apples full of worms. With our provision of eggs depleted, we bought a bucket full of them at a garage and filled up a five-litre plastic bottle with soap from a forty-five-gallon drum. Lastly, we looked for a post office. I had written a letter to my parents, giving them an address in a marina in Fort de France, Martinique, where Marc was planning for us to dock. I hoped Peter had answered my last letter, in which I wrote: 'Love isn't like money you put in the bank waiting for interest!' I mentioned I didn't intend to wait for him eternally. It had been five months since we had said *Au Revoir* in Cannes after working on a superyacht, he as a deckhand and I as a cook. I thought of the song *'Dis'* by French singer Barbara.

'Je ne suis pas de celles qui meurent de chagrin,
'I'm not one of these women who die of sorrow,
je n'ai pas la vertue des femmes de marins.'
I don't have the virtue of a sailor's wife.'

The lyrics resonated with how I felt, and I prayed my parents would forward Peter's letter if he had written one. They would often leave my mail in a drawer until I came home. I knew Peter and I were meant for each other, but the delay in receiving his letter could seal our fate.

Marc decided we would remain in Cape Verde for a few days while he and the skipper checked the yacht's equipment and worked out their navigation strategies before the extended passage to Martinique. Depending on the wind, the pair calculated we could spend thirteen to fourteen days at sea. After lunch, Jean-Marie volunteered to chaperone Jeanne and me while we explored the area. He seemed restless. Marc must have insisted he came on this trip. Jean-Marie didn't seem overly interested in sailing, but surely it must have been more exciting than working in a supermarket sorting out deliveries.

We set off along the pier and down a rubble road. There was hardly any greenery in this desolate environment, swept by constant winds from the Sahara. The beaches, however, could have competed with any exotic holiday brochures of multi-shaded turquoise waters gracing the golden shores.

We spread our towels on a beach, then watched the young, athletic fishermen hauling their catch. They seemed in a trance, manoeuvring their nets and singing in synchronised rhythm, while an array of fish with luminous silver bellies jumped in the air, desperate to find their way back to sea.

'Look at those bodies,' Jeanne exclaimed, pointing towards one of the fishermen. 'I could bite into that one like a chocolate truffle,'

'Jeanne, I exclaimed, 'If you spread your scent, they might pick it up!' Maybe it was the heat that had ignited such lust in her, and I found myself suddenly feeling it, too. We were like two mermaids landing ashore, ready to seduce some fishermen.

Jean-Marie broke the spell when he said, 'Come on, let's get back. Marc and the others might start worrying about us.' Had he noticed the fire of desire in Jeanne and me? Would we have abandoned ourselves in the arms of two total strangers if he hadn't been there?

The returned walk uphill along the stony ground hammered my libido to a pulp, bringing me back to my senses. As we walked along the quayside, I suddenly thought, 'I must be hallucinating.' The chance of meeting somebody I knew in Cape Verde had seemed remote until I recognised Arlette stepping off the German yacht moored against the pier. *'There can be no escape from this woman.'*

Arlette rushed towards me like a long-lost friend. 'I'm relieved to see a friendly face,' she cried. 'I've had such an awful crossing. I need to talk to someone. Can I come aboard for a minute?'

She looked as if someone had ruffled her feathers.

'Give me time to ask Marc's permission first,' I replied, feeling hard-pressed. The crew had retreated to their quarters. Arlette came aboard. I took her to the aft cabin and offered her some coffee. She asked if she could smoke.

'No,' I said.

'I'm glad we've bumped into each other again,' Arlette continued. At last, I've got someone to share my troubles with. I can't bear the German skipper anymore. He kept hassling me for sex, and I loathe the man. On top of that, I ran out of rolling paper halfway through the trip. I was so desperate that I made a pipe out of a potato. But you haven't heard the worst.'

'It sounds as if you had a tough time,' I replied, wondering where this was leading.

'Do you think I could join *Aubade* as an extra crew?' she asked, looking like a begging puppy.

'Can't the men on your boat help?' I retorted.

'They don't want to antagonise the captain. He had his eyes on me throughout the journey, and nobody dared interfere.'

Her insistence angered me. She would have dropped the subject if she could have read my face. We were six on board already, with only one bunk left in the skipper's cabin. Besides, Arlette and I weren't exactly bosom pals. She was less than helpful when our paths crossed in Los Cristianos.

Furthermore, it was up to Marc to decide if she could join us. Would the skipper gladly share his cabin with Arlette? At least there was no spare bunk for a poltergeist to move her shackles to another cabin.

'You've no idea of the nightmare I've gone through,' Arlette resumed. 'The captain miscalculated his waypoints, and we didn't know where we were. We also had a fire in the galley. One of the crew members left something burning in the bottom of a pan, and the place filled with smoke. I was scared out of my wits that the boat would go up in flames.'

Was Arlette telling the truth? I suspected there might have been more than one reason why she wanted to jump ship. Maybe the other men had tried their ways with her after she had given them her unique handshake! Despite my reluctance, I offered to speak to Marc. I couldn't very well let Arlette drown. I should at least throw her the *proverbial* lifebuoy. Knowing her, she would rather be saved by a muscular lifeguard.

When I asked Marc about Arlette, he said unashamedly, 'She isn't charming enough to have around,' but insisted it was up to me to decide if she should join us. He added, 'They employ Swiss guards at the Vatican, so I can trust your judgment being Swiss.

How could I get out of this one? If I took pity on Arlette and it proved a wrong move, nobody could ask her to take a running jump halfway across the Atlantic Ocean. What a choice to have to make. Either way, someone was bound to suffer, maybe everyone. We were, after all, in the same boat.

4. Four Aces

Arlette boarded *Aubade* a few hours before we cast off, bringing the crew to seven. At least she was spared the game of musical cabins when she settled in the skipper's quarters. There could be mutiny if Arlette misbehaved. She might even be the fledgling cuckoo pushing Jeanne and me out of the nest. Christophe lifted the anchor, and we all stood on deck like warriors, ready to do battle against the mighty ocean for the next two thousand miles.

After weaving through a floating graveyard of old rusting cargo ships and tankers anchored in the bay, starkly contrasting with the sun's glistening reflection on the water, Marc unfurled the headsail; Christophe hoisted the main before switching the engine off. Then, as we headed out into the big blue, I started to sing:

Deep in the Sea are riches beyond compare,
if you're looking for safety, it is on the shore,
sailing is a love affair
Deep in the sea are riches beyond compare,
sailing is a love affair.

I thought of my father. His only adventure out to sea was on a cruise ship exploring the Mediterranean. I doubted he could relate to wind and sails. To a mariner, this is poetry in motion. Papa's real passion was football. When I was little, he would drag me to matches every Sunday, where I learned the true meaning of boredom. 'When will the game be over?' I would ask him imploringly. He continually ignored my question until I persisted. Then, he gave me money to buy an Orangina to shut me up. When the bottle of fizz was empty, I would tug at his jacket sleeves again. Finally, he would point at the ninety-minute clock on the side of the pitch and explain the game would end when the hour hand on the big clock reached the top. I thought a snail could get to China and back before then.

When I told my father I wanted to become a professional classical singer, he retorted, 'You have delusions of grandeur.' Why did he have to quash my dream? But Papa had other ambitions for my sisters and me. He thought that after leaving school, we should take up a three-year apprenticeship in a watchmaking factory because we would be well-paid. Granddad had been a watchmaker, and Father must have felt we carried the gene in the family DNA.

Despite my father's cruel comment, I played with the idea that maybe one day, I might become a famous opera singer. Opera meant nothing to Papa. Petula Clarke was his favourite songstress. He loved her sensuous English accent when she sang in French:

'Coeur blessé torturé par tout le mal que tu m'as fait.'

'Broken heart, tortured by all the pain you've caused me.'

The lyrics spoke of his marriage. Although I was too young to understand relationships between grown-ups, I sensed my parents were hitting potholes on the marital road. *Maman* shouted a lot at my sisters and me, often for no reason. I never understood what she was saying. Maybe her words were lost in translation. Mother's native tongue was Swiss German. No matter what, Father would always say: 'Don't upset your mother; she has fragile nerves.'

Signs of something amiss began to show two days on from Cape Verde. Was it the result of too many cooks in the galley spoiling the broth? Arlette seemed keen to impress the crew with her cooking and boasted of a novel way of making pizzas, using a Pyrex dish to lay her dough in and filling the centre with cheese and tomatoes. I left her to it, happy to remove my apron and lose myself in the Big Blue. I took my notebook and wrote:

Feel the wind on the ocean wave in the wake of ships gone by, a thousand miles from the nearest land,
how awesome and grand.

When Arlette served her pizza dish for lunch, Marc said indignantly: 'I can't eat that; the pastry isn't cooked through.' Poor Arlette looked hurt and humiliated, having to toss her pizza to Neptune. She might not have had as much practice at the stove as me. I learned to put a spoon in a mixing bowl as soon as I could walk!

They say cooking is an art and baking science, but measuring anything on a moving boat is challenging. However, Jeanne's cakes always worked.

Jeanne spent more time in her cabin since Arlette's boarded *Aubade,* and Christophe appeared agitated. The responsibility of safely navigating an ocean must have taken its toll. If he got it wrong, we might end up off Cape Horn! Tension aboard was like seeing the lightning in a thunderstorm and counting the seconds before the coming thunder. Had Christophe succumbed to Arlette's advances? Whenever I saw Jeanne on deck or at mealtimes, she looked like a betrayed lover with her teeth clenched behind a barrage of words ready to burst out. I prayed that the pair wouldn't be left alone on deck, for if one pushed the other overboard in these marching waves, boat and crew could perish, trying to save the damsel who lost the duel of wits! Fortunately, the two rivals avoided each other. Both women must have known the danger of such a close encounter.

By then, we all felt lethargic, which might have been the underlying effect of seasickness or the realisation of our vulnerability and insignificance in the big ocean. Lying down in my cabin was like being on a waterbed with a partner continually tossing and turning, only I was alone. I knew someone who fell seasick the first night sleeping in his new waterbed.

Marc and Bernard were spending more time in their cabins. They complained they had run out of books from the boat's library. Maybe it was time for them to write a romantic novel. There was plenty of material to tap into amongst the crew.

Meanwhile, undeterred by previous failure, the skipper tried his luck at fishing again. Surprisingly, it wasn't long before we heard Marc shouting, 'It must be a big one.' The crew gathered in the cockpit to watch Christophe slowly winding the line around the bare wooden frame. I thought of *The Old Man and the Sea* by Hemingway, where the ageing fisherman struggles with a giant Marlin far out off the coast of Cuba.

Christophe's biceps looked stretched to the limit when he reeled in the big fish, which thrashed its tail from the end of the hook, fighting for life. Unlike *The Old Man and the Sea*, Christophe didn't need to slay five sharks to preserve his catch; he hit his prey on the head with a winch handle.

I rushed down below to get my camera and took a snapshot of him lifting the fish like a trophy. Shame on me for wanting to immortalise the death of an innocent creature, which, minutes before, was swimming free in the open ocean.

The skipper gutted it, and blood poured onto the teak deck. The sight of it made me queasy. I remembered the words of a farmer, 'People forget nature is a killing machine, eat or be eaten!' All this blood brought me back to the garage next to the butcher shop in my village of Auvernier when I was eight. I remembered the cow being led into the garage and the man in big rubber boots, wearing a heavy white apron, telling me to go home before he shut the garage door. I was a curious little girl, keen to understand what was happening. Next, I heard a gunshot, and it was a while before someone slid the door open. Then I saw the cow's carcass with hooks and chains hanging from the ceiling and the butcher hosing it down; his apron splashed with blood. My stomach turned with the pungent smell of warm flesh mixed with ammonia. The day before, the cow might have been grazing on a mountainside with a bell ringing around its neck. Now, it was no more than a hanging slab of meat.

The shining yellow and blue Dorada was cut into steaks and then barbecued. Its rich white flesh melted in the mouth, and we soon forgot the blood and gore on the teak deck. After lunch, Jeanne resumed her post as the ship's figurehead, her hair streaming in the wind. I joined her on the foredeck. 'Jeanne, you seem a lot quieter lately,' I remarked, trying hard to be casual.

'Well, I never thought I'd be so humiliated,' she retorted grimly.

'Has Bernard made advances to you?' I asked. I felt he could have swallowed her whole if his eyes had been his mouth.

'It's not about Bernard, but I don't feel like talking about it,' Jeanne said. 'I wish we hadn't encountered Arlette in São Vicente; I don't like her!'

'Sorry,' I said. 'It's all my fault.'

'No, not really. What else could you have done?'

Jeanne's eyes looked puffy and tired. I had told Arlette Jeanne and Christophe might be having an affair. Sadly, it didn't ward her off. Marc had mentioned Christophe's girlfriend was flying to Martinique for a holiday on *Aubade*. What would happen if she surprised us at the Club Mediterranée where we were headed? Would Arlette then be ousted from the skipper's cabin and told to leave? How would Jeanne react when Christophe's three-way betrayal finally got out into the open? Had he spoken of a girlfriend in Paris to her? As for Arlette, discretion wasn't an island she visited often, although she never talked about the skipper. Judging by how she continued spreading her charm amongst the men, I doubted she would feel guilty if she had transgressed.

Marc and Bernard, meanwhile, were enjoying gossiping like two old maids. What were they saying about the crew? Did they presume Jean-Marie and I were having an affair? How easy this would have been. He had asked me one night if I wanted a massage, and I said 'No.' He must have missed his wife, just as I longed for Peter. Being thrown together in a cubby hole, Jean-Marie and I could easily have rolled out of our sleeping bags and into each other's arms.

One day, Marc mentioned my passport, which stated 'divorced.' I told him I had had a four-month crash course in marriage, and by the tone of my voice, he understood I wasn't keen to talk about it. I had tragically made the monumental mistake of falling for a man who fascinated me because he was an artist. Three weeks before we were due to get married, something awful happened.

I was late that day after visiting my friend Héloise, who had decided to accompany me back home to where my fiancé and I lived. She wanted to see Stephen's paintings. Arriving two hours later than promised got him into a vicious temper, and he lashed out at me. A punch in my stomach and a black eye got Heloise and me fleeing from the flat in shock.

The following day, I had to explain to my colleagues in the office how I got a black eye. 'I hit the corner of a table by accident.' I said, trying hard to be convincing. While some women might feel embarrassed about a love bite on their necks, I was ashamed of bearing the brunt of my fiancé's anger. I wasn't sure they believed my story but didn't pursue the subject.

I stayed at Heloise's for a few days. Stephen kept calling me at the office to apologise, but I refused to speak to him. Then, one day, I succumbed and agreed to meet him on Wimbledon Common. Heloise's flat was near there.

I really should have ended the relationship there and then, but Stephen had gone down on bended knee, swearing on his mother's heart that it would never happen again, then declaring: 'I'm frightened that someone will snatch you away. I love you so much.' It was flattering for a naive nineteen-year-old who had come to London as an au pair to learn English.

'Finally, I said, 'I will marry you.' And we cried into each other's arms. But what was I thinking? Would I be marrying another born Edvard Munch? Sources claim that when the artist and his fiançé Tulla Larsen quarrelled at his summer house in Aagaardsstrand, a revolver went off during the fray, wounding Munch's hand. The incident inspired him to create two paintings: *The Death of Marat* and *The Death of Marat II*.

Back in the flat Stephen and I shared, I looked for the floral wedding dress I had made with the help of a neighbour. I couldn't find it anywhere. When I asked my 'groom-to-be' if he knew where it was, he confessed he had torn it to shreds after I left. I should have heard warning bells loud and clear and packed my bags there and then. But I put it down to Stephen's artistic temperament and the stress before the wedding, convinced that it was all my fault.

We married at a South London Registry Office on a gloomy July day. A handful of friends attended, but Heloise didn't come. I expected my friends Brian and Jean, but one of their children was ill. Only their father came.

After the Registry Office, our best man Matthew (Stephen's brother) agreed to drop Brian off at our wedding reception outside London.

As we sat in the rear seat of Matthew's car, my groom started to nip my arm while whispering indignantly down my ear, 'Why did you invite him?' He was referring to Brian. I couldn't believe this was happening on my wedding day. Had I just signed up for a life of marital hell?

After we dropped Brian off, Stephen's anger worsened. He took my wrist and started to press hard on it. I screamed with pain, which prompted him to release me. I begged Matthew to stop the car. When he did, I stepped out and fled like a captured bird let free. Stephen ran after me. 'We are already late for the reception,' he said as if he was scolding an unreasonable child. I thought, 'This must be a bad dream.' He took me by the hand, gently bringing his broken-hearted bride back to the car, and we drove on. Matthew never spoke.

We arrived late at the reception. The guests had been worried about us. After that, it was all a blur until my mother-in-law asked me, 'Will you be strong enough to cope with my son?' She had that condescending expression, which seemed to say, 'You poor girl!' She must have known something was wrong with him. Why had she not talked to me about it when Stephen and I stayed at her house in Devon? I told myself it wasn't her fault; it was mine to deny her son's dysfunctional behaviour, which had as many moods as the colours on his palette, from rosy pink to deep black splashed aggressively on the canvas of our relationship. It must have been my sense of worthlessness that had landed me into a dark hole of abuse, and I didn't know who to turn to.

Stephen's control tightened. He dictated how I should dress and what I did with my money. I broke away from all my friends because of his jealousy. He didn't enjoy my singing, so I took up the piano. For some reason, hitting the wrong keys never bothered him. I lived in permanent fear that he might lose his temper if he got frustrated because his career as a painter wasn't going his way. Each time he raised his voice, I would run down the stairs and wait on the landing until he had quietened down. Then, one day, I needed to return the guitar I had borrowed from Heloise. Before I left, Stephen made me promise to come straight back, but how could I resist spending time with my friend? The afternoon flew by. When I noticed I would be late home, I heard the warning signs loud and clear and thought, 'I can't live my life like this anymore. I need to get out.'

I never returned home that night and only went to the flat once, knowing that Stephen would be at work. I packed some clothes into a bag and left whatever we owned together. Like my wedding dress, my heart was in tatters.

Many miles had flown under the keel since leaving the pokey flat I had occupied in London. I was now living the adventure of a lifetime, sailing across the Atlantic Ocean to the Tropics on a splendid yacht. However, life afloat clearly contained all the ingredients of secrets and betrayal for writing a romantic thriller, though I wouldn't be directly involved this time. Meanwhile, Jeanne and Arlette managed to keep their distance, but I could hear muted words flying around like threats. Poor Jeanne must have wondered why Christophe had favoured a woman far less attractive than herself. Was her ego feeling deeply wounded?

She had fallen for a novice with blue eyes and candid charm. Shouldn't Christophe, at least, have tried to remain faithful during our passage to the Caribbean? For Marc and Bernard, this love triangle across the ocean waves must have sharpened their tongues. Their cabins were opposite each other, making it ideal for them to observe *the déroulement* of Arlette and Christophe's suspected affair and that of the stunning Jeanne. Maybe the two were amused and envious, seeing two women fighting over him. Life on an uneven keel can make people very irrational. Was a crime of passion about to happen? I could already see the headlines:

The police have interrogated the owner and crew of a French yacht on arrival in Martinique following the disappearance of a young female crew.

Apart from being a heartbreaker, Arlette dabbled at predicting the future. After lunch, one day, she offered to read Marc's cards. He jumped at this with a grin, indicating, 'It's just a bit of fun.' Bernard was curious enough to wait his turn. I left them to it.

When I saw Arlette playing a game of Patience on her own in the communal aft cabin, I asked her if she would read my cards. She didn't seem overly keen. I wondered why. Was there something terrible about to happen in my life? ‘Please,’ I pleaded. 'If you don’t, I shall worry about it.’

‘I don’t want to,’ she insisted.

‘Why not?’

‘I don’t know!’

‘Come on,’ I urged her.

She relented and handed me the pack of cards.

‘Shuffle them,’ she said impatiently.

I felt as if I was gambling my life away when I handed the pack back to her. My heart was beating fast as if I had been standing on a mile-high platform about to bungee jump.

Arlette spread fifty-two cards across the table, then said, ‘Select one.’

I carefully picked one up, turned it over and then looked back at Arlette as if my fate lay in her hands. The first card was the Ace of Hearts. I thought, ‘An Ace is good, especially if it’s a heart. Does it mean I’m lucky in love?’

‘Select another card,’ she commanded, interrupting my guessing game. Why was she so agitated? I turned over the Ace of Diamonds. She yelled, ‘Pick another one.’ It was the Ace of Clubs. Arlette looked shocked and perplexed. ‘One more,’ she barked.

The fourth card was the Ace of Spades!

‘I’ve never seen anything like this in all my life,’ Arlette exclaimed. ‘This is spooky.’

‘Is this good or terrible?’ I asked, starting to regret the whole thing.

'Choose another three cards, and I'll tell you what I see,' Arlette insisted with a face that looked far from the comedienne she was but more like a judge with a black cloth on her head about to give out a death sentence.

The fifth card was the King of Hearts, the sixth, the Queen of Hearts, and the seventh, the Ten of Hearts!

'Well,' she said, 'The Ace of Diamonds tells me you'll get a letter that'll change your life.'

'It's a fortuneteller's cliché,' I riposted. 'You can't go wrong with your prediction. Everyone gets letters.'

Arlette ignored my comment and continued. 'This man truly loves you. You'll be happy together.'

'If you're talking about Peter, I'm not sure. Nothing in the world would deter him from building a boat. It could be years before he sets sail or invites me to join him.'

'I think you'll get a letter that'll change everything. Maybe it's waiting for you in Martinique.'

Arlette gathered her cards and resumed her game of *Patience*. I went to join the others on deck to reflect upon such serendipity.

'Good reading?' Marc asked as I sat next to him in the cockpit.

'I got the cards a 'Mississippi Gambling Man' can only dream of when he coins the cash on the table and says to his fellow gamblers, "Read them and weep." You won't believe it; I raised four aces in a row.'

'Were you wearing long sleeves?' Marc asked.

I giggled.

He smirked, 'I've never heard of someone cheating at a reading. Were you trying to manipulate destiny?'

'My bikini hasn't got sleeves,' I replied with a grin.

'I must admit, Arlette might have something,' he continued. 'She mentioned my relationship with my girlfriend Amandine. She was right about her mother being ill and her sister going through a divorce. This stuff is unreal!'

Bernard, on the other hand, wasn't convinced. Maybe he didn't like it when Arlette told him his wife knew about his affairs and hated him for it.

Arlette's prediction took me way back to when I lived in London. One day, a friend offered to tell me about my future. She told me I would meet someone and live in a small English northern town. She also predicted we would marry and spend years on the water. Maybe the letter Arlette mentioned was waiting for me in Martinique. Still, I didn't hold much faith because my parents usually left my mail in a drawer until my next visit, which could be a year away, with Peter's letter languishing in the pile.

The mood aboard *Aubade* lightened when the skipper announced we could be in Martinique in forty-eight hours. Excitedly, Marc said he would treat us all to a feast at the *Club Méditerranée*, famous for their sumptuous buffet. After sixteen days at sea, we were now living on tinned food. Then Jeanne announced that she would be jumping ship as soon as we docked in Martinique.

'I thought you were sailing with us to the Grenadines,' I remarked.

'I am through with *Aubade*,' she snapped.

'What has upset you so much?'

'Christophe is into somebody else as soon as he gets the eye. Watch out, Monique. Arlette has sharp elbows! She might try to push you off the boat next!'

'I'm sorry, Jeanne.' I ventured, trying hard to avoid blaming Christophe in case Jeanne succumbed to his charm again and forgave him. Then Arlette would be forced to go while Jeanne finished her cruise with us. I thought the deep undertow could drag someone under, but who?

5. After the High Seas

The Rock rose high out of clear turquoise waters. With its salt-encrusted surface sparkling in the sunlight, they named it the Diamond Rock. It was hard to imagine the 175-metre-high basalt island once being the siege of bloody battles between the French and the English.

When we approached the *Club Méditerranée,* Marc radioed to request permission to berth at Buccaneer's Creek. The water there was like an azure-stained glass window, and I almost expected the surface to shatter when Christophe dropped the anchor from the bow. Over the side was a vast aquarium of wonders, with species of all colours and shapes amongst translucent algae. Around us were lush vegetation, giant agave, red bougainvillaeas, and hibiscus. I felt the Cinderella in me had joined the ball; this time, she wouldn't lose her slipper!

Everyone by then was eager to get ashore. As I stepped from the dinghy onto the wooden jetty, it felt like a heaving deck. The Atlantic Ocean was pulsating through me. Luckily, we soon found a bar where we all perched ourselves on high stools. At least I had the counter to hang on to. Arlette wasn't with us. She was sulking and told us she needed time on her own.

Marc ordered a round of *planters.* I took a sip from the tall glass that contained more than a *soupçon* of rum. The barman asked Marc to sign the crew in as visitors for the day, and he paid in advance for the *Club Méditerranée's* lavish buffet.

'It's going to be an expensive day for me,' Marc said. 'It's my treat. I want you to enjoy it.' We clinked glasses. He gave a speech and praised Christophe for having safely skippered the yacht to the Caribbean. We finished our cocktails and walked into the open pavilion for the gourmet feast.

What a sumptuous spread to take in, with tables assembled in a circle like a Western wagon train about to be attacked. Each stand had a theme. A swordfish head took centre stage on one, amongst various Caribbean fish, lobsters, crabs, shellfish, and crustaceans. A wild boar's head dominated the display of prime-cut meat, while pork and lamb were being cooked on spits and carved on demand. One could point at anything, either grilled, baked, or barbecued. It was a feast of gastronomic artistry with side dishes of cooked vegetables cut into multiple shapes and lettuces of all kinds creatively trimmed. Fruits worldwide were arranged in a colourful mosaic, and multi-tiered cakes, fruit tarts, and gâteaux crowned this opulence.

It was a royal belt buster and a blow-out on a grand scale. Then, in the hub of this gastronomic wheel, I noticed the dark torso of a naked male mannequin lying face up on a white linen-covered table. His manhood was accentuated by a large aubergine and two lemons. I thought the rum in my cocktail must be causing me hallucinations. Surely, there couldn't be a man in flesh and blood amongst all this culinary excess? Wouldn't that be stretching the exotic too far? I focussed more intently and caught him blinking. What a stallion of a man. I wondered if Arlette would have squeezed his lemons had she been with us!

The crew dispersed armed with plates and a big appetite. Meanwhile, the beautiful Jeanne was nowhere to be seen. *Aubade's* real-life figurehead had deserted us. We all felt as if we were actors in the film *La Grande Bouffe*, Blow-Out, where four friends meet for a weekend to eat themselves to death. We almost did that in a few hours.

After the French food extravaganza, we took a stroll and caught sight of Jeanne in the club's garden. She was striding hand in hand with a stunning-looking, tall, blond man. When Jeanne approached Marc, she looked as defiant as a gladiator addressing the Emperor after slaying a lion. She announced she would be collecting her belongings in the late afternoon. 'Don't be so hasty, Jeanne,' Marc pleaded. 'You're entitled to another two weeks on *Aubade*.'

'I'm through with Christophe,' Jeanne replied.

'Think about it,' Marc pleaded like a captain facing a mutinous crew. 'We're casting off tomorrow afternoon for Fort-de-France and will be sailing to Guadeloupe, Bequia and Mustique after that. You'll miss a lot.'

'I'll pick up my things around six,' Jeanne retorted. Then, turning on her heels, she and her companion disappeared into the crowd. Would Marc blame Arlette for what happened and worry about the skipper's girlfriend arriving amidst the bloody battle of aching hearts? Christophe's two affairs had seriously rocked the boat! There seemed to be something perverse about him spreading havoc amongst the ladies. Who knows what Marc and Bernard made of this? I could imagine them gossiping like two babbling old spinsters knitting by the guillotine. What a foolish decision I had taken to rescue Arlette. I felt my good deed had turned sour.

Jeanne hailed the crew from the beach after six, and Christophe set off in the dinghy to collect her. I saw him stepping ashore and raising his arms as if Jeanne were pointing a gun at him. Arlette was perched on the bowsprit, observing the sequence of events with glee. By leaving *Aubade,* Jeanne was playing right into her hands. With Arlette's rival eliminated, her status as Christophe's rightful lover would be fully established. But she may still have to confront Christophe's girlfriend, whose presence aboard would jeopardise Arlette's position with the skipper. I believed she was capable of doing anything to circumvent that.

Christophe ferried the outraged Jeanne back aboard *Aubade.* As she disappeared down below, Marc asked from the cockpit, 'How are you, Jeanne?'

'Very well,' she answered constrainedly before rushing to her cabin to pack as if she were late for a plane.

'You'll miss the sailing,' Marc cried out.

'I have other offers from the club,' she responded. Bernard shouted from the companionway,
'Come on, Jeanne, we all love you. You can't abandon us like this.'

'Well, you'll just have to ask Arlette to sweeten you up,' Jeanne called back from her cabin. 'She's good at dishing out her affections.'

I felt gutted to see Jeanne go. I waved her *Adieu* as Christophe rowed her ashore. I thought of the day Peter left me in Cannes to sail *Ellis* back to England - his burning ambition to build his steel yacht *Capricorn* had torn us apart. I tried telephoning him before setting off on *Aubade* to the Caribbean, and unfortunately, his mother answered the call. I told her how much I loved her son, hoping for some comforting words, but she said, 'I think you ought to find someone else; Peter isn't ready for another relationship.' Her comment felt as though she had pulled the trigger of a double-barrelled shotgun and shattered my emotions with the blast. Peter had mentioned that whenever a waitress showed interest in him at the boarding house his mother once ran, she would find a way to dismiss her. She never approved of Peter's ex-wife, Elisabeth, or me. Despite her warning, I was far from ready to accept what had come out of the mouth of a thousand daggers.

Leaving Jeanne to her new intrigue, *Aubade* and her crew set sail to Fort de France, the largest city in the *French Antilles*. We had a fair wind on the way. When we approached the harbour, we saw the Schoelcher Library building, which stood as a landmark with its elegant, innovative metal structure, supporting a multicoloured basilica and Byzantine glass dome. The architect Henry Pick constructed the building honouring Victor Schoelcher, who dedicated his life to opposing slavery.

Once moored at the marina, we caught a taxi to the supermarket. Everyone was surprised at how much we bought, including toilet paper. *Aubade's* waterline disappeared by the time we had stored it all away.

Guadeloupe, Bequia, and Mustique were our next destinations. On the way, a gale-force wind whipped up from nowhere, and the horizon vanished under the torrential rain. *Aubade* heeled alarmingly in the gust. The prospect of capsizing crossed my mind. We all hung to the stanchions like limpets on a rock, thoroughly drenched in the deluge. Then, when *Aubade* rounded up to the wind, the sails flapped like demented semaphores. The gale only lasted a few minutes, enough to shake up the crew. Christophe and Jean-Marie quickly dropped the headsail and mainsail. By that time, the wind had abated altogether. The skipper hoisted the sails again, and we resumed our course as if nothing had happened. 'You should be more vigilant next time,' Marc told the crew. 'Try to react as soon as you spot the dark line of a squall to avoid a knockdown.'

Our next port of call was Guadeloupe. The island, shaped like a butterfly, has mountains, turquoise lagoons, and mangroves. On the opposite side of the spectrum, the city's main shopping centre looked like a mini Cannes, with its Gucci boutiques and expensive restaurants, all very close to basic shacks where the locals lived.

We anchored in Bequia next to two other foreign yachts. Overlooking us from the clifftop was a lonely brown shack. I imagined Peter and me living there with the Caribbean Sea and the newly-built *Capricorn* gently rocking in the bay.

On the millionaire's island of Mustique, Jean-Marie, Arlette, and I hitched a lift to visit the place. It wasn't long before an English woman in a brand-new Range Rover pulled over. She might have been a film star or a famous singer, but she didn't let on. I lost count of how many mega-mansions we saw on this luscious green island with a no-paparazzi policy.

Returning to Martinique, we docked at Portbou Marina near Fort de France. Marc was returning to Paris to check on his supermarket. He would be gone for three weeks. Bernard and Jean-Marie were leaving too, and Marc's girlfriend Amandine and her sister Yvonne would soon join the love-ship for a holiday. He asked me to help his guests during their stay. In return, he promised to pay for all my expenses. Luckily, this meant my savings would stretch beyond my calculations. As for Arlette, was she hoping Christophe would dissuade his girlfriend from flying to Martinique so that she could be the skipper's sea maiden?

Amandine and Yvonne arrived by taxi the day after Marc, Jean-Marie, and Bernard flew back to Paris. Christophe helped the two sisters aboard with their luggage. I showed the women to their cabins and left them to unpack. They joined us on deck shortly afterwards. I served them coffee and fresh patisserie I had bought that morning. Arlette was out for the afternoon.

Amandine's presence was like a blanket of comfort, and I thought if I were a cat, I would leap on her lap. She was blonde in her forties with a rebellious fringe and a generous waist. Her sister, Yvonne, was tall and thin. She had long black hair, which hung like a curtain that was hard to pull back. Her blue eyes spoke of lost love. Arlette had seen a divorce when she read Marc's cards.

When Arlette returned later that afternoon, she greeted our new arrivals like gatecrashers to a party. She quickly retreated into the forward cabin with Christophe in tow. He excused himself by saying he had urgent things to do. We all looked at each other. Marc had already marked their card. But how deep were Arlette's claws into Christophe?

Two days later, Christophe announced, with the voice of a deckhand informing passengers of the next ferry departure, that Arlette was leaving. He must have decided to save the Good Ship *Aubade* and his relationship with his girlfriend in Paris. As Arlette stepped ashore the following day, she growled, 'I'll never worry about your survival. You play “the innocent” when, all along, you manipulate people. You should be the one to go, not me!’ Her outburst took the wind out of my sails. Had she forgotten I rescued her from the German yacht in Cape Verde? Marc only consented to accept her on board because I pleaded her case. From now on, she would have to row her own boat. Although Arlette was small but muscly, one could imagine her capable of throwing a man over her shoulders and carrying him upstairs. No matter what, I couldn’t help feeling sorry for her. Christophe had played with two women like unwanted stowaways he could jettison overboard whenever it suited him.

I mulled over Arlette’s words when she read my cards and said, ‘You’re going to get a letter that’ll change your life.’ Would something be there waiting for me at Portbou Marina?

When I arrived at the office late that day, I frantically sieved through a graveyard of unclaimed letters, which reminded me of times I had come home to abandoned mail in one of my father’s desk drawers. Was Peter’s letter lost in that pile?

I continued searching through the pigeonholes from A to Z, feeling increasingly despondent. What good did it do picking up four Aces, one after the other? I might have pulled the Joker instead. I was like *Noah,* waiting for the return of his dove, unwilling to surrender my disappointment. With a last glimmer of hope, I skimmed through all the local announcements and advertisements for ‘crew wanted’ on the noticeboard. Then, just as I was about to walk away feeling defeated, I saw a partially covered envelope marked *Express* with a Swiss stamp on it. I noticed my name and recognised my mother's tight handwriting. It would be the first letter she had ever sent me. I suddenly felt as if I was on fire. Had something awful happened?

6. The Letter

My legs were shaking when I rushed out of the marina office; it was as if I'd been at the epicentre of an earthquake. I found a bench nearby and collapsed in a heap. Could Mother have written to say she was thinking of me? She wasn't the affectionate type. Whenever I tried to hug her, she would recoil like a cobra about to strike. I doubted she'd tell me about her poor health either. She could be on her deathbed and still say to everyone, 'I'm alright.' Her courage in coping with adversity was admirable.

I hesitated before opening the letter. Then, with the theatrical move it deserved, I delved inside, ready to surrender to whatever fate lay in store.

At first glance, the content wasn't what I expected. My mother had sent me a greeting card with a pink rose (*Maman* was called Rosa), which read, *'Herzlichen Grüssen, deine Mama.'* 'Best Wishes, Mama.' It felt strange that she had used German. (She always spoke French to us.) With the card was an envelope. I immediately recognised Peter's handwriting.

I unfolded the letter and saw HELP written across the first page. Was he sending me a MAYDAY? I read on, excited and perplexed.

Peter wasn't a man who expressed his feelings with ease. I would often quiz him about how he felt about me. 'I'm passionately fond of you,' he'd say. It was frustrating. This time, however, his words were passionate, especially those that remained unsaid.

'Here's a happy soul,' Amandine noted when I returned to *Aubade*. She was sitting in the cockpit with a book. She couldn't have missed that glow on my face and the letter I was clutching in my hand. Keen to disguise my emotions, I pointed at the novel she was holding. 'Proust can be hard to read,' I remarked. 'Poor man, he spent most of his life in bed, writing.'

'But what a genius. Now tell me about your news. You look like your happiness barometer has shot right off the scale.'

'My boyfriend has written, begging me to return to him.'

'Ah, the man you said left you in Cannes. Surely, you aren't running back to him as soon as he asks you to?'

'I should let him linger. I know he took his time to declare his love.'

'Don't make it easy. Let him yearn for you.'

Amandine was right. I could enjoy a few more months sunning myself in paradise while remaining aboard *Aubade* until the crew sailed her back to France. But if Peter had received my letter before he wrote to me, he might have concluded that I was through with him. Maman must have sensed she held my future in her hands when she forwarded his letter to the Caribbean.

I only have vague memories of my early childhood, crawling under the table, picking up strands of wool as *maman* beavered away at her knitting machine, making baby clothes for a boutique in the village. Sometimes, a tall man with jet-black hair came to visit us. Once, he brought me a cuddly toy as a present. I kept the small bunny for years because I felt sorry for it, looking so sad. Sometime later, I learned from our neighbour, Madame Heineichen, that she cared for me when I was a baby. My sister Micheline, who was five years older, and Nicole, who was three, looked after me, too. One day, noticing my nappies were wet, Nicole decided to hold me on top of the wood-burning stove to dry them, and when I cried because I started to burn, Micheline, on hearing me, rushed to my rescue.

Nicole was amused when she related the event to me years later. However, I never forgot sitting on the spare bed in our playroom, asking her why our mother wasn't home. 'She works long hours at the hotel and can't be with us,' she explained. I felt a pang in my heart and a deep sense of abandonment.

Our mother's past seemed as shrouded in mystery as her dark-tinted glasses. Behind them, one couldn't see the colour of her eyes. The world must have looked dark and grey to her. One day, as I went into my parents' bedroom to fetch something from one of the drawers, I came across a small silver box hidden under a neat pile of starched hankies. I knew prying was naughty, but I couldn't help myself. I needed to find out what was inside. I struggled to open the box and winced when I caught my tiny fingernails under the clasp to release the lid. I unfolded the silky pink cotton wool and gasped at what I saw. What was an eye doing there, and who did it belong to? Worse still, it stared at me without blinking as if wanting to scold me for breaking a secret. I quickly covered it, shut the lid, replaced the box under the hankies, and ran out of the room as if I had been bewitched.

Yet, despite my fright, I returned to my parents' bedroom the following day to take a closer look. I opened the box again and removed the soft pink cotton wool, though this time, I hovered over the eye with my finger and touched it, expecting a soft, wet, slimy texture. Surprisingly, the surface under my fingertip felt smooth and cold, like marble. I half-expected the eye to wink at me. It was all too strange for a naive eight-year-old to comprehend. Therefore, the mystery of the eye remained unsolved for some time.

Years later, I learned Maman had lost her right eye when she was nine years old because of an infection, which didn't get treated in time. I wondered if she blamed her parents for their negligence. She would often say how much more she could have done with her life if this had never happened. My father told me he never knew Mother wore a glass eye until after they were married. I wondered what hurt him the most. Was it that his wife didn't tell him or that he never noticed it in the first place? There was something else which bothered him. He would have to look after our mother if she lost her sight.

I snapped out of that episode and reminded myself that it belonged to the past in 'picture postcard' Switzerland. I was now in the tropics on a yacht, lulled by the gentle motion of the Caribbean Sea, and there was Peter in England, promising me love, devotion, and a life of adventure roaming the seas.

I couldn't wait.

Over breakfast the following day, I told Amandine I would call Peter. I knew leaving this paradise for the freezing north of England in February was a crazy idea, and what if we no longer felt the same for each other?

My hands were shaking when I dialled his number from a telephone box. I could hear my heart beating like a drum summoning the advance on a battlefield. Would Peter be home? England was six hours ahead. I heard the ringtone and the payphone swallowing the coins; it was like playing a 'one-arm bandit,' hoping my jackpot would be him at the other end of the line.

'Bonjour, it's Monique,' I said. 'I received your letter.'

'I got yours, too. Our letters must have crossed. Are you about to tell me to take a long walk off a short pier, or should I send you the money for your flight?'

I giggled, then replied, 'You're straight to the point, so I shall be too. You don't need to send me money. I'll look into the flight situation and let you know. Is there a train from London to Scarborough?'

'Yes, you'll need to get to Kings Cross railway station and take a train to York. Call me before you leave, and I'll meet you on the platform. I can't wait to see you.'

The beeps went. My Jungfrau mountain of coins had vanished, leaving us no chance for romantic words. Peter's letter had travelled from red pillow boxes to snow-capped mountains, then to the land of palm trees, where it found me. What serendipity. Arlette would never know!

Three weeks later, I said my goodbyes, hugged the warm-loving Amandine, the sad Yvonne and the seductive skipper Christophe and wished them fair winds back to France. What a pity I would miss Marc's return from Paris by a day. I bid farewell to the floating carriage that had whisked me to the Caribbean - Peter had found Cinderella's slipper - in my case, it was a 'yellow wellie.'

The Boeing 747 was ready to take off, bound for London Heathrow Airport. I was grateful to be sitting alone by the window. Nobody would notice my agitation. I was leaving the beautiful island of Martinique for the freezing North Yorkshire Coast to run into the arms of a man I hadn't seen in months. Would my romantic vision of Peter be shattered when we met again? And how would it be for him? Was he clutching at the illusion of love in his time of need?

The aeroplane's speed increased on the runway, and as it continued its race across the tarmac, I suddenly heard the engines going into reverse thrust and the Boeing slowing down. Were the princess's coach wheels about to fall off on her way to the ball?

Next came the radio announcement:

'Ladies and Gentlemen, due to a technical problem, we are returning to the terminal. Passengers will be accompanied to a departure lounge awaiting further information. We apologise for the inconvenience caused and assure you that we'll do our utmost to minimise further delay.'

Were the powers above trying to warn me by aborting my departure? All passengers disembarked and headed for the terminal building. An hour went by, and we waited packed inside a stuffy hall. Tempers began to fray like an ill wind. By then, everyone had consumed several free soft drinks and started to demand answers. It was another half an hour before the final announcement came.

Ladies and gentlemen, we would like to inform you that a bus is waiting outside the terminal to take you to a hotel for the night. The airline will cover all expenses. In addition, each passenger will receive a complimentary voucher for their evening meal and breakfast. You are now requested to collect your luggage at baggage reclaim number 5. The flight departure is scheduled for tomorrow at the same time. Again, we are sorry for the technical problems experienced, and on behalf of Caribbean Airways, we wish our passengers an excellent stay at Hotel Valménière.

Fate was holding me in Martinique. I thought of the song *I Was Born Under a Wanderin' Star,* which I sang silently while camping under the stars in Los Cristianos. It seemed a long time since I had set off to sail across an ocean to the Caribbean. I settled in a deckchair outside my five-star hotel room, watching the palm trees swaying in the breeze. I thought of my family. Both my sisters were now married with two daughters each. I didn't envy their lives, even though mine was rocky and unpredictable. Micheline strongly disapproved of my lifestyle. Being the better-educated one in the family, she thought I was wasting my potential. 'Look at Grandfather,' she once remarked, 'he never had a fixed abode, touring around Switzerland on his bicycle, repairing clocks and watches.' Although Micheline had married a top executive working for a large corporation, I suspected she wasn't entirely happy.

I thought of Nicole and pictured myself sitting on a swing as she threw me a ball, shouting, 'Catch.' I was too little to appreciate that I could fall if I let go of the ropes, but I wanted to impress her by catching the ball. I landed right on my stomach on the swing's steel frame. It hurt so much I could hardly breathe. Maybe Nicole believed I had a talent for juggling. She warned me, 'Don't tell Father about it. If you do, I'll make you pay for it later,'

There were times I denounced her to Papa. It was my only means of defence. Years later, Nicole admitted her cruelty towards me. 'I can't believe what I did to you,' she would say, laughing it off. Sadly, she never stopped tormenting me. When I took umbrage, she would retort, 'I'm only joking.' To her, I was too dainty and needed toughening up. She was probably right.

Papa had favoured me over my sisters, maybe because I was the youngest. Micheline was quiet and timid, unlike Nicole, who was a tomboy. One night, she returned home late after playing football with the boys. Father was furious. He started to slap Nicole's bottom with his leather belt. Micheline and I screamed, 'Papa *arrête - stop.*' Our bedroom, with posters of kittens on the walls, frilly blue satin bedspreads and teddy bears sitting on pillows holding vigil, was suddenly a scene of violence perpetrated against one of its innocent occupants.

Our father's fury was terrifying. Nicole begged him to stop. It seemed all pleas only intensified the lashes. Finally, he let go, looped his belt back around his trousers, and stomped out of the room, leaving us stunned. He had never lifted a hand on us before but shamefully lost control that night. It was inconceivable. Maybe the years of poor treatment he underwent at the Catholic orphanage, his own father's abandonment, and his wife's betrayal took their toll, and Nicole sadly had to bear the brunt. So, she chastised me to release her anger from being the sacrificial lamb for our father's frustrations? Being three and a half years older, she must have resented looking after me while *Maman* worked at the Hotel du Lac. It wasn't cool for a tomboy to bring her little sister to mingle with older boys. Whenever they played 'hide and seek,' Nicole deliberately forgot to look for me. I would run after them, feeling rejected and helpless when I realised their wicked game. Nicole shouldn't have been responsible for me at such a young age.

Our parents even put her in charge of the tin cauldron used on the gas stove, where all our white garments were boiled and washed weekly. I received strict instructions to keep away. The cauldron was big enough to sit in if I drew my knees to my chin - not that I had any such intention. Surely Nicole wouldn't put me in it during bath time? When she lifted the lid off, I imagined a genie rising from the steam, ready to grant me three wishes. Mine would be to learn to play the guitar, not to dry dishes again, and certainly not to clean cupboards on our day off from school.

Washing those whites involved the use of long wooden tongs. Nicole would lift our father's vests to check for any remaining stains. Each one looked like a wet bandage for an elephant with a broken trunk. I enjoyed watching the bubbles reflecting the colours of the rainbow as they cascaded over the rim, making the flames dance and then splutter before blowing out, leaving the kitchen smelling like rotting eggs. I often reminded Nicole not to turn the gas too high like Maman had warned her. 'I'll put you on the wood stove as I did once to dry your nappies,' she countered. 'And this time, no one will lift you off when you cry!'

'Does Mother know about what you did to me when I was a baby?'

She didn't respond.

'Next time I'm at confession,' I declared, 'I'll tell the priest to speak to God and suggest he might want to turn the gas up when he washes his white robes. Then, with the cauldron boiling over, the bubbles will put the fires out in hell, and there'll be no more horrible people in the world, and that includes you.'

'The devil might throw little children like you in the fire to keep it alight,' Nicole replied. 'God doesn't wash his robes; the Angels do it for Him, you stupid girl!' She had that look which said, 'Don't push me.' Nicole was like a box of firecrackers; she only needed to hear one wrong word to ignite the fuse.

There came a day when the gas was far too high, and the steam pushed the cauldron lid off. Nicole was standing close by and burnt herself. She ran around the kitchen frantically, holding her face. I asked her what was wrong, and she shouted, 'Leave me alone.'

I rushed down the stairs to the bakery where my Godmother, Odette, worked. By then, the postman had completed his rounds and had his habitual croissant and coffee in the back room. Hearing of Nicole's accident, he offered to take her on his moped to the doctor's surgery in the next village.

My sister returned home with her face covered in bandages. All I could see were two eyes staring ahead. It was unnerving. She looked like a soldier wounded on a battlefield. Despite her ordeal, she acted like it was just one of those things and boasted about her ride on the moped with the postman. It was a miracle that she was spared being scarred for life.

I tossed about through the night, unable to sleep despite the luxurious bed of the Valménière Hotel. I was at a pivotal point, aged twenty-nine, about to fly into the arms of a man whose burning ambition was to sail across oceans in pursuit of contentment. A palmist once said, 'You're not meant to be happy in this life.' My reaction to such a damning prediction was to burst into laughter, and I couldn't stop, determined to prove her wrong.

The following day, all the passengers clapped enthusiastically when we heard the hydraulics retracting the undercarriage and the aeroplane gaining height. I thought of one of Edith Piaf's songs I enjoy singing, *Sans Amour On est Rien du Tout - Without Love, We are Nothing*. Peter spoke of a lifestyle chancing providence on the high seas. Would our aims clash with my pursuit of success in the music business? Somebody said, 'Shangri-La' isn't a destination but a journey.' Was I strong enough for the challenge?

7. Scarborough Fayre

We stood on St Oliver's Mount, looking at the town below. From high up in the distance, the illuminated St Mary's church (the resting place of one of the Brontë sisters) took centre stage. Above it, the thirteenth-century castle appeared to be holding vigil over the sea, while the old town dwellings looked as if they clung desperately to the sloping ramparts. Perched on the central pier was the lighthouse reflecting its guiding light over the water. I prayed, 'May Lord Neptune grant the skipper and his *Edelweiss* safe passage across the oceans.'

I heard Peter whispering in my ear, 'Let's go. You don't want to catch a cold.' He kissed me tenderly, took my hand and led me back to the car. Then we drove off.

On our way back down, we rounded several hairpin bends through the wooded area. Peter explained that he had competed on these roads during his racing days.

'Have you won many trophies?' I asked as I sank deeper into the comfortable leather seat of the old Jaguar.

'A few when I was younger,' but not all for motor racing,' he replied, chuckling.

'Now, it's all coming out,' I said sarcastically.

When we reached the seafront, we passed the iconic Victorian Grand Hotel with its ornate façades, the fishing harbour and the Marine Drive. Finally, we stopped outside the last row of terraced houses, which marked the end of a long road. Peter had explained we would be staying at his mother's house while she was in Australia, visiting her daughter Eileen. I once met her at his sister's home in Winchester before she moved abroad. I remembered a tall woman with curly grey hair wearing a tailored jacket and skirt. I felt she still carried the demeanour of the landlady she once was.

Meeting Peter on the train platform felt like a fairytale until we entered his mother's house. The woman had cast such a dark shadow on my love for her son, yet she had redeemed herself by letting us live in her home. I looked at the yellowy-brown carpet in the lounge, the oversized sofa, and the armchairs, which appeared to be stifling the space, and I thought, who was I to pass judgment on somebody's interior? Peter made tea, and we sat on the floor awkwardly like two teenagers on a first date. So much water had floated under our keels since we parted. He was the first to break the silence.

'What happened aboard the ship Kovalam after you joined the crew in the Côte d'Azur?'

'It wasn't much fun working on the ship,' I said. 'The French owners had a rather colonial attitude towards the crew, but the husband had gentle manners, given he was an arms dealer. However, his platinum-blonde wife was vain and contemptuous. She treated their poodle like a golden child. She never made eye contact with me. She must have thought talking to the cook was beneath her. During our stay in the Balearics, she told the Polish-born captain to convey a message to me: "Tell your exuberant cook to keep her distance when we take a swim over the side." The woman couldn't bear the idea of sharing the sea with a mere mortal like me. Maybe she was afraid I might contaminate her?

The crew, the captain, the engineer, two deckhands, the stewardess, and I outnumbered the owners and their guests. The captain was in his mid-fifties and looked weather-beaten. He never showed me mercy, seeing me beavering away in the kitchen with little help from the petite Spanish stewardess Conchita, who spent more time 'in the horizontal' with the athletic Canadian engineer than doing any work. She told me they were trying for a baby. When the owners left, they didn't even say goodbye, and I felt the full impact of their total disregard for the crew. Something in me died that day.

Thankfully, Tangiers was the highlight of our cruise after the Balearics. It was where the owners left *Kovalam*.

Then, we had an Egyptian family chartering the yacht. They came with their male secretary and governess. I couldn't have managed without her help in the kitchen. She showed me the best way to cook fish and seafood to her employers' taste and how to stir their coffee to create the perfect foam. The family were wonderful to me, and it wasn't just because they enjoyed my singing.

'We finished our cruise in Malta. Luckily, the captain didn't keep all my wages. The engineer once hinted he suspected him of embezzling money due to us.'

'Now, I understand why the chef you replaced left the yacht,' Peter remarked. 'He wouldn't have gone along with having to cook and wash the dishes.'

My mind flashed back to the gin palace *Jesty,* where Peter and I had worked as crew before I joined the *Kovalam.* 'Do you remember that fatal day on the Île Sainte-Marguerite?' I asked. 'We could have been crushed to death when the cradle collapsed and the boat rolled over.'

'I wonder what happened to the superyacht after we left,' Peter resumed. 'Did they ever find a crane big enough to lift her from the beach? Maybe it was a total write-off. I guess we'll never know.'

We woke up early. I drew the curtains, looked out the window, and saw the Yorkshire sky ready to tumble onto the row of terraced houses opposite. I thought of one of Jacques Brel's songs, *Le Plat Pays Qui est le mien*, in which he talks about the Belgian skies being so moody that a canal hung itself in despair.

After breakfast, we drove to the foreshore, where we saw children and adults skipping in a row over long fishermen's ropes that stretched the entire road width with line swingers at either end. They were re-enacting an old custom: *Shrove Tuesday* - Pancake Day. Traffic would be halted until somebody tripped, and the rope was laid on the ground. Only then would cars be allowed to move on, as far as the next group, who would try to keep the drivers waiting as long as they could before they were too tired to continue skipping. If motorists were foolish enough to go along the promenade that day, they would run the full gauntlet from Blands Cliff to the beginning of Eastborough, a stretch of one hundred and seventy-four yards. Although I shared the people's excitement, mine was one of anticipation.

Burniston was only a few miles north of Scarborough. En route, Peter forewarned me from expecting *Capricorn* ready to be launched.

What a massive understatement! At first glance, the structure looked like the most oversized boat-shaped colander I had ever seen. Our 'yacht-to-be' (a rusty skeleton of a boat hanging from a building frame) stood in a paddock, flanked by a dairy farm with the moors stretching beyond. *Capricorn* wasn't at all what I had imagined her to be. Peter noticed my dismay and chirped, 'I can hear the tide gurgling around the hull.'

I didn't know what to think and couldn't imagine *Capricorn* ferrying us across the Atlantic Ocean to America. Looking at her, I felt it would be years before we set sail. How was I going to fit into this mammoth project? Had I made a terrible mistake? I remembered the woman in Martinique who was perplexed as to why I was leaving a luxurious yacht to go and help someone build his own in the depths of the English winter. Admittedly, I had nurtured the most unrealistic vision of boat-building while sipping my tropical cocktail aboard *Aubade* under a hot Caribbean sun. For a moment, I thought, 'Why don't I fly back to Martinique and resume my adventure there? However, I believed destiny had thrust Peter and me together, drawn by the same desire for freedom, favouring the luxury of boundless time over security and money in the bank. I knew whatever lay ahead would be tough. Did I have the strength and willpower to share such an endeavour? The bitter cold February morning glared at me ruthlessly, and I adjusted the collar of my jacket in defiance.

8. Brogues and Brown Hen

Looking at *Capricorn's* rusty shell, I wondered how I could help. I wasn't used to manual work. Maybe I should have thought of it earlier. Peter must have noticed my concern when he took my hand and led me to his workshop in one of the outbuildings. He put the kettle on and unfolded *Capricorn's* plans on his workbench. The yacht seemed impressive on paper, but her specification in feet meant little to me. I grew up using metric measures. Still, I noted:

Overall length 33 foot
Beam 12 foot
Waterline length 27 foot
Draft 4"7' foot
Mast 50 foot

Capricorn was a steel adaptation of Joshua Slocum's *Spray*. Being the first yachtsman to circumnavigate the world single-handedly at the turn of the nineteenth century, Slocum, in his book, claimed he never touched the tiller during his three-thousand-mile passage across the Pacific. As he lay on his bunk, sick and unable to move, the ghost of the navigator on the '*Pintar*', who reputably accompanied Christopher Columbus aboard the *Santa Maria*, suddenly appeared to him. Slocum believed the ghost steered his boat until he was well enough to regain command. His story has seduced hundreds of amateur boatbuilders worldwide, and many are still building the *spray* design today, showing as much individuality in their construction. Peter, for one, was so inspired by Slocum's adventures that he dismissed the French design he had initially chosen to build *Capricorn*.

Alex and his wife Audrey owned the land where the boat stood. They lived in a cottage close by and had agreed for us to put a caravan on their grounds until we finished building our boat. Luckily, it overlooked open fields. It had a lounge and kitchen, all in one. The bedroom was small but accommodated a double bed and wardrobe. Peter fitted a shower in our storage area, and there was an outside toilet nearby. (I could see the need for a potty under the bed.) We transformed the interior with new upholstery, matching curtains and some varnish on the wood. It was 'home sweet home' to me once I ignored my inner voice hammering the words: 'How can you sink so low, living in a caravan!' I was amused when a BT engineer came to install our landline. He had such a puzzled look on his face. Maybe he never fitted one in these places before.

Marie-Allen, Audrey's pet hen, roamed around the paddock, carefree. She had escaped from Audrey's cousin's farm. They had wanted to wring her neck and feed her to the guard dogs because she no longer laid eggs. Then fate brought tragedy when the cousin's son was crushed under a combine harvester. After his death, the family decided to sell up. The dogs went to new homes while Marie-Allen remained alone on the deserted farm until Audrey took her under her wing.

The brown-feathered hen followed me everywhere, clucking loudly by my side, which made me giggle like a schoolgirl. She trundled down to the village shop with me and waited outside, pecking at worms on the grass verge. Strangely for a hen, she loved chocolate and knew when she was in for a treat. She had a penchant for other things, too. One day, the barnyard cat dropped a field mouse in the grass in front of Alex and his black Labrador, who were taking a walk. Whilst the tabby cat calmly sat on his haunches with his eyes riveted on the mouse, waiting for it to run away, Marie-Allen, who must have been observing the scene, suddenly arched her wings, propelled herself towards it, and pounced on it. The cat, the dog, Alex, and I watched Marie-Allen in astonishment, strutting away with the creature dangling from her beak. Then, as she gained some distance from us, she stopped, tilted her head back, opened her gullet wide, and swallowed the mouse whole. Marie-Allen was, without a doubt, a hen with attitude.

Sometime later, as an April Fool's joke, Alex and Audrey's son Brian cheekily placed a goose egg in the nesting box of their other chickens. His parents pretended not to notice the size of the egg and left it for one of the hens to sit on. Surprisingly, it hatched into a fluffy gosling, which became Audrey's favourite pet. She left her protégé to roam free.

Of course, this little bundle of joy soon grew into a sizeable bird and ran into the field, head down, flapping its wings and screeching like a banshee to defend its territory. It was hard to imagine the once cute little gosling becoming so aggressive. When Peter told Alex about it chasing us, he let it wander in the adjacent field. Audrey didn't object. The goose had already pecked her when she shooed it away from her vegetable garden.

A few days later, while standing on *Capricorn's* deck with a bird's eye view over the field, Peter noticed the goose had vanished. Alex was relieved; each time he took the dog for a walk up the paddock, the bird would attack them both. Maybe a fox snatched it?

Unlike the territorial goose, I shied away from Audrey as I believed she barely tolerated our presence. She once shouted at me when she heard me playing a classical tune on my guitar. Perhaps she thought I'd better help Peter finish the yacht than serenade him. Furthermore, the boat was spoiling her view over the field. Unlike her, Alex enjoyed seeing an ambitious project in his backyard. Both Alex and Peter shared similar skills and admiration for each other. Alex also did joinery work on the bungalow Peter built while he was still married to his first wife, Elisabeth.

In August, my father came to visit us. I had booked one of Audrey's B & B rooms for him to stay. Poor Papa was shocked when he saw the caravan and the rusty structure of a boat in the field. But that wasn't all. He had this thing about relationships outside one's nationality. He once told my sisters and me, 'If you bring an Italian boyfriend home, I'll push him down the stairs.' He resented the many Italians working in Switzerland in the late 1960s. Nicole helped soften Father's attitude when she introduced her French boyfriend to him. Papa thought he was too loud. My eldest sister Micheline married a Swiss German, but he couldn't hold that against her, given Mother was Swiss German too. However, it didn't stop him saying, 'They have square heads.' Then, when I brought Peter home, he declared the English were a strange breed and mean at tipping. He must have heard it from Mother when she was working at the local hotel. Papa admired *Churchill,* though. Was it because he smoked big cigars like him?

I was enjoying my life, although I had never anticipated that space would become such a luxury. *Alice in*

Wonderland drank the potion to shrink her size so she could follow the white rabbit. For Peter and me, the elixir was a mindset. Adapting to a space no bigger than a minibus was the price we were prepared to pay for our epic adventure ahead. I felt Switzerland never allowed me wide horizons because mountains always got in the way of the bigger picture. I had walked on glaciers and scaled rocky outcrops, but I loved the sea above all.

I owed the experience of mountaineering to 'pock-mark faced' Monsieur Despland, who took his sons and me on expeditions when I was a teenager. (I had no idea of the liaison between my mother and him then.) Ironically, I developed a crush on his younger son François, who had sparkling blue eyes and big lips like Mick Jagger. François was nine years older than me. It was all very innocent. We only ever kissed on the cheek once or twice, but the earth moved each time. My sister Micheline had a brief affair with the elder son, Pierre-Yves. He was handsome and knew it. I thought novelist Emile Zola would have had a field day with our family's intrigues.

Yet, unbeknown to me, tragedy was unfolding in our household. Papa was forty when he developed sciatica and was forced to give up most of his vineyards. He was so worried he wouldn't get another job to support the family and remembered him saying, 'I'm good for nothing.' One day, Papa went to the attic, where he stored wood for our open fire. He also kept his rifle and ammunition up there, ready for immediate mobilisation as an army reservist. Nicole must have thought it strange that he would spend such a long time in the attic and wondered if he had a *malaise*?' So, she rushed up the stairs to go and check on him.

When she opened the door, she saw Papa with the barrel of his rifle under his chin and his finger on the trigger. She screamed in horror, 'Please don't do this.' Her plea stopped him just in time. It would have been too late if it had been another second or two.

Papa dropped the rifle, and Nicole flung her arms around him. He sobbed like a little boy. For a man who could only tickle our ears to show his affection, the barrage of emotions must have proven too much to contain. How desperate he must have been when he loaded his army rifle, ready to take his own life.

Nicole kept it all to herself for some time. She only revealed it to me during one of my visits home. Maybe she needed to unburden herself. How would I ever come to terms with my father's attempted suicide? I loved him more than he would ever know. I often found excuses not to go out with my friends because I didn't want him to be alone at home. Mother was always out working. I thought of the guitar he bought me as a present. How could he have known that his gift would pave the way for me to become a singer-songwriter?

Papa partly rebuilt his life when he found work at a plastic components factory and made his way up to becoming a foreman. It must have felt like a prison sentence for a man who loved working outside. Luckily, he still owned a small vineyard and an allotment. He buried himself in work to escape his unhappiness. Yet, he had interrupted everything to come and visit me in Yorkshire. Mother didn't like flying. I doubted she would have come anyway.

Everything about England was bizarre to Papa. 'Why do they drive on the wrong side of the road and drink warm beer?' he would remark. From his Swiss perspective, he saw Scarborough as an impoverished town. I wondered what he would have made of Middlesborough and other industrial English cities. I defended my newly adopted country with enthusiasm. I thought about how much I preferred *Fawlty Towers,* England, to a homogenised, sterilised country where everything ran to the tick-tock of the cuckoo clock. My father's world was picture postcard Switzerland with geraniums in window boxes, immaculate streets with no dustbins in view, vineyards, mountains and lakes. Therefore, Scarborough's magnificent north and south bays, its Norman castle, the beautiful Victorian Spa ballroom and the outdoor concert place where violinist Max Jaffa played with his three-piece quartet every summer season failed to impress him. He commented about people's shabby shoes and clothes. Papa only wore quality clothes and brogues bought in specialised shops. The working class in Switzerland enjoyed a good standard of living in the 1980s. Maybe he couldn't understand why I had left my home country.

During his stay, Papa heard me sing in two of my hotel venues, and although he may have been proud of me, he still said, 'They are *oldies* you're singing to,' as if it didn't count. When I appeared live on television for the Swiss entry to the Eurovision Song Contest in 1983. I asked him what he thought of my performance. He said he forgot about it that day and was watching football. Sometimes, his indifference worked to my advantage, especially when I asked him to sign letters I wrote on his behalf, excusing myself from attending school. I always chose a moment when he was engrossed in a match on television. and would point to where he needed to sign. He never read the content beforehand.

Surprisingly, for such a dispassionate man, Papa loved ballroom dancing. The Viennese waltz was his favourite. How proud he was to dance with me at the Grand Hotel in Scarborough. A Country and Western group was playing that night. Over a snooker game in a pub the following day, he asked me if Peter and I were considering starting a family. I wanted to say, '*Capricorn* is our baby, born from molten metal poured out of a crucible and flattened with rollers at the steel foundry.' But what was the use? Boats and water were alien to Papa. He could better relate to the quality of his wine or which football team he hoped would win. When I offered him a glass of our home-brewed parsley wine, which had the colour of ginger ale, he must have thought, by the look on his face, that we were about to poison him. When he took a sip, he spluttered, 'It's like lemonade.' Our forthcoming adventure was just as unreal to him as making wine without grapes. No doubt, he must have lamented about the loss of *Swiss* etiquette when I served wine in odd glasses, and to crown it all, I was speaking a language he didn't understand.

We drove Papa to Manchester airport a few days later. He wore a tweed cap over brushed back, jet black hair, a checkered shirt that stretched its buttons and a sports jacket with epaulettes on the shoulders. I kissed him goodbye, thinking how much I loved him despite everything. He had been a boy brought up in a nun's orphanage. To him, God had died that night in the darkness of a cold dormitory, grieving his mother's passing and his father's abandonment. Would he come to England again for *Capricorn's* launch? I could read the loneliness in his eyes, which felt like a stabbing pain in my heart.

I watched him disappear into the departure hall. I knew I had alienated Papa by adopting a new country and another culture. Still, there was no turning back. I had left my Swiss mountains for the sea, stepping into Peter's dream of sailing across the Atlantic to America, where I hoped to fulfil my deepest aspirations. While I was flotsam on an ocean of ambitions as a singer-songwriter, my love for Peter pulled me like the moon on the tide. I thought of the words in one of Gladys Knight and the Pips' songs, 'I'd rather live in his world than live without him in mine.'

9. Iron Ships and Wooden Men

'Bloody Hell, *Iron Ships and Wooden Men*,' the driver exclaimed as he jumped out of his cab. The tattooed Schwarzenegger of a man with unruly hair in a ponytail, jean shorts and high-laced leather boots had delivered the repartee like a ham actor. Peter and I looked at each other, amused. The man had played with the quote, *Wooden Ships and Iron Men,* from Nelson's days, showing his knowledge of history.

'I never expected to see this thing at 41A Burniston Road,' the driver remarked, nodding at our rusty skeleton of a boat. 'Where do you want these, *Admiral*? And do you have a forklift truck?'

'No, sorry!' Peter replied awkwardly. 'But, can we slide the steel sheets off, one at a time?'

'If you're up to it.'

I thought it was madness for two men without a forklift to unload six heavy steel plates off the lorry bed. It was a task fit for champion weightlifters, but they were ready to test their metal. With leather gauntlets reaching their elbows, the pair began to slide the 5' x 10' sheets off the truck, each hitting the ground like the blade of a guillotine. If either of the men were to lose concentration, they could have their toes chopped off. Tirelessly, they laboured until the last sheet of steel was unloaded.

'Is this thing going to float?' *Schwarzenegger* asked while soaking up the sweat on his forehead with his forearm.

'Are you launching this lump in Peasholm Boating Lake? That's something I want to see. When is it happening?'

'June,' Peter replied, 'but I'm not telling you which June!'

The driver chuckled.

Peter was used to being ridiculed. Most people thought the boat would never see the sea. The man's attention suddenly shifted to me. I must have looked a sight in overalls and yellow wellies, with a rag wrapped around my head. Had my attire been khaki-coloured, someone could have mistaken me for a wounded soldier from the trenches repairing a tank; only mine was dismantling the old Perkins engine, cleaning each part like someone scouring a neglected toilet.

'Sorry, miss, I took you for an enslaved cabin boy,' the man said, staring at me intently. 'If I were you, I'd be a mutineer and cast your tyrant adrift like Captain Bligh!'

I nodded, although I didn't fully understand the gist of his comment. The driver was about to leave and despite his sarcasm, Admiral Peter gave him a generous tip to buy a bottle of rum in compensation for the lack of a forklift truck.

So, how did Peter start building his steel sailing boat, and what tools did he need? From his shopping list, he bought two oxygen-acetylene bottles plus a cutting torch, a welding plant, chains, block and tackle, large steel plates, a set of plans, and, last and foremost, a big sledgehammer. His mighty capacity to work long hours was taking care of the rest. And there was me, ready to support him whenever I could. So, each time he struck an arc with his rods, I coated the bare steel on the inside hull with anti-rust paint. Then, after I had finished an area, I returned to the caravan and rehearsed for my evening concerts. I was like Cinderella doing her chores before going to the ball.

After Peter had welded the final piece of steel plate in position to form the hull, shot-blasting came next. It was torture to hear the diesel-driven compressor roaring, followed by what sounded like thousands of bullets hitting the steel hull. The shattered grit formed a black cloud that engulfed the site and the adjacent buildings. Then, when the contractor removed his leather suit of armour and 'diving bell' helmet, linked to a pipe that delivered air, his face dripped with rivulets of sweat and grimy dust.

What a way to earn a living!

Peter and I had often wondered what neighbours in the nearby bungalows made of our cottage industry boatyard. We figured out that afternoon when a man yelled from behind the tall bushes. 'Look at my sodding cap. It was white when I came out to cut the grass. Now it's black like *bloody* coal.'

When Peter approached the hedge to check who had been shouting, he saw, through a gap in the foliage, an elderly man doing a kind of war dance while pointing towards his bungalow. 'My window sills are covered as well,' he remarked, red-faced.

Peter apologised and promised to clean his windows, frames, and sills within the hour. He even offered to wash his cap. The man didn't respond. He stomped off, threw his cap on the grass, and slammed the back door behind him.

Armed with a bucket of soapy water, a squeegee and chamois leather, Peter swapped his boatbuilding hat for that of a window cleaner. There were four bungalows in a row covered with black dust. Peter first cleaned the white-capped man's windows and sills, then refilled his bucket before knocking on the neighbouring property. A sweet old lady appeared at the doorway, looking puzzled. Peter apologised for the noise caused by the shot-blasting and pointed to her blackened window sills, which he had come to clean. 'I've already got a window cleaner,' the woman said but thanked him before shutting the door. He did them anyway.

A blonde woman holding a baby appeared on the threshold of the next bungalow. Peter explained why he rang the bell. 'You don't need to clean my windows,' she declared but offered him a cup of tea as he set to.

No one was home in the last bungalow, but that didn't stop Peter from fulfilling his good deed. And as if that wasn't enough, we had several tons of spent blasting grit piled beneath our boat. Meanwhile, another contractor was standing by to spray paint on *Capricorn*'s hull and decks before the evening dew could cause flash rust on the gleaming silver hull.

Besides boat-building, I continued pursuing my musical career. Singing in the Northern clubs was like being in a den of hungry wolves ready to tear their prey apart. Before the performance, there was no time to practise with the resident keyboard player or drummer. One evening, I asked the female organist if she wanted my 'dots.' She replied, 'No love, I can't read music, just start, and I'll join in.' Luckily, she was formidable and anticipated everything I played on the guitar. Audiences expected the same level of professionalism as on television shows. There was no place either to show fear on those stages, or the audience would devour the performer alive,

Live music took place between bingo sessions. On one occasion, I was in full flow when my microphone suddenly died on me, and before I could investigate the problem, the concert secretary was announcing through the house PA system that the pies had arrived. Then, he switched my microphone back on, and I resumed my rendition of 'Don't Cry for Me Argentina.'

In another club, the concert secretary said pointedly, 'You know, we once paid Tom Jones off after his first spot.'

It must have happened before he became famous. Was this night's performance an omen for my career?

'This place is nicknamed the graveyard club,' he declared proudly.

'Is this because you are so tough that entertainers die on stage?' I said, with 'tongue in check.'

'No, our club is next to the graveyard.'

The audience that evening must have risen from their graves, determined to make the most of my performance. As we left that evening, the concert secretary said, *'Ee lass, thee can come back anytime thy wants.'*

I received sound advice from a comedian while sharing a dressing room one evening. Commenting on his performance, I expressed my surprise at how insulting he was to his audience. Yet people were on the edge of their seats laughing. 'They lap it up,' he said. 'If your spot is dragging because people are not listening to you, try my technique; just tell them off. You'll be amazed how they'll behave after that!'

Singing in hotels was a welcome respite from the trenches of the northern workingmen's clubs. Having to wear an invisible armour to face audiences was weighing me down. Even David would have found it hard to confront one Goliath after another. Therefore, I needed a shield to protect myself against the slings and arrows of outrageous audiences.

Another contribution to financing Peter's and my dreams was to teach French. The pupils I taught individually were studying for their O'Levels. One of them was an ambitious ballerina who never did her homework. Even though I tailored my lessons to suit the language of ballet, she was more interested in which coloured varnish to apply to her beautifully manicured nails. Then, a smartly dressed businessman came for a lesson. He took his suit jacket off and loosened his tie. Before he went any further, I asked him if he spoke much French. We got through the lesson; he paid me, but I never saw him again. Later, I rephrased my advertisement in the local newspaper from *'French Lessons Available' to 'French Tuition, Children Welcome.'*

Even though Peter had various well-paid contract work as an engineer, the boat-building kitty kept disappearing like water down the plughole. Regrettably, the plug of reason had long come off the chain. If *Capricorn* were to meet the tide at Scarborough Harbour in June, we would have to sail out of the 'money doldrums.'

One day, out of the blue, a company offered Peter a short contract in Egypt. He went for his yellow fever vaccination, but the work offer fell through at the last minute. That was when I decided to contact my school friend Françoise. We grew up in the same village of Boudry. Françoise had left home to move to Geneva to pursue her dream of owning a nightclub. When I telephoned her and explained I was looking for work, she offered me a job singing in her club.

For Peter, *Capricorn* was the mission while I was the Lady Hamilton, leaving her homebound *Admiral* with a glimmer of hope at what bounty she would bring back. I had no idea how Peter felt about our parting. He was an island too rocky for anyone to approach. I was sure he would work, eat and sleep while I was gone. He never shied away from working a sixteen-hour shift seven days a week, but I feared for his state of well-being the most.

As we drove to Manchester Airport that drab morning in January, my spirit plummeted. I wondered how many more hardships our love would endure before being washed up once again on the shores of the brokenhearted.

10. Banknotes and Shrimp Boats

I had pictured Françoise with a generous waist and short, curly blond hair. But when she walked towards me, I thought how much she had changed. She was now a slim brunette with hair down to her waist. She also had a cute nose, which I once remembered as being rather prominent. Dressed in black leather trousers and a zipped jacket accentuating the curve of her generous bosom, Françoise had the allure of one of James Bond's girls. Her plastic surgeon could have afforded gold door handles on his Rolls Royce after she had settled her surgery bills!

We greeted each other with the customary 'kiss on each cheek,' and then I said hello to the dark-skinned man standing by Françoise's side. He was in his late thirties and wore a blue suit. He looked at me with shifty eyes. I noticed he had a bulge in his breast pocket. Was he a bodyguard?

'Let me introduce my boyfriend Enzo,' Françoise announced cheerfully. I felt several days of stubble growth when his lips brushed my cheeks. He grabbed my guitar case, Françoise carried my luggage, and we exited Geneva Airport.

It was a twenty-minute drive to Françoise's flat. Enzo parked the blue Mercedes in front of a high-rise retro-style building while she and I walked towards the plate glass door entrance, which opened into a small hallway. When Enzo caught up, we took the small lift to the second floor and crammed together awkwardly. We entered the narrow corridor to Françoise's flat, and she directed me straight into her lounge.

At first glance, I thought I must be in the wrong country. I had half-expected a cuckoo clock somewhere in the room and was surprised when I saw the mural of a jungle scene covering the full length of a wall. Even more puzzling was the life-sized tiger with teeth in the corner of the room, looking as if it could pounce at any moment. More welcoming, though, was the ceramic Dalmatian with puppies by its side, beckoning me for a pat through its pleading eyes. There was a treasure chest by the window between two fake palm trees. I wondered what was inside - maybe a skeleton or some Spanish doubloons!

Françoise prepared us a cocktail. She filled the glasses with tropical fruits, alcohol, and red squash, which fitted the ambience. During the conversation, she pointed through the window to her nightclub, which was only a stone's throw away. From the outside, it mimicked the frontage of a shop with a red velvet curtain drawn across its main window. Neon lights were flashing the name, *The Exotic Champagne Bar*. When we finished our cocktails, Françoise and I walked into the club.

At first glance, the place looked smaller than I had imagined, although a large mirror across the wall gave the illusion of a more expansive setting. I noticed the red carpet looking tired, with heavy footfall in some parts, and there was an odour of sweat, perfume, and stale alcohol hanging heavily in the gloomy air. Horseshoe-shaped beige leather settees surrounded small round tables. Adjacent to the seating areas was a long bar with a line of high stools.

Beyond were more tables and upholstered benches, but where was the stage? I couldn't imagine myself singing in Françoise's nightclub. Maybe I should have joined Auntie Frida and Uncle Albert; they performed in top hotels in Luzern, but I don't yodel.

The pair looked impressive in their Swiss costumes. Auntie Frida wore a long black velvet dress with a laced apron over it, a white puff-sleeved blouse and embroidered lace-up bodice. A white bonnet accentuated her jet-black hair. White stockings and buckled shoes completed her perfect ensemble. Uncle Albert, slightly bald, donned short leather trousers with braces, a long-sleeved shirt, a black velvet jacket, half-length socks, and shiny shoes. Together, they yodelled and danced, accompanied by an accordionist playing traditional Swiss tunes. Auntie Frieda spoke English with an American accent and a guttural Swiss-German twang. At the end of each show, they taught American tourists how to yodel and perform various dance moves. They also demonstrated how to blow a mountain horn. The instrument looked cumbersome, with its mouthpiece a metre and a half away from the far end that rested on the ground. The audience loved to try it, giggling and laughing between each blow. They enjoyed the entire show so much that they wanted to package up Auntie Friday and Uncle Albert and transport them to the States.

What seduced me about Françoise was her zest for life. She believed everything was achievable, and I loved that. She dreamed of owning a nightclub, and there it was.

She led me to a sizeable kitchen at the back of the premises to sort out the flowers. There were birds of paradise, white and pink lilies, and ruby red anthuriums. We trimmed and rinsed each stem before rearranging the flowers in vases.

'I can't see any room for a singer here,' I remarked as we placed them in various alcoves around the club. At least the flowers were exotic!

'I'm sure we can work something out,' she replied. 'There are other clubs. I've approached a few on your behalf, but one thing at a time. We're opening in an hour, and I could do with your help tonight if you don't mind. My barmaid, Evelyne, is off sick.'

Françoise knew hotels and restaurants had once been my playpens. As a child, my mother would keep an eye on me while she worked at the Hotel du Lac. As they prepared the next banquet in the large dining room, I often tinkled on the piano, to the staff's annoyance. On laundry day, I ran in and out under rows of bleached white bedsheets drying in the open air by the lake. Maman would shout, 'Don't touch them; you'll get them dirty with your hands.' Then, during high school, I worked as a silver-service waitress and was a natural like my mother. However, I wasn't used to popping champagne corks. It is a skill, after all. Françoise gave me a uniform to wear. I reluctantly squeezed into the short skirt and donned the low-cleavage white blouse, lace-up bodice and fishnet stockings. In this attire, I looked like a waitress from a beer cellar in a Benny Hill sketch! How far removed from the overall I had practically lived in while helping Peter.

Françoise noticed my unease and said, 'We all dress the same. Every month, I create a new theme, design the outfits, and my seamstress makes them.' Her uniforms were more erotic than exotic! Her club's name had conjured fruit-feathered headdresses with long flowing gowns in the style of *Carmen Miranda*. What a fool I had been. Still, I continued imagining all the Swiss banknotes I could earn singing in clubs Françoise had lined up for me. The future seemed as exciting as bubbles of champagne in a glass.

In my new role as a barmaid, I observed customers entering the club, choosing a hostess sitting at the bar, and then ordering a bottle of champagne to share with her in the seating areas. Françoise's club would have been the ideal environment to base a novel, but I wasn't here to write one.

A week later, she and Enzo took me to a top nightclub in town. It was an impressive place with a big stage, a dance floor, tables, and chairs set out in a cabaret theatre style. Françoise chose a table, and a waiter brought us Moët champagne without her having ordered it first. She must have been a regular customer. The waiter popped the cork with expertise, and I watched him pour the champagne into our glasses. Before he left, Françoise asked him if the manager was available. 'He is having a night off,' he replied.

We clinked glasses, then Françoise said, 'I've spoken to the manager on your behalf. He seemed interested in auditioning you, but there's plenty of time.' She saw my face drop. I felt like a captain on a ship navigating without a chart. I couldn't see myself singing my Streisand cover songs after a strip-tease routine and intense disco music. It seemed Françoise's sense of reality belonged to another world. I blamed myself for being such a dreamer of fairytales. I had seen her counting the empty bottles of champagne, the piles of banknotes and the list with the numbers tallied to each hostess. It seemed the young women were on commission. With Françoise's week of takings, we could have fitted out the inside of *Capricorn* and more. But how did the hostesses remain sober, drinking all that champagne?

I found out one evening when Françoise showed me how to place a glass of ginger ale next to the hostess's drink at the bar counter, 'do the switch,' then pour the champagne down the sink when the customer isn't looking. I repeated this manoeuvre several times during my shift. In the seating areas, the hostesses had to resort to clever manoeuvres when emptying their champagne glasses into vases or down an air vent behind the seats without the customer noticing.

On one occasion, a regular customer ordered a magnum of champagne and invited Françoise and three hostesses to join him. For himself, he ordered a double whisky. Then, for some reason, he asked to sample Françoise's glass of champagne. (As instructed, I had filled an empty magnum with ginger ale beforehand.) Even though the customer seemed heavily intoxicated, I thought Françoise would be in trouble. I watched her handing the customer her glass without a care. The man took a sip. 'To be frank, I'm not a connoisseur. I prefer my whisky and soda,' he said before returning the glass to Françoise.

Surely, he must have tasted the difference. Maybe he didn't want to lose face or create a scene in front of the ladies, having already paid handsomely for a litre and a half of bubbles. Another customer at the bar, who had only just ordered champagne for one of the hostesses, approached the man's table and said, pointing at the magnum, 'I don't believe this is champagne.'

What prompted him to question it? Was he envious of the man's attention, with four attractive young women leaning on his shoulders? Françoise quickly challenged him. Her steely eyes gave nothing away when she plucked a hundred franc note from her cleavage, slammed the money on the table like a poker player and announced, 'If it's ginger ale, you'll get the hundred, but when you taste the champagne, you'll owe me.'

The man's prying eyes veered between the magnum and the money. He stared into Françoise's piercing eyes, looking for a sign to wipe out any flicker of doubt. His fate seemed sealed, having challenged the woman to a duel 'with pistols at dawn.' The man conceded at the last minute and said, 'Okay, lady, I won't push the issue this time. He turned on his heels and left the establishment, slamming the door shut behind him.

I must remember not to play poker with Françoise, seeing she has bluffed with a 'pair of twos' and won.

The woman was running an all-female enterprise with no bouncers on the premises. When I asked about it, she said boastfully, 'I'm a black belt in Judo.' (I had seen her wearing her *Judogi* at her father's home once).

Then, one evening, I understood what Françoise meant when a customer tried to argue with her, accusing the hostesses of being *des filles de joie.* Without hesitation, Françoise's reply was a fist to his jaw. What happened next surprised everyone, including her. The man hit her back, right on the nose, nearly undoing her plastic surgeon's work. But she didn't leave it at that. She picked herself up and grabbed a bottle by the neck. The customer swiftly exited before she could crown him with it.

The barmaid kept missing work, so I took over. I was now sharing a flat round the corner with two of Françoise's staff. Isabelle was French, tall, fit, well-spoken and witty. She went to the gym and knew how to look after her skin. She didn't eat the greasy restaurant food delivered to the club early every evening. I was putting on weight.

With her wages at the club, Isabelle was buying a villa in Tuscany. She showed me a photograph of the place, with a swimming pool, and said she was planning to move there in a few years. She must have been earning extra on the side to pay the mortgage every month. Isabelle told me her mother still scrubbed floors for a living. It made her cry each time she looked at her hands. Yet, when Isabelle bought her some luxuries, her mother would say: 'I don't need anything, love.'

So Isabelle promised herself never to struggle like her mother. She hardly slept in the flat and always spent her days off away. I didn't ask her where she went, but she spoke of a boyfriend or even two who were spoiling her, although she confessed to never getting emotionally involved with anyone.

Jeannette was the other flatmate, a petite, bubbly blonde from a small village in county Vaud. She looked like *Heidi,* 'the girl from the mountains,' with plaited hair. When her Spanish boyfriend had a drink at the bar, she seemed less flirtatious with the customers. No wonder he spied on her every move.

Tilly, one of the hostesses living over the French border, was the most popular amongst the customers. She wore no makeup, was tall and busty, with short dark hair. Tilly made men laugh and played each one like an angler reeling in a marlin before throwing it back. The other hostess, Sacha, came from Alsace. She didn't have a place of her own but always had someone to stay with. She said, 'I must pay for my children's education.' Her husband, built like a bouncer, would arrive the night before her days off to collect her. It was odd that he always took pictures of her wearing the club's latest outfits.

The brutal reality finally hit me one evening after closing time. I found myself walking through the tunnel of doom. I worked in a bar where men paid money for a champagne pop to talk to a girl. Did they need to measure their manhood by what they spent for a woman's company? However, if a hostess did anything besides drinking champagne, giggling and talking on the premises, Françoise would show them the door. I was puzzled about why lawyers and judges visited a place like that. Françoise told me they liked the fact that no one laid judgment on them.

One evening, she announced she had booked a photographer to do a promotional photo shoot in the flat. She thought I needed a new image to advance my career as a singer. Her enthusiasm and charisma still played such tricks on me that I almost believed I could climb the Jungfrau Mountain with a step ladder!

Under her supervision, I posed in the lounge by the life-sized tiger, then in her blue bedroom by her fierce leopard that had teeth nearly as long as my index finger. Françoise had also designed my outfit. With my long, curly blond wig and high heels with buckles, I looked like virtuous, sweet Jane in *'Pride and Prejudice.'* Maybe Françoise had found me a part in some movie or wanted me to join her in a pantomime.

Undoubtedly, Françoise possessed a unique way of relating to the world. Little did I know this extravaganza would cost me nearly a month's salary. Maybe it was her ploy to keep me captive while I continued riding on her carousel of fantasies and grandiose promises. It had all begun so innocently, and now I was embroiled in murky waters. Françoise must have seen my enthusiasm drowning in champagne. When I talked about returning to England, she came up with the idea of a well-paid job for Peter. Given the delicate nature of the work, she insisted she had to offer it to an outsider, who would sworn her to secrecy. As Françoise believed she was a saviour of souls, she would bring Peter over from England to stop me from drifting into the doldrums of despair. I told Peter about

Françoise's proposal. The money was too enticing for him to refuse. The boat had eaten all our building kitty.

The first time Peter flew to Geneva Airport was when he visited me during his leave working in Iraq. This time, it would be different. For months, I had seen him in overalls covered in holes, his face hidden inside a welder's protective mask. When we met in the arrival lounge, I had forgotten how smart Peter looked in a suit. We hugged and kissed, ignoring the crowd.

The following day, he began working on the 'secret device' based on Françoise's diagram, but he had to promise never to divulge anything to anyone. Françoise could lose her customers or licence if he leaked information to the press.

There were narrow wooden shelves behind the leather-covered settees where Peter started to build dummy air vents with special channels made of the same leather cloth. He designed them so customers wouldn't hear liquid trickling into the catchment bowls when the girls poured their champagne down the vents. The receptacles underneath the sofas would then be emptied and rinsed with detergent daily, saving Françoise a fortune on deodorant and fabric cleaners. Moreover, she would save her hostesses from becoming alcoholics despite themselves.

One evening, two lively Americans arrived at the club. Max was a tall version of Marlon Brando with a wicked sense of humour, and Steve was a chubby version of Al Capone. They were regular visitors, judging by how

Françoise welcomed them. The men dealt in foreign currencies and used one of the Holiday Inns as their mobile office when in town. Françoise asked me if I would give them a private concert at her flat.

The men's enthusiasm for my music seemed genuine. I sang my heart out that night but didn't include *No Regrets* by Edith Piaf because I had plenty of my own. Max was particularly impressed by my rendition of *Country Roads* and asked, 'How would you like to sing in my chain of restaurants in Houston, Texas? Many singers can sing country songs but not with a French accent like yours. It would be a novelty! I could get you on radio and television and offer Peter a job as a skipper on a ship.' (Peter had mentioned delivering a 60-foot trimaran from Amsterdam to the Canary Islands.)

'While Monique is singing in Max's restaurants, you can work for me,' Steve continued. 'I plan to buy an Ex-US Navy patrol vessel and turn it into a shrimp boat with fitted refrigeration. We could fish off the Columbian Coast, then speed back to Houston and deliver fresh shrimps to Max's restaurants. I've got a fast method of C them. All you need to do is put the shrimps through an old-fashioned mangle, which cracks the shells off.' Max had the idea of buying a decommissioned Frigate that he would ram onto the beach and turn into a permanent restaurant. Like Françoise, the two Americans were drawing us into a merry-go-round.

The following weekend, the men invited us to stay overnight to discuss their proposals further. In the afternoon, we caught a tram to the Swiss-French border.

We must have been mad, but Peter and I couldn't resist missing the excitement. We cleared the checkpoint on foot and walked a further quarter of a mile to our rendezvous meeting. From there, the men would collect us.

We arrived just in time when an old maroon Volvo Estate pulled up with Max at the wheel. How odd that the Americans wouldn't meet us at the Swiss-French border or near the checkpoint. Max was all chirpy. He asked us to step into the car and made a witty remark about the state of the seats, which looked like a dog had chewed some of the upholstery in anger. On the way, we passed several expensive properties alongside the lake with impressive driveways and tall ornamental iron gates. Surprisingly, all had shutters over their windows, which made them look eerie.

We pulled into a gravel driveway in front of an elegant two-storey villa. Strangely, the shutters were also closed. We followed Steve into a large hallway with a twin-sweeping staircase, then into a lounge the size of a ballroom. The room looked starkly sparse, with only two basic upright chairs, a striped deckchair, and a television in a corner. The fireplace, with a log-burning stove, was a welcome sight. Max had mentioned renting a villa on the French side of Lake Geneva. At least the location fitted. However, we couldn't help wondering whether the Americans had broken into the mansion and were squatting. Then, when we saw Max exciting the kitchen, with our two flatmates Jeannette, the 'Heidi girl' and the 'stray cat' Sacha in tow, drinks in hand, I looked at Peter. Was he thinking the same as me?

We could smell trouble amidst the inviting aroma of tomato sauce and herbs wafting in the air. Max had cooked spaghetti bolognese for all of us. We ate on our laps in front of the fireplace, although Sacha and I sat on the floor on pillows. Peter's unease and mine wore off after a few glasses of wine. We laughed and joked until Steve started to yawn, and we all turned in.

Max took us to a guest bedroom that could have accommodated a large family. It had a wardrobe in a corner, which dwarfed the place. The double bed had no bedside tables; the wallpaper, matching the bedcover, indicated some designers had left their touch! The only other furniture in the room was an upright chair, which someone must have thrown in as an afterthought. At least there was an ensuite bathroom. Max bade us goodnight, and Peter closed the door after him.

The room was as cold as a fridge. We decided to sleep in our clothes and be ready to make a quick getaway. I got into bed and was relieved that the sheets were clean. Peter peeked inside the wardrobe. The empty clothes hangers rattled. At least he didn't find a skeleton inside. The only item there was a propped-up tennis racquet in a frame. I never asked him why he hooked the chair underneath the doorknob until I noticed there was no lock. As a little boy, Peter had learned this trick, fending off a family friend who tried to force his way into his bedroom.

Lying in the large bed, we listened to every creaking sound. At least we had a tennis racquet in case somebody attacked us, although it didn't make sense that anyone would. Still, it was going to be a very long night.

Thankfully, we woke up to see a glint of light streaming through a gap in the wooden shutters. We quickly got up and walked downstairs. Max greeted us like two old friends when we entered the kitchen for a glass of water. 'I'll make coffee,' he chirped 'and then Steve can drive you and the girls back to where I picked you up yesterday,'

Everyone seemed in a hurry to finish their coffee and leave. Steve gave the girls and us a lift to near the border then we walked through customs and caught the tram back to town. By now, Peter and I were on edge. On payday, I told Françoise we wanted to take a few days off to visit my family. She agreed.

I didn't jump for joy when Max offered me a job singing in his restaurants; I wasn't desperate enough to want to fly to America to be on stage. Although I had found a venue at a fringe theatre, I was now tired of looking for new places and had stopped trusting Françoise's promises. She was finally showing her true colours, fluctuating between helpful and aggressive. Maybe the pills she took to keep her weight down affected her mood. She didn't like my empathy towards her staff, who bitterly complained about her. They called her *the witch* behind her back, and I fought hard to defend her. I remembered Françoise caring for her father when he was ill and looking after her two younger half-brothers. Alas, money had corrupted her good nature. Then, there was the creepy villa by Lake Geneva, which seemed like a villain's lair. It was highly suspicious that we had to walk more than a quarter of a mile from the customs post before being picked up. And when Max and

Steve mentioned we would need to carry some of their excess luggage when flying over to the States, we thought, 'They want to use us as drug or currency mules.' How naive did they think we were? Why would Max need a high-speed shrimp boat with special refrigeration, fishing off the Columbian coast? It sounded more like a drug-running operation, using shrimp fishing as a cover. And why did they need a fast vessel? Was it to outrun the coastguard cutters? By then, Peter and I knew too much and needed to disappear. We packed everything we owned and left Geneva.

When we arrived at my parent's house, I found the key under the mat as usual. Peter and I made ourselves at home. Later, we called the Hilton Hotel and asked to speak to Max. We used a public phone so the Americans couldn't trace the call. Peter told Max we had to return to England because of family commitments. 'Don't be so hasty,' Max insisted. 'Please reconsider our offer. Come and meet us at the hotel before you go.'

'Okay, we'll see you there,' Peter answered. I called Françoise next to explain we were flying back to England. She was furious at the news. Her language was so blue that I could see steam emerging from the handset. She was shouting: 'There'll be consequences.'

No one had ever threatened me before, and it was unsettling. But what could she do to us? Then, when my sister Nicole mentioned her boss was looking for a waitress in his restaurant, I jumped at the opportunity. We needed more money for the boat.

Peter flew back to England to resume work on *Capricorn*. When we said our goodbyes again, we had no idea how long we would be apart this time.

11. Viking Ritual

As the plane landed at Heathrow Airport, my heart thudded at the sound of the undercarriage hitting the tarmac. I pictured myself in Peter's arms. If only I were with him now.

At King's Cross Railway Station, there was a train leaving for York in less than an hour, allowing me time to buy a ticket and call Peter. While I stood on the platform waiting, I thought of my mother. She always insisted on accompanying me to the railway station and would cry when I kissed her goodbye. I couldn't understand why. She never made time for me during my visits.

I remembered the many nights I heard her gasping for breath during one of her asthma attacks. Her choking sounded like the death knell of ringing bells, which terrified me. When she was down, it wasn't unusual to hear her say, 'I'll throw myself in the lake and end it all,' Although the threat was extreme, my sisters and I never took it seriously. A while later, I learned Maman had received electric shocks to treat her depression.

But now wasn't the time to rekindle the past on the eve of a new start with Peter, sailing our ocean-going yacht into the blue. *Capricorn* was our 'baby.' She was conceived entirely out of recycled material. The steel for the deck and hull originated from scrap metal and unwanted stock, including three tons of steel punching ballast for the keel. Most of the material was from Ward Brothers, where Peter had once worked as a welder. The wood for the interior construction came off ships discharging timber in the Port of Hull. Peter had bought several cubic metres of Iroko (dunnage packing material). This wood is a poor man's teak but has the advantage of being rot-resistant. The grain, however, can change direction several times in every plank, making it challenging to work with.

The engine was an old three-cylinder 35 HP Perkins. When Peter checked the block number with the manufacturers, their records showed it came off the assembly line in 1961. They gave us the last copy of their workshop manual free of charge and wished us the best of luck. Our forty-four-foot mast came from Kemps's obsolete stock; the sails, including the deck fittings and blocks, were second-hand. All other chandlery items were bartered at Beaulieu boat jumbles.

Maybe we should have called *Capricorn* '*Second-Hand Rose*.'

Peter used a thousand welding rods and several tons of steel to meet *Neptune's demands* and the wrath of *Anemoi*, the Greek God of the four winds. To achieve a smooth finish on the hull, he dressed the welds with a grinder equivalent in length to the height of Nelson's column.

Furnishings were new, including our custom-made double mattress. A manufacturer in York had agreed to make the 6'6" x 5'4" mattress. When it arrived, we carried it up the three-and-a-half metre scaffolding steps onto the deck, which proved a mammoth task, with its springs fighting against us on the way. Once we reached the wheelhouse, we lifted, pushed and squeezed it through the narrow passage leading to the after-cabin, which felt like we were trying to fit an elephant into a small compound. Then, by the time we had tamed the 'beast and flopped it onto the bed, we were ready to collapse. But it wasn't long before Peter hollered, 'I've miscalculated the footwell.' The mattress was protruding into the aft-looker at the bottom of the berth. For once, my lips were sealed.

'I can't leave it at that,' Peter said. 'It would be too much of a squeeze for our feet. I'll have to modify the bulkhead, cut the footwell and re-weld it.' We retrieved the mattress, carted it back to the caravan, and slept on it that night, forgoing candles and chilled champagne to inaugurate our first night aboard *Capricorn.*

The launching date was approaching, and we still had no trailer to transport *Capricorn.* Peter's friend, Tim, who owned a pub in Scarborough, hatched a plan. His yacht was in his backyard, on a WWII bomb-carrier trailer. Nobody knew how he came to own it. Maybe a customer had settled a heavy bar tab with it. Tim hadn't sailed for the last two summers and was ready to sell his boat. He told Peter, 'If you give me three days of work on my boat, making it ship-shape, you can have the trailer once I've sold it.'

Peter agreed.

The crane driver, Ian, arrived a few days before the launch. He was returning a favour, willing to lift *Capricorn* onto the WWII trailer at a peppercorn price. (Peter's mother had helped finance the start of his father's business before he took over.)

It was Ian's second lift, which meant he had already covered his travelling expenses. But there was a problem. he had no lifting straps, only the hook and chains he had used earlier. The lift was now jeopardised until Peter suddenly remembered the ocean-liner-size mooring ropes his friend Ken had bought at the Yacht Club's auction while he was bidding for a dinghy on Peter's behalf. Ken must have thought Peter was building the sister ship to the *QE2!*

When Ian saw the massive plaited nylon ropes, he sucked air through his pursed lips and said, 'These will stretch a lot, but I'll admit they look hardy for the job. 'You will have to tie ropes 'fore and aft' and then onto each strap, in case *Capricorn* doesn't align when I lift her. I've seen boats roll out of ropes like these faster than a bank robber on roller skates!'

Ian had a point. It was impossible to guess *Capricorn's* balance point on the straps, but Peter told him to proceed. I heard the crane's engine roar like a warning sign. Ian took the slack off the ropes, increased the revs and pressed on.

She didn't budge even though the straps had already been stretching substantially. Then, we heard a clatter, and the chocks that had been holding our boat up three feet above the ground suddenly collapsed like dominoes. *Capricorn* was now swinging nose down in mid-air like a demented pendulum threatening to tip the crane over while Peter hung on to his boat with one line to the stern and another to the bow, frantically trying to steady her. Although it looked like a circus act, nobody was laughing. It was as if the lion tamer had forgotten to close the cage door, and we were holding our breath!

When *Capricorn* finally stopped her dangerous sway, Peter lined her up to the trailer, and Ian lowered her down in place perfectly. But if the rope hadn't tied 'for and aft' to the lifting straps, *Capricorn* could have rolled out of the slings, dropped to the ground, and toppled over.

What a way to be shipwrecked without ever getting her keel wet! Thankfully, it didn't happen. However, Peter later confessed that our dream of sailing away together could have been crushed a few months earlier. With icy decks and icicles hanging from the keel, he had accidentally slipped over the side. As he plummeted three and a half metres to the frozen ground, he suddenly remembered his Judo training when he was sixteen and broke his fall, with his forearms hitting the ground first. He believed his Judo stance saved him from injuring his spine or breaking his neck.

Keeping the vision of water lapping against *Capricorn's* hull for five years had nurtured Peter's dream. Friends had often asked, 'Will your boat float, Pete?'

'If she doesn't, I'll go down with the ship,' was his reply. At times, I wondered, as I knelt on the cold steel of the hull, painting the bilges, why I had left the Caribbean for all the hardship of boatbuilding. It was a brutal environment for someone like me who plucked strings on the guitar, wrote romantic songs and chased rainbows.

Next, we had to get *Capricorn* down to the sea - a five-mile drive away. We also needed to inform the police of our convoy. I heard Peter talking to the traffic sergeant over the phone, 'I've just finished building a steel boat in Burniston and am calling to inform you that at 8 am on 3 June, I'll be towing it down to Scarborough Harbour.'

'Fine,' the officer said. 'Is the trailer over ten feet wide?'

'It's exactly that.'

'Okay! But does the trailer have brakes?' There was a pause. The policeman repeated his question impatiently.

'No,' Peter replied. Then, improvising, he said, 'I'll have a four-wheel-drive tractor with tyres half-filled with water for extra grip and a second tractor chained to the back as overrun brakes.'

'Thank you for this information,' the officer replied. 'Given the trailer isn't over ten feet and the second tractor covers the brakes issue, you won't need an escort. I've noted the time and route of your journey.' (Peter had forgotten to inform the officer that *Capricorn* was two feet wider than the trailer).

We left Burniston on a grey morning. Charcoal maker and supplier John, in his Morris 1000 pick-up, was leading our strange convoy, flashing an orange light on the cab top. Following closely behind was a forestry tractor with four enormous wheels, towing a trailer with our shiny white steel hull and mast strapped horizontally across the deck. Chained at the back, with Peter driving, was a small tractor he had borrowed from his friend Mitch, who owned a builder's yard. Bringing up the rear was a black and orange Citroën 2cv with our friend Andrew and myself. Behind us was a vintage Austin Princess belonging to Roy, followed by our landlord, Alex, in his white van, and Alistair, driving his milk truck. He owned the dairy farm next to where *Capricorn* had stood for five years. Alistair delivered gold-top pints of milk to the surrounding area, including ourselves.

On the way, the Morris 1000, ahead, blocked the road at each junction to hold the traffic back until we had passed. Surprisingly, nobody blew their horn. Perhaps they were too stunned by our comical convoy!
We trundled along the Marine Drive, past the base of the Norman Castle, before reaching the public slipway, which ran parallel to the road. From then on, the task became more challenging. George, a skilful tractor driver, would need to reverse the trailer onto the slipway with *Capricorn's* stern facing the harbour. An additional 90-degree turn was required to align it before descending the ramp. The stakes were high. A mistake could result in our boat tipping over the edge and dropping fifteen feet into the mud - a less graceful launch for *Capricorn!* However, George could achieve the correct alignment by inching forward and allowing us to control the boat's descent down the slipway.

At this point, Alistair, accustomed to manoeuvring all types of trailers, took the reins. He turned *Capricorn* ninety degrees towards the bottom of the slipway with the help of all the convoy drivers and a few onlookers, using the turn-table tow bar as a tiller. He came so close to the crab stalls that he could have downed dishes of cockles and mussels just by leaning over from his seat as he slowly went past. Then, we all pushed *Capricorn* until gravity took over, and the tractor carried the weight. Finally, the trailer crept at a crawling pace towards the bottom of the slipway. Two men were leading the rear with chocks to be placed under the wheels in case the manoeuvre suddenly got out of control. Then, we waited for the incoming tide to float *Capricorn* off the trailer.

Meanwhile, all hands were on deck to erect the mast. This was one occasion when many hands didn't make light work. Peter and I had erected the mast with block and tackle a week before to check if the rigging was all the proper length before lowering it for our journey down to the sea.

Then came the grand moment for Peter and me to baptise *Capricorn*, all dressed in flags. I popped the cork of a champagne bottle, shaking it and showering the bow. We didn't break the glass against the hull as customary. (Who would sweep it up? Besides, we wanted to drink the champagne). It was a momentous day. The triumphant look on Peter's face was my ultimate reward.

A young boy leaning over the railings had been observing the scene. Looking puzzled, he asked, 'Why is the deck covered in branches and leaves?'

'It's an ancient ritual,' Peter explained. 'It dates back to the Viking *Scarfie,* who gave his name to Scarborough.

When the Vikings used to launch their boats, they covered the deck with foliage to ensure they would always return safely to land.'

The boy seemed satisfied with the fairytale. Peter had omitted to tell him this forest on our deck was due to the unscheduled pruning of an avenue of trees we had met on the way because of the boat's height on the trailer.

Then, as we watched the tide lapping close to *Capricorn's* waterline, I could hear the words on everybody's lips: 'Is she going to float?'

Finally, she drifted free from the trailer and gently bobbed on the water. It was one of the proudest events in Peter's life and mine! Well-wishers boarded *Capricorn,* like marauding pirates, keen to partake in this short and inaugural journey to the yacht harbour, which was only just around the corner. Our friend Ted counted we had one and a half tons of bodies aboard. I started singing:

The ocean blue is waiting for you,
put some miles under your keel and follow the dream…

12. Yellow Wellies and Stilettos

'Are Those Boots Made For Walkin?' the woman asked, pointing at my yellow wellingtons.

'She'll be singing it next!' I mused.

'Are you a novelty act in our line-up?' she continued.

'Yes, but don't tell anybody I've got a fetish for *wellies*.'

I must have looked as out of place as a fisherman dressed in foul-weather gear at a cocktail party when I walked across the threshold of the elegant dressing room. Its thick red carpet must have supported the footfall of many artists on their journeys to fame.

'I'm Gloria,' the woman chirruped.

The name suited her perfectly. I watched her spreading foundation cream over her face like a plasterer with his trowel, smoothing his handiwork on a wall. It made me laugh, and I nearly pushed my lip gloss up my nose, putting my makeup on. There was no hiding under those naked bulbs in front of the large dressing-room mirror in the Scarborough Royal Opera House.

Everything about the pin-up girl displayed sexual arrogance, including the sequinned V-neck leotard that struggled to contain her large breasts from going on a reconnaissance mission. Her musk and jasmine perfume infused the air so strongly that I wondered if she had accidentally sprayed the whole bottle on herself. I caught her looking at my embroidered waistcoat and pouting her blood-red lips seductively. Then she asked with a smile that almost cracked her makeup, 'Do you yodel?'

'Yes, mostly when I call my captain to pick me up from the quayside.'

'Sounds interesting. Tell me more later. I'm due on stage any minute now.'

Would Gloria believe I had walked across the muddy harbour bed moments earlier, wearing my Swiss costume, to come and perform at the Royal Opera House? I was curious about her performance, and when I asked her, she declared, as casually as if she was telling me her favourite ice cream flavour, 'I'm the magician's assistant, who gets sawn in half.'

I wanted to say: 'break a leg' when she left the dressing room to answer the curtain call. The plimsoll line of her skirt floated higher than my petticoat. She even looked at ease in her gold, pencil-heeled stilettos, which to me would have felt like walking on stilts.

While performing at the Opera House offered glamour and excitement, being in our boat and dealing with weather and tide was challenging. Although we weren't strictly cut off from the world anchored a hundred yards away from the quayside, sometimes it felt like it. In the morning, when the tide was in, I rowed Peter ashore for him to get to work. Once on land, he waited until I was safely back aboard *Capricorn*, then, we would blow each other a kiss goodbye before he drove off in his car. In the evening, he might row me ashore, or if the tide were out, I would trudge across the mud in my wellies and up a vertical ladder to reach the pier. From there, it was a short walk uphill to my venue.

So, I needed to calculate my every move from when I stepped off the boat to how long I would be away. At times, the rising tide deceived me when I rowed across to the dinghy pontoon, and I had to drag my tender along the sticky mud and then tie it amongst the other boats to ensure it was afloat on my return. Negotiating the fifteen-foot vertical ladder affixed to the harbour wall featured strongly in my routine, carrying shopping or laundry bags in one hand while hanging on to each rung in turn with the other. Then, I had to quickly let go before grabbing the next rung. Missing it would mean leaving a cartoon impression of myself spread-eagled in the mud. I prayed I would master the art of becoming a yachtswoman. If all else failed, I could run away and join the circus.

Since launching *Capricorn* in June, there had been no end of gales. I often wondered what people thought when they saw me stepping ashore, all dishevelled. I must have looked like *Grace Darling* after she rode out in an open boat and rescued several seamen from the shipwrecked *Forfarshire* in 1838.

Deep down, I was *a reluctant sailor*. It was one thing to embark on a boat for a short spell but quite another to surrender my life to the mercy of the sea. Yet, I was ready to follow Peter across oceans, come what may. There were times I wished he had been a passionate gardener. Ploughing the soil would have been far more manageable than riding waves in a boat.

Capricorn was being challenged, too. She settled on her retractable legs at low tide or floated with them dangling below the surface.

The idea of retractable legs was born on the back of a beer mat with the help of Peter's friend, pub owner Tim. Their 'two-legged' invention has been featured in a few yachting magazines, bearing the caption, 'How do you like Peter's legs?'

'Didn't I say when I met Peter: 'What a shapely pair of legs on a man!'

Meanwhile, I had appeared on various television shows, won several talent competitions, and built a repertoire of over a hundred and twenty songs. I could sing and play ballads, country songs, rock and jazz numbers. With this in mind, I believed there would be audiences for me to entertain anywhere in the world we happened to be.

One evening, as we prepared for our performance, Gloria said, 'How romantic it must be to sail away with the man you love. It's not fun being stuck inside a box, waiting to be cut in half every night. Can I come with you?'

'You might get bored travelling at the speed of a cyclist riding uphill. There's seasickness and rough weather; it can be scary.'

'I'm used to fear. How long will you be gone?'

'I don't know.'

'I think you're brave. I hope you won't regret leaving show business.

I shrugged my shoulders, knowing I was now the skipper's wife *'in fair weather or storm.'*

Peter and I had exchanged vows at The Registry Office in Auvernier, where I was born. I remembered *Maman* asking me to choose a day she wasn't working so she could attend the wedding. Only Mother could make such a request. Two days before the event, my father was rushed to hospital. Then my sister Nicole and I fell out. She was accusing me of playing with Father's life. 'Papa is dying,' she stated with such anger that I thought she would hit me. 'You are giving him false hope that he will recover.'

One has to believe in miracles for them to happen.

Then I don't know what came over Nicole when she said, 'Peter is making the biggest mistake of his life marrying you.'

So, only my mother, my school friend Silvia, and her husband Daniel were to attend the ceremony. When we arrived at the Registry Office, the registrar greeted us. He looked sombre, and I thought he must have run out of time to put on 'his happy face.' As he expected to marry a national to a foreigner, he immediately assumed Daniel, who was black, was my husband-to-be. I quickly clarified the issue by pointing to the blond, blue-eyed Englishman.

Once we knew where we stood, the ceremony began. It was a sterile-looking room that didn't seem congenial to joyful marriage events. As Peter spoke little French, he needed to be prompted to pronounce the word *Oui* at the right time. It was a tense moment, given that the registrar could refuse to marry us because Peter needed to understand enough of the language to know what he would be signing for. Mother, Silvia, Daniel and I whispered the *Oui* so audibly across the room that a whole church congregation could have heard us. The entire affair was like a pantomime. It is a wonder that the registrar, who never looked up from his paper during the ceremony, didn't marry the witnesses to hedge his bet that he got the right couple!

After we left the Registry Office, *Maman* invited us for a drink at the hotel where she had worked when we were children. We sat at the table with our glasses of bubbly and a few amuse-bouches. Mother proposed a toast to wish us good health and happiness. Before she left to visit

Father at the hospital, she put a one hundred franc note on the table and said: 'Drink to my good health.' And that was her wedding present to us.

Back in Scarborough, we asked Reverend Samuel at St Mary's Protestant Church if he would bless our marriage on *Capricorn.* 'Blessings should take place in a church,' he stated.

'The boat is our home,' Peter explained. 'We plan to sail it across oceans.'

Reverend Samuel thought again. As part of his Parish duties, he blessed the Scarborough fishing fleet on a chosen day each year. He arrived late once, and the boats had already gone, but he blessed them anyway. Finally, he agreed to do the same for us.

That day, *Capricorn* became a floating church for the blessing of two people who were embarking on a voyage of a lifetime. Peter looked elegant in a suit, standing next to me in a pink gypsy dress ensemble. With the extra weight on board, the boat's waterline disappeared. I doubted our former landlords, Alex and Audrey, Roy and Liz, Peter's mother and the couple staying with her ever noticed. I had requested my favourite hymn, *'All things bright and beautiful,'* and Reverend Samuel led us without any accompaniment. It was an exciting cacophony sung in various keys. I couldn't stop giggling. Then, we generously toasted the occasion with bubbly and savoured a small buffet. Peter and I cut into the two-tier wedding cake his mother had made.

At the end of the summer season, all the entertainers at the Royal Opera House arranged to celebrate our last performance with wine and nibbles at the bar after the show. When we left early in the morning, glamorous Gloria hugged Peter and me like long-lost friends and wished us happy adventures.

When we woke up a few hours later, Peter and I couldn't remember whether we had rowed back to the boat or walked across the seabed. But, seeing the footprints over our decks and our wellies caked in sludge, it was clear we had trodden across the mud. I wondered if we would have risked swimming across the harbour to return aboard had the dinghy been afloat left tied up alongside *Capricorn*.

Departure day was approaching while I continued promoting my career. One day, I contacted Tyne Tees Television to ask if they would consider featuring a modern sailing troubadour setting off into the blue. They jumped at the idea.

It was a dull day when a film crew arrived. They parked their vehicles on the lighthouse pier. An alluring red-haired female presenter introduced herself, then explained she would do a short interview before I sang something and suggested we sit in the cockpit. I was wearing a red and white striped V-neck T-shirt and shorts. Although we were into July, it wasn't overly warm. The interview began with the obvious questions: 'How long did it take you to build the boat?' 'Where are you sailing to, and how long for?'

'It took us five years to build *Capricorn*,' I said. 'We're sailing to America without a return date,' When the woman prompted me, I picked up my guitar and began singing: 'Sail Away Today.' As I broke into the chorus, we suddenly heard some hammering noise, which clanged like a cracked bell across the harbour. Peter rushed to ask his former workmates who were repairing a fishing boat to stop making a noise for ten minutes. When all went quiet, I continued with my song:

Some people dream of flying to the moon,
others like to dream in their room,
but all I want to do is sail away with you.

After my rendition, Peter and I cast off with the cameras still running. He engaged the engine into gear, and we slowly motored through the narrow harbour mouth. Once in the bay, he hoisted the sails and tacked at close quarters so the two cameramen could take a better shot of me sitting on deck with my guitar. I doubted the crew knew the skilful manoeuvres the skipper had to deploy to tack close-hauled in such a narrow space. It would be devastating for us if *Capricorn* accidentally hit the harbour wall. I had had a crash course tacking in Peter's 25-foot *Ellis* on the Guadalquivir River in Portugal, coming so close to the banks that I could have picked some flowers before tacking out again. Little *Ellis* was able to turn on a six-pence, unlike *Capricorn*. With her weight and long keel, she went from one tack to another much more sedately, but she could cope with all conditions, Peter believed, including hurricanes.

When we painted the first undercoat on the hull battleship grey colour (because the price was right), people asked: 'Are you building a yacht or a submarine?' And now our shiny white *Capricorn* was heeling right over to starboard, heading for the harbour mole, with her sails as tight as my guitar strings. The film crew might have thought we were about to collide against it with a bang. What a spectacle this would have been on camera! Thankfully, we bore away just in time. It was sweet music to our ears when we heard the camera crew finally say on our last tack, 'That's a wrap.' They told us the sequence would be shown in 'Look North' next Thursday at 6 pm.

My last singing venue was at Scarborough Burniston Barracks. That evening, Peter radioed *Maxi Taxi* to pick us up from the harbour, using our Citizen Band radio, which was the rage in the 1980s. Users enjoyed inventing silly jargon such as *eyeballing you sometimes* and other ridiculous names. Ours was *Tin Can.* Nobody would respond unless operators used the CB language and gave their call sign.

When we called *Maxi Taxi,* no one answered despite following the correct procedure. Someone must have thought it was a hoax. Then, after some 'to-ing and fro-ing' over the airwaves, a man finally responded. He agreed to collect us from Scarborough Harbour and take us to Burniston Army Barracks.

He arrived just as we reached the top of the vertical ladder to the pier like a raiding party. The driver stepped out of his vehicle and walked towards us, staring at my Swiss costume, yellow wellies, and guitar case. He looked confused. I handed it to him, and when he placed it in the boot, he asked, 'Is this a machine gun?'

'It's a standard issue for the Swiss Navy,' I said.

He forced a smile.

En route to the venue, we collected my PA system at Peter's mother's house. After we had loaded our equipment, the driver asked again, 'Is it really Burniston Army Barracks you want me to drive you to?'

'Yes,' I confirmed.

As we approached the entrance to the barracks, a *squaddy* with a truncheon and a torch asked, 'Who goes there?' Was England the only country in the world in 1985 where soldiers defended their barracks without a gun? Peter wound the window down and announced, 'My wife is the artiste for the officers' mess party.'

'Oh! When she finishes with the officers, would she come to our privates' mess and draw us?' the soldier asked.

'She is an artist; she sings,' Peter explained.

'Oh great, even better that she can sing and draw. We look forward to seeing her later on.'

It was hard to keep a straight face when Peter asked him for directions to the officer's mess. The soldier saluted and then lifted the barrier.

We drove through the barracks and across the parade ground. The entrance was under the clock tower. Peter said, looking at me, 'England can sleep easy tonight because the soldier who asked "Who goes there" is ready to protect his country with his sharp wit and truncheon!'

When we walked into the officers' mess, the bar steward showed us where to set up my PA system. From the far end of a corridor, we could hear the Military Brass Band performing for the officers in the dining room. They must have just finished their seven-course dinner. Someone came to tell us they were passing the port and cigars and would be at the bar shortly for the rest of the night's entertainment. It wasn't long before the place filled with officers dressed in dark blue uniforms with gold crowns on their epaulettes and row after row of medals on their chests. They also wore spurs that jingled around the room like a Salvation Army mass band of tambourines. Peter started singing quietly to me:

'My brother Sylvester had a row of forty medals on his chest,
big chest. It would take all the Army
and the Navy to put the wind-up, Sylvester.'

As a child, he heard this song in the pub his parents ran after some customers were downing their sixth pints.

General Fitzpatrick introduced me to the audience, and then, while in full flow, I noticed a pint of beer being passed from hand to hand around the outside of the room, which ended at Peter's table. Was it some army ritual? I went to the ladies during the interval to powder my nose and apply more lipstick. When I returned for my second set, Peter told me Major Hamilton Foxton wanted to play the spoons to accompany me to a Country Western song, preferably. How could I refuse?

The officer nodded to the bar steward, who brought a chair and placed it beside me. Everyone cheered when

Major Hamilton Foxton strode across the floor, medals, spurs, and all; his head held high as if he was about to challenge the mess to a duel. He took up his position, and I broke into the *Gambler* by Kenny Rogers. Spoons bounced on his knees, elbow and head, with their gleaming silver flashing in the spotlights. Major Hamilton Foxton had the mastery of Uri Geller, though he never tried to bend a spoon.

The audience raved at his outstanding performance, and the night was a triumph for everyone. Peter quickly packed my PA system away while I collected my money at the bar and bid goodnight to the officers. By then, *Maxi Taxi* had arrived and was waiting on the parade ground. We carried our equipment to the vehicle like two battle-weary soldiers, dragging cannons behind them after retreating. That night, we learned some of the officers' mess fundamental rules:

Rule number 41: *Guests cannot sit with an empty glass or cross the floor during a live performance.*

Rule number 42: *Nobody leaves the officers' mess sober on a Saturday night!*

On our return journey, we dropped the PA at Peter's mother's house, where I exchanged my stilettos for 'wellies.' Then, *Maxi Taxi* deposited us back at the Harbour. I wondered who was the most relieved. He smiled when Peter gave him a generous tip.

As the tide was out, we descended the muddy steps to the seabed and plopped across the mud in a zigzag fashion while singing, *What shall we do with the drunken sailor?* Then, we helped each other up the ladder onto *Capricorn's* deck, where we rendered the last verse, *'Put us in the scuppers with our hosepipe on us till we're sober,'* so loudly that it would have drowned out the lighthouse foghorn. Peter said: 'I wonder if that Scarborough Yacht Club might get us arrested for lowering the tone of his flotilla by being drunk and disorderly while in charge of yellow *wellies*?'

13. The Dream a Tide Away

It wasn't every day one cast off into the unknown with no safety net or return date in mind, pitting oneself at the mercy of the North Sea, the Atlantic Ocean, the Mediterranean, and the World. We had worked so hard for this moment that it didn't seem real. There was no one on the quayside to wave us goodbye. (The skipper and I are superstitious, so we kept our departure quiet.) Hundreds of people had waved the *Titanic* goodbye on her maiden voyage. For us, there was little chance we would be sailing near icebergs unless we got our navigation drastically wrong.

Poised at the tiller, I slowly motored out of the narrow entrance, feeling as proud as Boudicca would have been when she paraded in her chariot in front of her tribes before a battle. Except there was no crowd to bid us farewell nor a 'bloody' battle to be fought; the weather would be the force to reckon with.

A pale sun had broken through the heavy-laden sky, and there was a chill in the air. Peter hoisted the mainsail and the jib before we headed out into the open sea. The wind was light at first, but it steadily increased. *Capricorn* ploughed through the churning waves at a good pace. A fishing boat astern was struggling to overtake us. Considering we were carrying a hundred and forty gallons of water, the same amount in diesel, plus tools, bicycles, a PA system and a sewing machine, our boat's performance was impressive. But how did we fit all our chattels in a space no bigger than a minibus?

Off Flamborough Head, the wind gradually veered in the opposite direction. Peter switched the engine on and dropped the headsail. The Yorkshire Coast makes for lumpy seas with wind against tide. *Capricorn* was now rearing up like a wild horse with each mounting wave. Still, nothing could dampen my spirit at the start of our voyage, not even wind-driven spray slapping my face or water trickling down my neck, chilling me to the bone. The skipper looked pensive standing in the cockpit while young Tom, who had joined us for the journey, was resting in the forward cabin, ready for his next watch.

Little Tom was Liz and Roy's son. We had watched him grow up during the building of *Capricorn*. He was struggling at school, and his only interest was sailing. So Roy asked the headmaster for a special authorisation to allow his fifteen-year-old son to take time off school. His father believed Peter would make a yachtsman out of him.

Tom understood the dynamics of wind and sail and loved the sea. He would never be mutiny material. He was helpful, adaptable and willing to learn the ropes. His only rebellious streak was his Medusa-style blond curly hair. I was pleased we had him as an additional crew. I knew Peter could handle *Capricorn* single-handedly, but I was still *a reluctant sailor.*

When I remarked we were late in the season to set off, Peter said, 'We could yet have an Indian summer.' It was early October, and there was no sign of the elusive sunshine and warmth he had talked about. The sea was now building. Peter rechecked the shipping forecast. A wind force of four to five was developing into a gale. We were twenty miles from Spurn Point, which could take five or six hours to reach, pounding into head seas. We opted for Bridlington, five miles away, with the wind up our tail and a following sea.

I pushed the tiller hard to port, choosing a lull in the swell while Peter hoisted the jib. By then, Tom had emerged on deck in his wet-weather gear. He must have sensed something was happening for us to turn back.

The tide was ebbing fast when we reached the harbour entrance an hour later. Luckily, there was enough water to get in. It wouldn't have been a great start to our journey having to sail back to Scarborough.

Once inside Bridlington Harbour, we dropped the sails and laid *Capricorn* against the quayside. Peter tied a rope from the mast to the shore to stop her falling away from the pier when the harbour dried out.

It was late in the afternoon when the tide fully receded, just enough to see the surface of the mud. Then Peter slowly lowered the starboard leg to steady the boat, expecting it to settle at the same level as the keel, but with the weight, he suddenly lost his grip, and the leg slid from the deck through its casing and disappeared into the bottomless sludge.

Our retractable legs were vital for *Capricorn* to take the ground evenly in harbours that dry out at low tide. There were several anchorages and harbours like this one along the Brittany Coast, where we planned to sail. Peter looked distraught. Then, when he tried to sound the bottom of the seabed with a pole, he discovered *Capricorn* was floating in two metres of liquid mud. No wonder boat owners aren't allowed to remain aboard their vessels moored in the middle of Bridlington Harbour at low tide because the only way of rescue in an emergency would be by helicopter. The Harbour Master had allowed us to stay on board because we were moored to the quayside.

When he came to collect harbour dues, he said, 'You were lucky you got in and didn't hit the remains of the two-masted concrete sailing yacht with your keel. The vessel came in at low tide to shelter from a storm, but she bounced her keel on the solid rock floor in the entrance and cracked her hull in half. When the storm tailed off, there was nothing of her left to re-float. We had to use explosives to blow up her pounded hull to ensure safe navigation in and out of the harbour.' Peter must have been relieved that he built *Capricorn* in steel rather than ferro-cement. By then, it was getting too late to solve the problem in the dark; we had our supper and opted for an early night.

We woke up with the breaking dawn, and the three of us sallied on deck. The incoming tide hadn't reached *Capricorn* when Peter stepped into the dinghy floating on oozing mud. If he fell overboard, it would be like being thrown into an Irish bog, never to be seen again. He seemed unfazed. Tom passed him the boat hook, and he plunged it into the mire. The two-metre-long shaft rapidly disappeared, and so did his arm, right up to his armpit. Finding King John's lost treasure in the Wash Estuary might have been less of an endeavour. Undeterred, Peter pursued his search. It was guesswork where the leg could have landed in the mud, but being heavy, he hoped it could have fallen under the aperture. He decided to concentrate his effort there first.

I thought of all the near-misses Peter had experienced on his 25-foot sailing boat, *Ellis of Tamar* when he collided with a 65.000-ton cargo ship in fog in the English Channel, lost his mast alone in the deep Atlantic Ocean in a storm, and much more. For him, floating in mud in a dinghy should be like sailing on a duck pond. Still, he couldn't afford to make a sudden move and tip it over. However, finding the leg in the thick ooze seemed as unlikely as seeing two identical snowflakes in the Sahara Desert, but miracles happen. Tom and I watched the skipper intently while I prayed. It could have been comical if I wasn't so concerned for Peter.

Tom and I watched the skipper intently while I prayed. It could have been comical if I wasn't so concerned for Peter. Then, as Tom and I looked on anxiously, we suddenly heard him shout, 'I've got it.' *Ah, the power of prayer.*

Still, we remained wishful as we watched Peter pull the boat hook up, carefully 'hand over hand' so that the leg wouldn't jump off and go walkabout. It must have looked farcical for people walking down the quayside to see Tom's chest on the deck, head and arms over the tow-rail, and me sitting on his legs as if I was stopping a lemming from jumping off a cliff. He then seized the boat hook, which allowed the skipper to secure the leg into the dinghy and tie a rope around it. I pulled Tom back on board by his belt, hoping he would remain in his trousers. Then, he and Peter hauled the oozing leg on deck. Seeing thick mud dripping from their arms, I said, 'You've had a free beauty treatment.' Neither of them appreciated the joke. I thought to myself, a pig sty would have smelt sweeter!

Peter treated the ordeal like a challenge, after which he and Tom had a warm shower at the Royal Bridlington Yacht Club. Later, he arranged for *Capricorn* to dry out on the careening grid and hoisted the leg back into position through the hull.

The predicted force eight wind developed into a battering storm nine. The sea boiled like water in a cauldron. It would have been hell being caught out at sea in this. We were still weather-bound the second day. Peter called his mother and invited her for lunch in a café. We ate fish and chips overlooking *Capricorn* moored in the harbour. The torrential rain drumming against the bay window filled the silence between us. Whenever I visited my mother-in-law at her home, she had the television blaring in the background. Perhaps it helped dispel the awkwardness that existed between us. She may have been angry at me for taking her son away. When Peter announced we were getting married, she said, 'Whatever for?' But she sat in the audience when I sang at various hotels in Scarborough. I always included her favourite song, *Streets of London*. She must have liked me a little, although I didn't understand why she never signed her name when she gave me a birthday card.

The weather finally improved, and we made for Spurn Point on an overnight passage. Then, as we entered the Humber Estuary, a spectacular red sunrise graced us. A strong wind had picked up. The billowing sails bathed in crimson light confirmed the saying: *Red sky in the morning, sailor's warning.* With a following swell and a tide in full flood, *Capricorn* crashed into the troughs with her bow engulfed in spray. During the gusts, she surfed down the back of steep waves. It was exhilarating. However, the Humber River is a treacherous place with its shifting sandbanks. Many ships have foundered in these waters. Therefore, keeping within the channel and picking up buoys on the way was imperative to avoid a similar fate.

When we reached the entrance of Hull's old commercial docks, now a marina, the incoming tide was running fast across the harbour mouth. Peter must have seen the furrows on my brow when he said, 'It will look alarming when I steer the boat close to the mole wall, but don't worry, the current will push us sideways into the middle of the entrance at the last minute.'

I stood in the cockpit with my hands cemented to one of the stanchions and my heart about to jump out of my mouth, and before I knew it, we shot through the entrance like a matchstick down a storm drain. Once inside the lock waiting chamber, the water was as still as the *VI of Swords* in the Tarot cards, where one sees the ferryman in an open boat rowing a woman and child away from troubled waters into a mill pond. We rounded *Capricorn* into the wind and dropped the sails.

We were storm-stayed in Hull for a few days. While waiting, we hired a professional adjustor to swing our compass. I needed more than a few corrective magnets to re-adjust mine. No doubt curious, two Customs Officers visited us when they saw our Swiss flag flying from the port side cross-tree. Had they known their flag etiquette, they would have realised our ensign indicated a Swiss National onboard, not the arrival of a foreign vessel. We wouldn't be hoisting the Swiss flag again to avoid confusion.

We intended to anchor in Wells-next-the-Sea, but the tide was wrong, so we headed for Lowestoft instead. On the way, we punched into head seas, with wind against tide, throwing us about like a ping-pong ball. Then, the depth dropped off dramatically as we approached the harbour entrance from a northerly direction. If we ran aground in those waters, our voyage to the sun would be well and truly scuppered. Peter looked concerned. He told me to call the Harbour Master on the VHF radio and ask him where we could find deeper water.

'Just come on in,' the watch-keeper said as if we had rung his doorbell and he was inviting us into his home. Had he ever entered Lowestoft in a boat in such adverse conditions? The least he could have done was to guide us away from the shallows. Maybe he was too engrossed watching *Eastenders* to bother about us.

Meanwhile, Tom and I watched Peter from inside the wheelhouse, bracing himself against the violent motion, one hand clasping the tiller, the other gripping the handrail whilst *Capricorn* bounced about like an origami paper boat. Down below, everything rattled and banged. *Sailing is supposed to be fun - it shouldn't be like riding a steer that is trying to throw you off!*

I looked at Tom's face by the dim glow of the red table navigation light. Was he frightened like me? Then, suddenly, we saw Peter altering course, making for a southerly approach towards the harbour entrance. The cross-tide was rushing across the outer mole like a flooded river. What if he got it wrong this time?

Once again, he made a dash for the entrance, and we came so close to the harbour wall that my heart almost stopped. But, as Peter had predicted, the tide swiftly swept us into the middle of the entrance just like that! We tied up to a black floating fender the size of our 33-foot *Capricorn,* normally used by large vessels.

Now that we had been granted the rite of passage to safety, we needed something sweet and strong to recover from the ordeal, so I prepared hot chocolate with a generous splash of brandy. When I handed the skipper his mug, I said, 'Sailing is like trying to commit suicide when you don't really want to die.' I immediately regretted my damning comment and said, to redeem myself, 'I guess the weather will improve once we get to the Med.'

Peter didn't comment.

On our way to Dover Harbour, we finally sampled the elusive Indian summer Peter had wished for, and I exchanged my foul-weather gear for a bikini. The sun was hot, and the sky a Mediterranean blue. It was as if summer had decided to have its last blast of glory. We anchored in the harbour, sat in the cockpit and ate spaghetti with tuna in a tomato sauce. Then we retired early to our bunks, hoping *Capricorn's* gentle pitching would lull us to sleep. A light breeze was forecast for the night, which was unlikely to whip up a lumpy sea.

Two hours passed, and I was still awake. By now, the pitching had become a roll. It wasn't the romantic workout between the sheets one might have imagined. For a start, Peter was fast asleep on the inside of our double berth. And if either of us accidentally fell out of the conjugal bunk, I would be the one to hit the cabin sole first. After all, I had chosen to sleep on the outside. By now, our boat was like a rodeo horse, fiercely bucking without a lull in between. Even our spring mattress couldn't absorb the shock. So I held on tight to my duvet with knees and fists clenched, alarmed at the prospect of a night of this. I started counting sheep, which didn't work. I tried white horses, but I frightened myself thinking of rough seas. In vain, I prayed for slumberland in a bed that didn't move. It was no use waking the skipper up and crying, 'I want to go home.' Our boat was our home. If I sent a '*May Day*' to Dover Coastguard: *Wife in distress on a boat at anchor urgently needs a hotel room,* would they respond to a matrimonial tiff? Finally, Peter woke up. By then, my nerves were like a mooring line, too tight for a falling tide.

'I knew this was a bad decision,' he said in a guilty voice. 'We should have paid and gone to a marina.'

My face was a storm. How lucky Peter was such an expert rodeo rider or a heavy-duty sleeper like Tom, who remained deep in slumber.

'I'll go and see if I can ease the motion,' Peter announced. *How does he think he can calm the troubled waters?* I heard him on deck, letting out some chain. Minutes later, the lurching stopped, and the beast was tamed. *My skipper might try walking on water next!*

'I should have done this before,' he said when he climbed back into bed. I thought, 'Why didn't you?' But I was curious enough to ask how he had managed to stop the violent rolling. He explained he had put a rope around the chain and led it to the stern, creating a triangle he could fine-tune to bring *Capricorn* broadside to the wind and head on to the swell.

Amazingly, my crib became a gentle pitch. What a shame we had to catch the tide within the next two hours. 'You can stay in bed,' Peter offered. I was still bad-tempered but not mad enough to cast him off in a dinghy like *Mr Christian*.

When we left Dover Harbour under sail, the sea was as smooth as a bowling green. I woke up after we were well on our way to Southampton.

14. Our Bermuda Triangle

Are we lost?' I cried. The words had sprung out of my mouth before I realised what I was saying. Light rain had been forecast, but not fog. The veil of mist was so thick I could have sewn a button on it. And that wasn't all. Our navigation equipment had failed us, starting with the temperature gauge on our reconditioned Perkins engine. The radio direction finder (RDF) (the device that receives bearings from a radio beacon) and the speedometer, which registers speed and distances covered through the water, had also stopped working. The impeller must have fouled with seaweed.

With its forty-foot tides and perilous currents, the Channel Islands were a dangerous place to sail in these conditions. Without navigation aids or landmarks, the skipper could only rely on the last running fix he had plotted on the chart; the rest would depend on his intuition. He had made this crossing three times before in other sailing yachts and found he didn't need to allow for tide because if the boat were pushed northward by the current, the next tide would bring it back on course and vice-versa. Because of the solid wall of fog, Peter called Guernsey coastguard on the VHF radio to ask if they could verify his position. They told him they would contact Cherbourg and get a triangulated fix between them. Shortly after, the coastguard radioed back with a position.

'They've got it wrong,' Peter told Tom and me, poised in the cockpit with our senses on high alert. We couldn't see anything or hear the sound of a foghorn. Another vessel might have been out there. Peter suspected our VHF radio could also be faulty. Despite the coastguard's findings, which put us a long way to the west, he continued on our initial heading, and it wasn't long before Guernsey's lighthouse loomed out of the mist. Had the navigation been left to me, we might have been heading for Norway or shipwrecked on rocks.

It was early evening when we anchored into Guernsey's outer harbour, where we waited for the tide to float us through the lock gates into sheltered waters. By then, I had no desire to celebrate my birthday, even though I had bought a cake for the occasion before we left Southampton. Peter surprised me when he placed it on the saloon table with a few candles. Seeing me sulking, he said, 'Maybe we should sell the boat?'

'Don't be silly,' I replied, feeling he was overreacting. He was never seasick. It must have been hard for him to understand how low-spirited one can get when suffering from *le mal de mer*. 'No pain, no gain,' as the saying goes. I reminded myself that it had been my choice not to sit in an armchair with remote control buttons, watching other people's adventures on a screen. Although we had endured endless mishaps since we set off, we were living our own.

Luckily, we cleared the tidal lock before midnight, moored to a pontoon in St Peter's Marina, and retired to our cabins.

We woke up to a beautiful sunny day. I called my friend Nobby Clarke, who had retired on the island. He was a Naval Commander on an anti-submarine frigate during WWII and one of the charterers on *Spirit of Labrador*. Whenever he saw me beavering away in the galley, cooking 'cordon bleu' meals for the group of WWII German and British veterans, he would insist on helping me with the dishes.

Nobby gave us a grand tour of Guernsey in his car. Seeing thirty-foot high islands swallowed up, only to re-appear at low tide in an endless cycle, reminded me of French writer Victor Hugo's description of the Channel Islands: *Les Îles de la Manche sont des morceaux de France tombés dans la mer et ramassés par l'Angleterre* - The Channel Islands are pieces of France that fell into the sea before being picked up by England.

We could have stayed on this enchanting island much longer, but winter was fast approaching. I kissed my friend Nobby goodbye, sad that we would probably never see each other again.

The Island of Bréhat was our landfall into French waters. We zigzagged our way through a fortress of craggy rocks leading into a bay that could have sheltered us from a hurricane, not that we were expecting one! We dropped anchor and sat in the cockpit, watching the sunset. Bathed in the hazy golden light, I felt inspired about the future and began writing a new song:

Deep in the sea are riches beyond compare,
but if you're looking for safety,
it is on the shore; sailing is a love affair.

Peter lowered the retractable legs as *Capricorn's* keel touched the seabed. 'If you hadn't retrieved the leg from the mud in Bridlington Harbour, you would have had to make a peg leg like Long John Silver,' I remarked over dinner.

'Or hop ashore with a crutch,' Peter replied.

The next stop was the fishing port of Roscoff. It was high tide and still daylight when we arrived. Peter had visited the place five years earlier in *Ellis* and sailed into the harbour in the dark, at low tide, dodging his way through the rock-strewn channel. People partying on their boats had clapped and cheered him, shouting: '*Bravo l'Anglais.*'

We sailed to Aberwrach Harbour next. The entrance was festooned with high rock pinnacles covered in multi-coloured seaweeds. The rockery at Kew Gardens would have looked like a pile of pebbles by comparison.

On our way to Le Conquet, the sea resembled a millpond. The gentle breeze hardly filled the jib. Rocks appeared and disappeared on either side of the channel while imposing lighthouses bellowed like moaning cows. Their sound, muffled in the low mist, created such an eeriness in the harsh marine environment. Whatever the weather, the sea isn't a place for complacency, below or above deck. Peter always insisted on us wearing our harnesses, which we tied to a lifeline. The legendary French yachtsman Eric Taberly had fallen foul during a freak moment when he was caught off-guard.

On that fatal day, competing in the Fife Regatta, Taberly was by the mast with two crew, about to drop the gaff-rigged sail. He leaned against the boom and tried to put a line around it to secure the mainsail. He had done this manoeuvre a hundred times, but in the wild swell, the 'gaff' suddenly swung across the deck with such force that it struck him across the chest. Taberly was propelled backwards and over the side. The crew heard him shout something before he disappeared into the raging waves. He had no lifejacket, no torch, and no hand flares. His body was recovered two weeks later in the Irish Sea.

Lulled into quiet contemplation by a gentle sea, we found ourselves ten minutes late to meet the tide. 'We'll put the engine on,' the skipper said. 'We're only 1.5 miles away from Le Conquet.' Had we known, we wouldn't have indulged so casually in the most treacherous channel on the coast of Brittany. None of us was prepared when the floodgates opened upon us. The tide was like a torrent rushing past *Capricorn's* hull. Peter increased the revs on the engine. Looking at her impressive bow wave, it seemed we could be in Le Conquet in no time at that speed, or so we thought. Then, the skipper realised that the leading channel marker buoy we had passed a few minutes ago was now overtaking us. It's just as well Peter is a man who never panics, because we were now being swept backwards towards the rocks faster than our engine revs could propel us forward at full throttle. Then, suddenly, the engine stalled. Was the Channel du Four to be our Bermuda Triangle?

Capricorn and her crew were now in the jaws of a vicious tide, with no engine or wind to hoist the sails. As we careered closer to the rocks, the prospect of a shipwreck seemed inevitable. I stared at Peter's face, trying to read his mind. What was he planning next to get us out of this? Both Tom and I trusted him with our lives and knew that with his deep knowledge of the sea, our skipper would take the appropriate action. He did just that when he leapt to the bow and let the anchor go. We heard every link of the two-hundred-and-fifty-foot chain rattle out of the locker and plunge towards the seabed thirty feet below. As the anchor struck the bottom, it rumbled over boulders, and with a shudder, the chain suddenly became a solid bar as straight as a rod. With seven knots of tide rushing past her hull, *Capricorn* created such a mighty bow wave that it felt as if we were underway, yet the anchor was stopping us from being swept onto rocks, at least for now.

Peter checked the engine while Tom and I remained on watch. His diagnosis was swift: it had overheated. We couldn't have read the signs because the temperature gauge had given up on our way to Guernsey. Therefore, we would have to sail into Lorient to buy another one.

The tide started to ease while we waited for the engine to cool. Peter tried the ignition key. There was an anxious moment until we heard the healthy roar of the motor. Next came the mammoth task for him to winch in all that chain by hand. I took the tiller, and he shouted instructions for me to head towards the anchor to lessen the weight of the chain while he lifted it. We had bought the anchor winch at Beaulieu jumble, but it proved laboriously slow, especially in our predicament. We would need to add another item to our wish list.

By the time Peter had hauled all the chain, he was ready to collapse. The blisters on his hands had burst, and he was bleeding badly. I left Tom at the tiller, rushed below deck to get our first aid kit, and nursed his injuries. Then, we motored at a snail's pace for an hour, slogging towards Le Conquet.

Once through the entrance, we passed a local fisherman in a large open boat. I asked him where he thought it best to anchor our 1.5-metre draft sailing yacht. He pointed astern, twenty metres behind him. We dropped the hook where he suggested.

Why trust local knowledge?

We pitched non-stop through the night with the swell, and if that wasn't enough, at low tide, *Capricorn's* keel bumped the seabed with every trough. My teeth rattled, and my stomach turned with each thud and I wasn't the only one.

Thankfully, the concrete trampoline effect on the seabed was short-lived, and we got some sleep with the incoming tide. I wondered if the French fisherman was still smarting over the hundred-year war with England!

Many sea shanties have been written over the years, evoking the saltwater memories of sailors navigating the iconic *Pointe* du *Raz*. Located between the Isle of Sein and Pointe du Raz, the tide between the straits can funnel up to eleven knots through its narrow channel, creating violent seas in blustery winds. Bounced by *La Jument* lighthouse, the Raz has been the theatre of many tragic stories. Countless vessels have been lost through the centuries, swept and shipwrecked onto ragged rocks. It still happens today.

The Raz became legendary on the world stage when the photographer Jean Guichard took his renowned picture of a man, a lighthouse, and a wave. The story goes: Théodore Malgorn, one of *La Jument's* lighthouse keepers, was on duty when he heard a helicopter hovering overhead. He thought it had come to rescue him. He rushed downstairs, ready to be picked up. Then, as he stepped outside, he saw a giant wave about to engulf him. Malgorn rushed in and immediately shut the door behind him.

At significant risk to himself and the pilot, the photographer, Jean Guichard, took the ultimate shot of *La*

Jument lighthouse and the keeper in the storm. It made him famous, though Malgorn almost lost his life.

We chose a quiet day to sail through the Raz. *Capricorn* rose and dipped at ten knots over the ground; six were the tide pushing her. Then, before we knew it, the forty-eight-metre-high granite fortress of *La Jument* loomed abeam of us as a symbol of deliverance.

Lorient wasn't a place to linger as a tourist. We only stopped there to buy a new speedometer and temperature gauge at one of the chandlers. The French Navy heavily occupied the harbour and was still using the forbidding-looking WWII German concrete bombproof submarine pens.

We anchored overnight in Audierne and the Isle de Glénans before sailing for Belle Île (Belle-Île-en-Mer). The crew was close to mutiny on the way when *Capricorn's* yellow decks became covered in powdery snow. It was Peter's fault we were still in the Bay of Biscay in November. He wouldn't be shovelling snow now if he had finished building *Capricorn* four months earlier! I thought he should make a snowman, put on a sailor's hat and call him *Jolly Jack Frost!*

Yet, the skipper took his watch in the cockpit without a fuss, and Tom and I only came on deck for a quick sail change before returning to the wheelhouse. We were snug in our T-shirts, with the diesel heater blazing in the saloon. Outside, the temperature had plummeted to minus two degrees. Then, once we had moored by the harbour wall beneath the *Citadelle Vauban,* I redeemed myself and served Peter a lamb stew, which restored his spirit, not that he had lost it.

After lunch, we decided to explore the area. We headed for La Citadelle and walked up a steep hill to the gatehouse. The place was deserted, yet on the display board was written: *Ouvert au Public.* We took turns trying to open the heavily studded wooden door and found it locked. Frustrated by our effort, Peter grabbed the large hanging wrought-iron ring and hammered at the door.

No one answered.

We waited a while. Then, as we turned to go, we heard a heavy bolt being drawn back, followed by an eerie creak. Someone had opened the door just a few inches to reveal a pair of hands with gnarled knuckles pushing hard against the reluctant hinges. Then we saw a woman wearing a dark cloak, which almost covered her large black, pointed shoes. She stared at us with probing eyes from underneath her long, straggly hair and a beret pulled down over her forehead. The beak of her nose preceded her. She beckoned us in with a sweep of her arm and said, *'Vous venez voir le château?'* You are coming to see the castle.

'*Oui*,' I replied, feeling intimidated.

As we walked through the hefty studded door, we wondered where the woman had parked her broomstick. Was she a phantom or an eccentric tour guide wearing a strange costume? She handed me a leaflet with a map for us to follow, then disappeared. *Ghosts don't usually hand out pamphlets or play 'hide and seek!*

We saw her briefly again, standing in the centre of the vast parade ground and then peeping through the ramparts, observing us. Our bizarre encounter with the cloaked woman of *La Citadelle* was a welcome respite from all our misadventures.

Perhaps she wasn't the only ghost in the castle. Built in 1549, *La Citadelle* was occupied by the English from 1761 to 1763. In the 19th century, it was used as a penal colony for war and political prisoners before becoming a centre for Spanish Civil War refugees at the end of the 1930s.

At dawn, we left Belle-Île on an overnight passage to Royan. In the murk, I watched the breaking waves of the Atlantic Ocean, with our navigation lights reflecting red on the port side and green to starboard, while *Capricorn* rode the waves like a horse jumping over hurdles. The stars emerged from the horizon as we sailed into the night, while the disturbed effervescent algae in the boat's wake shone like emerald green crystals. The Atlantic swell would soon give way to ripples on the Canal du Midi, but not just yet. The River Gironde Estuary would be our next rite of passage to the Mediterranean. We couldn't wait.

15. The Soup Kitchen

The morning was crisp, the wind fierce enough to blow my yellow sou'wester hat off as we raced up the estuary to Royan with a following wind. *Capricorn* rose the steep ochre-coloured pinnacles before she slid down into the troughs. It felt as if we were on a never-ending splash ride at Disneyland. With the sails spread like angel wings, we could feel the acceleration of the water swishing past the hull. Seeing waves, yards away, crashing on the shallow banks was nerve-racking. From the cockpit, Tom and I kept a close eye on the compass and the buoyed channel while Peter was busy down below, rechecking our course on the chart. The Gironde Estuary, a seaway to Bordeaux, is infamous for its shifting sands and overfalls. It wasn't the place to enjoy a leisurely sail on a sunny Sunday afternoon. To avoid travelling in the dark, we stopped in Royan and arrived a few hours later, graced by the most spectacular orange sunset.

Royan had a lingering aura of despair from the days when the German Nazis flattened the city in WWII. It was entirely rebuilt, including the Cathedral of Notre Dame, which stood as a concrete postwar construction resembling the prow of a ship seen from miles around. Inside, the chancel, transept and nave were one cavernous open-plan interior. The exposed reinforcing bars had rust streaks bleeding through the structure as if they were there to represent all the bloodshed of WWII. The drabness of this sanctuary couldn't lift my spirit above the ashes of war. What a stark beginning for a baby to be christened in the rusting concrete font. I lit a candle on the altar rails, prayed for the newborns and paid homage to the dead.

From Royan, we motored upstream with the incoming tide. On the way, we saw skeletons of wrecks scattered along the river banks, lying there as a stark reminder for sailors to watch for shifting sandbanks and fast-flowing currents. We reached Bordeaux seven hours later, just as dusk fell and tied up to a working barge a stone's throw away from the historical *Pont de Pierre.* Its seventeen arches, fully lit, conveyed an air of festivity. (Legend has it that the arches depict the same number of letters as Napoléon Bonaparte.)

On the other side of the river, the sinister bomb-proof submarine pens appeared like a fairy castle with multi-coloured festive lights. Lying in my bunk, I could hear the gurgling of the river streaming past our hull. It felt as if *Capricorn* was underway. That night, I dreamed I was singing on stage wearing a green dress. How strange when I was practically living in my wet weather gear and wellies. Still, I wasn't the only one on this voyage to undergo deconstruction and reinvention. *Capricorn* would soon be transformed into a canal boat.

For some people, Monday is laundry day. For us, it would be unstepping a 45-foot mast. The skipper has an inventive mind for executing dangerous and strenuous manoeuvres, as this one happened to be. After careful preparation, with the aid of pulleys and two scaffolding poles, he lowered the mast like a Regimental Colour Sergeant dipping his flagstaff to salute the monarch. He made it look so easy but frightening for those watching.

For the past three hundred years, boats and barges have sailed from the Atlantic to the Mediterranean, back and forth, through the Gironde estuary and the Garonne. The Garonne rises in the Pyrenees and is the key river of southwest France with its fertile farmland and fine vineyards. Although very picturesque, the depth in this body of water can be critical in places.

It was dusk when we reached the Canal Latéral leading to Toulouse. We entered the lock and tied a rope to the steep ladder; then, I climbed the dark, sinister chamber to the top. There was a telephone booth there where one could contact the lock-keeper. I called, but no one replied. Staying inside the lock for the night wasn't an option as we would need to adjust the rope with the changing tide. It was tethered to a bollard twelve feet above our deck. So we reluctantly moored against a barge by the lock entrance.

The temperature had dropped dramatically by now. The decks and mooring ropes attached around the barge's bollards were frozen solid. Peter had to pour buckets of water from the river to thaw and release them. But, as soon as he put the pail down, the ice grabbed it. Seeing the inside of our cabin's aluminium frame hatches frosted was another shock. So much for all this talk about the butter getting softer, the further south one gets!

Then, the following morning, we heard *Capricorn's* bow breaking the ice when we exited the lock. For goodness sake, we were heading for the Mediterranean sun, not Iceland! And there were one hundred and thirteen locks left to weave through to Sète. Peter had cruised to Bordeaux in *Ellis* on his return to England one summer. Although he knew the ropes, he had never anticipated we would encounter such winter conditions.

We took turns at the tiller, although Peter and Tom insisted I did less. No doubt, they would have gladly swapped places to remain in the saloon with a hot stew simmering on the stove, but they were chivalrous.

As I steered *Capricorn* in the cold, I sometimes wondered if my meditative mood wasn't the early stage of hyperthermia. I wore so many layers on top of one another that I struggled with every move I made. My mind, on the other hand, was in overdrive, and I felt as if my emotional baggage was being stripped to bare threads. How long would I keep trying to patch up the past?

I was six years old when I told my Godmother, Odette, who ran the bakery on our ground floor, that I was leaving home for good. I had packed soap and a flannel inside my red doll's suitcase and was ready to go. She looked at me, grinning the whole width of her horse-like teeth, rocking her head from side to side and pursing her lips. Her eyes narrowed, and it was hard to guess what she was thinking. She grabbed her handbag, and I thought Odette might be looking for a handkerchief to wipe my tears. Instead, she took out her purse, extracted a twenty francs banknote and handed it to me.

'You'll need this for the journey,' she said.

A hug was all I wanted. Odette must have known I wasn't getting much attention at home. Still, this blonde purveyor of bread loaves with bright red lipstick and a devilish smile enjoyed making jokes at other people's expense, including me. She seemed to be made for the theatre, but God knows why she worked in a bakery!

I left the shop tearful with my head down and walked out of the village, staring pitifully at the empty road to the cemetery. I often went there to see my brother's grave. It had such lovely yellow pansies on it. I had heard Maman talking to Odette about her son Jean-Louis dying of cot death before I was born.

I had no idea of the time when I returned to the bakery. Odette didn't seem surprised to see me. She looked at me, waiting for a repartee, and when none came, she asked for her twenty francs. I handed it back to her, feeling I had achieved nothing when I tried to run away. But where could I have gone?

A few days later, Odette decided to strap one of her bras on top of my red cardigan.

'What are you doing?' I prompted, feeling perplexed. Surely, I was too young to wear a bra; besides, it was far too big. She ignored me and filled the two cups with tissue paper, then told me to knock at Madame Grolimund's door, show myself to her, and recite what she taught me. I looked at Odette with the eyes of a pleading puppy.

'Come on,' said Odette firmly, 'Madame Grolimund will be impressed by your accoutrement.'

The woman must have seen me at the bakery when she came to buy her bread. She wore 'jam-jar bottom' glasses. She was so tall and thin that I thought she must have gone through a mangle. She plaited her long hair and tied it around her head.

I left the bakery feeling awkward. Who would wear a bra on top of a cardigan? Still, I walked down the cobbled street to Madame Grolimund's house, just a few minutes away. My stomach was churning. When I got there, I rang the bell, feeling panicky. Would I regret what I was about to do? It didn't make sense. I heard some quickening footsteps from inside, which made me want to run away, but it was too late; Madame Grolimund had already opened the door. She looked down at me, surprised to see a child with a bra over her cardigan. Then, before she could ask me what I had come for, I pointed at my chest and said boldly, just as Odette had instructed me, 'Look, Madame Grolimund, my breasts are bigger than yours.'

In my defence, I hadn't fully grasped the meaning of this satire aimed at the flat-chested woman who never did me any wrong and certainly didn't need to be reminded of her lack of physical attributes by a six-year-old girl. Madame Grolimund slammed the door hard, leaving me lost and dejected.

I felt ashamed when I grasped Odette's tasteless prank on Madame Grolimund. She would never know how terrible I felt. When I told Odette about her shutting the door on me, she smirked, revelling in her perversity. How far would I go to please my godmother?

Sadly, Madame Grolimund never bought her bread from the bakery again, and Odette lost a customer. I could only hope she would forgive a naive little girl who never meant to do her any harm because she didn't know any better.

By midday, the ice on the canal had melted, leaving rows of trees reflecting on the water. The high branches spanned out from the banks, meeting in the middle like the vaulted ceiling of a cathedral. I felt as if we were in a time warp, and it was only upon approaching a lock that we stirred from the canal's hypnotic spell. Then, it was all hands on deck. Tom or I would jump off the boat before *Capricorn* entered the lock, stand on the quayside, grab the looped ropes and drop them over for-and-aft bollards. Then, Peter took the slack as the water rose. In the late afternoon, after the locks closed, we would tie up to a tree on the opposite side of the towpath to feel more secure at night.

We arrived in Toulouse a week later and moored at Port St Sauveur (Port St Saviour). Then I telephoned Les Bureaux de la Navigation to double-check our passage to Sète. I didn't expect the answer they gave me.

'There's been a drought,' the employee explained. 'The reservoirs which feed the Canal du Midi are empty.'

'But you confirmed a week ago that we could get to Sète.'

'We thought it might rain before you arrived. We don't have enough water to get you over the summit, four or five locks on from Toulouse.'

'How much rain do you need to fill your reservoirs up?'

'Three weeks, a month or more, I don't know,' the man said impatiently.

It would need more than a rain dance to float *Capricorn* to the Med. How ironic! We had left England because of the rain, and now we were praying for it. But how long would it take to fill the reservoirs and feed the canals? Only Jupiter knew! We were now stranded in Toulouse. Still, we had no intention of turning back and facing

Biscay in December. When Tom flew home, we began looking for work.

Our first port of call was the nearest job centre in the old town. I made an appointment with the receptionist for an interview. She asked us to bring our last two wage slips and be there at 2 pm the following day. (We hadn't kept any documents from our previous jobs.)

We presented ourselves at the centre promptly the next day and were ushered into a classroom where we sat at desks with other people. A young woman in a dark suit, holding papers, walked into the room. She handed each of us a form and a black pen. She explained how to complete it. The form didn't allow much room to write all our work experiences. Still, for now, I entered: 'secretarial skills - shorthand and accountancy, fluent in English and German, touch-type sixty words a minute.' For Peter, I wrote 'welder, joiner and engineer.' The woman returned to the room and collected the questionnaires as if they were examination papers. 'Your forms will be processed and sent back to you in a day or two,' she announced before returning to her office.

Our address was now 'Yacht *Capricorn* near Les Médecins sans Frontière, Port St Sauveur.' Peter had tied a letterbox to the boat hook and fastened it to one of the stanchions. To check if the process worked, we sent ourselves a postcard. It was delivered the following day. Didn't I say a boat hook for a sailor is the stick of salvation? After all, the skipper had retrieved *Capricorn's* leg in the mire of Bridlington harbour with it!

We called the office a week later after hearing nothing from them. A woman told us they had no vacancies and referred us to social services. I called them to make an appointment.

The building resembled a hospital's outpatient department, which provided dental and medical treatments for the poor and the unemployed. At the reception desk, a young woman queried the purpose of our visit.

'We've got an appointment with a social worker at 2.30 pm,' I explained. The woman picked up the phone and told us to wait. The lobby was busy with people of all ages. I noticed some women wore scarves, oddly held down with a knot under their chins, whilst the men were dressed in multiple overcoats and woolly hats pulled down over their ears. The smell of urine was overbearing. The harsh neon light spotlighted the resigned expression on the people's faces as they stared into space, waiting for their turn. I heard my father's words from beyond the veil. 'You've always had delusions of grandeur. Look at where you are now!'

Before we could decide where to sit, a heavily pregnant woman approached. 'Are you Madame and Monsieur Newby?' she asked.

'Yes,' I replied.

She motioned us to follow her to her office. Once we sat opposite her desk, we felt like schoolchildren with our backs straight, waiting for detention.

'What can I do for you?' the woman inquired. She had long auburn hair and kind hazel eyes.

'We're stranded on our boat in Toulouse because of a drought on the Canal du Midi. We have work promised to us in Mallorca, but we cannot get there now. We have also run out of money and are trying to find a job in Toulouse.'

The woman stared at me. I could see she wasn't sure of our story. She glanced at Peter, expecting him to explain himself. 'My husband is English,' I said. 'I'm sorry his French is limited.'

'What about family or friends? Couldn't they help you?'

'We don't like to burden them. Would you know of any jobs? We both have several skills to offer, but we are willing to clean, and my husband would even consider road-sweeping.'

'Impossible,' she answered. 'Those jobs are reserved for out-of-work ex-military personnel.'

Peter and I looked at each other, thinking, 'What a rewarding prospect for these Frenchmen who risked their lives to defend their country.'

'December is a difficult time,' the woman continued, 'but I'll come up with something. How do you keep warm on your boat?'

'We have a diesel heater.'

She scribbled a note for twenty litres of fuel and gave us directions on how to get to the filling station.

'If you like, you could stay in one of the hostels, but you'll be separated,' she stressed.

'No, we're fine,' I replied. This option would be the last resort.

'Now for food, we have *Les Restaurants du Coeur.*'

It sounded more poetic than soup kitchens, which was what she meant. French comedian *Coluche* founded these free restaurants because he believed nobody in his country should go hungry.

'If you don't like the idea of *Restaurants du Coeur,* I can give you a ration card. There are warehouses where you could collect free food to take home daily.'

The woman handed me a list of the places and then asked to be excused. She returned shortly after, carrying a large paper carrier bag. 'Here,' she announced, 'this will keep you going until you've sorted yourselves out. Good Luck!'

The food parcel contained everything from cooking oil to lentils, fresh coffee beans, and biscuits. Surprisingly, it also included a bottle of Beaujolais. The French wouldn't expect anyone to go without wine, even when the chips were down. Once outside, I cried out tearfully, 'Thank you, France. You wouldn't leave us hungry.'

We rounded the corner and saw three young women standing on the street. One shouted to an old man, as if he were deaf, 'Let's do it.'

'I'm married', he answered.

'So am I,' she replied.

We felt like we were on a stage set without a script.

The soup kitchen was a vast canteen with cheap *Formica* table-tops and basic stackable tubular chairs. There must have been well over sixty to eighty people in the place, mostly middle-aged, who must have been life's casualties, drop-outs and misfits. I thought they looked just like characters in Dickens's novels. It also had a powerful smell of boiled cabbage, disinfectant and body odour, which was nauseating.

We felt self-conscious standing at the serving counter with our trays, waiting to be served. A woman in a green apron filled our bowls with a thin soup with noodles and vegetables floating awkwardly on top. She cut us some chunks of bread, then pushed two plates of food towards us, with an insipid concoction that looked like meatballs in gravy and stodgy mashed potatoes. We thanked her. She never looked up.

We made for a table and sat opposite a man who seemed the tidiest. Peter dug into the food as if he hadn't eaten for a week, slurping down his soup and shovelling bread into his face. He played the role only too well. He couldn't have been that hungry. Amidst the charade, he lifted his little finger as he drank his cup of water, trying hard to humour me.

I managed a grin.

The situation didn't seem to distress him. For Peter, this must have been like a brief storm at sea whilst I was drowning in self-pity. I glared at the food on my plate and thought, 'I'm not going to like this.' I tried the soup, but it wouldn't go down. People were staring at me.

'The food is better in the evening,' the woman shouted from the next table. I nodded in acknowledgement, not wanting to strike up a conversation.

'Christmas lunch is very good,' she continued. I thought, Christmas here - NEVER.

'Aren't you hungry?' the man at our table asked. He had an air of *je ne sais quoi* about him. Was he a philosopher on a mission? I asked him where he lived. Maybe it was a silly question!

'Mais ma petite dame, à la belle étoile naturellement,' 'under the stars naturally,' the man answered casually. 'In winter, I live in a hostel. We have three meals a day and a colour television. I can't complain!'

He made it sound like a holiday! He explained he had been a truck driver before he lost his job. When his unemployment benefits ran out, he found himself on the street. What a thin thread between respectability and vagrancy!

Two English yachts were moored a few yards up the canal from us. Eric owned the 43-foot blue ferro-cement ketch built like a bathtub with two masts. He was tall and muscly, and when standing on deck, he had the demeanour of someone ready to repel borders.

In contrast, his friend Frank owned a flimsy plywood catamaran. He and Eric had travelled together in convoy from Bordeaux. Frank looked like a derelict *Popeye* with his pipe and nicotine-stained beard. One afternoon, he invited us on his boat for tea and cake. We were intrigued.

The first thing that struck us when we walked into Frank's saloon was the overpowering smell of paraffin. It must have been what he used for cooking and heating. He invited us to sit on horse-shoe settees by a table that had lost its lustre like the rest of the boat.

He went to make the tea. The galley was in one of the hulls. When Frank served us, he said, almost running out of puff, 'I can't believe how cold it is in the South of France.'

It appeared his paraffin heater wasn't keeping him warm. His face looked blue despite being dressed with, God knows, how many woolly jumpers on top of each other. Frank told us that the staff in cafés often refused to serve him as they mistook him for a tramp. It must have been humiliating and upsetting for him, given he was once a petty officer in the British Royal Navy on a WWII destroyer.

Frank offered us his homemade cake. I wondered what ingredients he had used, for the sweetness of sugar and raisins couldn't mask the taste of paraffin. Still, we ate it in appreciation for his effort. He explained that Eric and he would resume their travels to the Med together in the spring. Meanwhile, he was flying back to London, where he and his English wife now lived. He would spend the rest of the winter there.

'I am sure I'll get bored watching television all day,' he lamented.

'Better bored than dead,' I thought.

Frank attended the Anglican church regularly. He talked about Reverend Arthur Harvey, who was also a yachtsman.

'Do you have his telephone number?' Peter asked. 'Maybe we could give him a ring and invite him aboard *Capricorn* for a chat.'

Meanwhile, Eric was enjoying his stay in Toulouse. He had met a young French foreign legionnaire, fitting out a yacht a few yards down the canal from us. Eric had built his own boat and was happy to help Jacques with his. Surprisingly, for such a tough-looking man, Eric wrote love stories. Whenever he had guests, he'd ask them to sign the visitor's book and take Polaroid pictures of everyone. He must have been collecting characters for his plots. Eric had travelled Europe giving lectures on industrial central heating and stayed in five-star hotels, which might have provided the backdrops to his short stories. Perhaps we would appear in one. Peter's friend, Tim's mother, had written a tale about us in which she describes me standing on the quayside with my suitcases, watching my beloved sail away into the blue. What had prompted her to imagine such a dramatic end to our relationship when she didn't know me? But I thought if our marriage took a deep dive, would there be time to 'man the pumps' of reconciliation to save it?

16. The Gift

We heard a knock on the roof hatch and saw a man staring into the wheelhouse from under his black felt trilby hat, which was pulled down over his forehead. He looked menacing, especially with the collar of his long charcoal grey overcoat turned up. Had he come to make us an offer we couldn't refuse? Before we could evaluate the situation, the stranger said in a deep voice: 'You must be Monique and Peter.'

How did the man know our names?

'Your friend Frank, who has attended my services, mentioned you. I'm Reverend Arthur Harvey.'

I don't know what surprised us the most: his gangster-like appearance or the fact that he was a man of the cloth.

'Please, come inside,' Peter motioned. 'Make yourself at home.'

The Reverend had a mahogany complexion, dark hair, and a well-defined Marlon Brando nose. *Maybe he is the Godfather disguised as a reverend! He might ask us to deliver a special cargo on his behalf.*

He undid the top button of his coat, revealing his clerical collar, and laid it on the chart table with his hat. He looked around appraisingly and said, 'Your boat has a fresh feel. When I sail with friends, the cabins usually reek like rugby changing rooms.'

I smiled, relieved at his casual comment.

The Reverend made himself comfortable on the saloon settee. Peter asked if he would like coffee, tea or an aperitif. 'We only have whisky,' he added apologetically. Although it was just midday, the Reverend seemed partial to a tipple.

Peter joined him in a *wee dram* and proposed a toast to plain sailing as we clinked glasses.

'I've only sailed in the Balearics,' The Reverend continued. 'A group of us once chartered a *Moody*. My experience was either boredom or terror. In the Med, it's one or the other - no wind or too much of it.'

'That's the general consensus amongst *yachties*,' Peter conceded. The Yorkshire Coast inevitably slipped into the conversation and why we were in Toulouse.

'We are stranded on the Canal du Midi because of a drought and are both looking for work while waiting to get to the Med. I'm a singer-songwriter-guitarist,' I said, 'but I can do secretarial work, cooking, cleaning, etc. I've tried to perform in restaurants and hotels in Toulouse, but students from the Conservatoire de Musique cover those venues.'

'I could build a Noah's Ark if any of your flocks were worried about the rain coming,' Peter said jokingly. 'Perhaps some of your congregation might want repairs or painting done?'

'I'll put the word out,' the Reverend replied. 'Meeting people like you makes a real change. Most of my faithful are ex-pats or Americans working for the Airbus Industry. They usually complain about roof repair bills on their second homes or paying too much for their air tickets back home.'

Christmas came into the conversation. He asked if I would sing at his Carol Service and said, 'I've religious lyrics for *Morning Has Broken* by Cat Stevens, and maybe you could play *Greensleeves,* too.'

'Yes, I'd love to, Reverend,' I said excitedly.

'Please call me Arthur.'

I remember attending the Protestant Service near our home every Sunday as a nine-year-old, then walking two miles to the next village in time for Mass. Listening to choirs with their angelic voices was a step away from heaven. The rhythm of Latin spoken when the priest recited sacred words from the Holy Book was hypnotic. Most intriguing was when he oscillated his thurible down the aisle, wafting frankincense over his congregation. Yet, while I immersed myself in the promises of Heaven, Satan and Hell awoke my worst fears. First, there was Jesus on the cross. I thought of all the blood he lost before his passing. Then there was the confessional. It was most intimidating talking to the priest behind red curtains. However, his sympathetic voice felt as if he understood the temptations of a little girl when she shouted at her sisters or murdered a wasp. Then came repentance. The priest would ask me to recite a few *Ave Marias* for absolution. I felt I could fly like an Angel when I left the church.

I can still picture myself walking down the aisle on my Confirmation Day, wearing a new white lacy dress, a veil and white shoes, ready to seal my promise of devotion to God. I was so proud. My parents didn't attend the ceremony. They didn't believe in God. They only went to church for weddings and funerals because it was the right thing to do. Yet, they complained about the cost of my outfit. I never wore another white dress after that day.

When Arthur visited us the second time, he asked Peter if he would take the train to Bordeaux, pick up his old car and drive it back to Toulouse. 'You can borrow it, so you'll have transport to get about,' he offered. The church had bought Arthur a new car and agreed on a deal with the garage to keep the old one for himself. The vehicle required minor repairs, but he insisted Peter could do those if and when he had time.

Arthur was an Anglican vicar without a church, so he borrowed one for his Sunday service in Bordeaux or Toulouse. He would inform his faithful where to go at the last minute. He had booked a hall in a convent run by Catholic nuns for his Christmas Carol Service. We drove there on the day, knowing we had just enough petrol to return to St Sauveur.

Arthur greeted us warmly when we arrived at the convent. The hall had a stage and a piano. Chairs were set up in anticipation of a large congregation. A small group of men and women had gathered on the stage. The church filled, and the choir began to sing, accompanied on the piano by a middle-aged blonde wearing a flowery dress.

Midway through the carol service, I sang *Greensleeves,* followed by *Morning Has Broken.* Then, Arthur gave a sermon on 'giving' and 'receiving.' He stressed that 'receiving' was as important as 'giving.' His words resonated with our predicament. Peter felt guilty for putting me in a situation without money in a foreign country, and I was utterly ashamed for not handling it well. *The ego is like a tightrope that can break or sag.*

After the service, they offered tea and coffee in a meeting room adjacent to the hall. We mingled amongst the flock. Arthur came over and asked: 'Have you got an invitation for Christmas yet?'

'No,' we replied, surprised at his question.

'Give me a minute or two to sort this out.'

He returned triumphant, announcing he had found a family of five, keen to share their Christmas with us. 'They live fifteen kilometres outside town. You've got my car to drive yourselves there,' he confirmed with a smile.

A petite, dark-haired woman and a bold, stocky man walked towards us. 'Let me introduce you to Josephine and James. I leave you in good hands,' Arthur said before striding away to spread the cheer.

We shook hands, and then Josephine announced, 'We'd be delighted for you to come and share Christmas with us. We've two teenage daughters and a son.'

She flicked a strand of her long hair back in place, smiled and waited for our answer. The woman had a kindly face, but looking at her husband's steely eyes, I doubted he welcomed the idea. Still, Peter and I replied, 'We'd love to come.'

Josephine gave us their address and telephone number. 'See you on Christmas Day at about 11,' she beamed before the pair melted into the crowd.

Accepting their invitation presented us with a problem - we didn't have enough fuel to drive there or money to buy the family a present. We finished our tea. Then, a man with a pencil moustache approached us and said with an American accent, 'I enjoyed hearing you play the guitar and the unusual words in those familiar songs.'

'Thank you,' I replied proudly. Peter explained we were stranded in Toulouse in our boat and looking for work. 'Maybe you might have some rooms to paint or a garden to weed?' he ventured, smiling.

'No, sorry,' the American answered. There was an awkward silence. Then, Peter described how forging through the ice and discovering new places on the canal made us feel like pioneers. The man looked thoughtfully at him and said, 'I guess being on the pioneer trail, one is bound to hit some bumps along the way.'

Peter shrugged his shoulders and said, 'I guess so!'

'Why don't you have a meal on us,' the American offered. I watched him extract something from his wallet, slip it into Peter's hand, and then close his fingers as if he didn't want him to look at it now. A woman in her late fifties with short, curly hair was approaching. 'Sorry, Vern, we need to go,' she said. Then, turning towards us, she explained: 'We're expected at the American Embassy in half an hour for a dinner party.'

'Oh, yes,' Vern confirmed. 'Let me quickly introduce my wife. Marian, this is Peter and Monique.'

'Sorry, I've got to drag my husband away,' Marian urged. She took his hand and led him out of the room.

As they disappeared, Peter unclenched his fist to see what Vern had placed in his palm. When he thought it could be a contact number to arrange a date to have dinner together, he found a hundred-dollar bill folded with his visiting card.

All this good fortune at Christmas was overwhelming. It began with a bag of food topped with a bottle of Beaujolais and addresses of 'Restaurants du Coeur,' followed by the use of a car, free diesel to keep warm, an invitation to Christmas, and a $100 bill. Then, a string of invites from friends rolled in for the New Year. It was as if we were riding with Santa in his reindeer sleigh.

The soup kitchen now belonged to the past, although we still collected our daily food rations from a disused warehouse. In our shopping basket were eggs, a tin of cassoulets, one of meat, and some bread. These were ample to survive the day. In our circle of friends, nobody knew our situation. It would have been uncomfortable to tell them. Besides, it was a temporary setback. Toulouse was grey, cold, and damp, but the lamp posts were festooned with coloured lights, and the shop window displays heralded the glory of Christmas. All this glitter symbolised our good fortune, yet my pride had endured a blow, and I couldn't brush off the lingering feeling of worthlessness. The change in me threw Peter, but we covered our discord in the company of friends. Meanwhile, I found solace in Sunday mass, where I prayed to God or the Divine Source to help me rediscover the woman I once was or dreamed of becoming.

Josephine and James's country house was a thirty-mile return journey from Toulouse, nestled in the small village of Brouilly. The family lived in a two-storey residence built in the early 1920s with its own grounds. The property may have once been owned by a wealthy *Toulousain* merchant seeking a quieter life.

We rang the bell and waited. I was nervous while Peter was his usual quiet self. A tall youth wearing a bright rugby shirt and two brunettes dressed in short skirts and festive T-shirts answered the door. They had a look of expectation on their faces as if we had followed *yonder star* to their abode, but we didn't have frankincense and myrrh, just a white Christmas rose in a pot. Their father, who was hovering behind them, appeared irritated. He shook our hands, studying us intently. Was he worried about the safety of his silverware?

Josephine's affable greeting dispelled our unease. I handed her our gift, which she deposited by the tall Christmas tree adorned with multi-coloured baubles and fairy lights.

James took our coats, Josephine beckoned us into the lounge, and we sat on the white upholstered settee by the bay window overlooking an extensive vegetable garden. Josephine asked us if we would like a sherry, and her husband, James, returned with two generous glasses. The conversation became animated. We mentioned being caught in fog in the Channel Islands, our narrow escape from being shipwrecked in the Chenal du Four, and being stranded in Toulouse. Everyone hung onto our every word, and their comments made us feel like heroes. However, the friction between father and son was palpable. I caught James's disapproving glance aimed at Matthew, who looked back at him with exasperation. Had we been invited to defuse discord?

The girls were cheerful and invested in us. They played *Fuire Le Bonheur*—Running away from Happiness by English singer Jane Birkin. The song overwhelmed me with its unusual poetic lyrics and stirring melody, and her singing was breathtaking.

Sally, the youngest, took the lyrics off the album cover and wrote them on a piece of paper for me. I translated a few words:

To believe in God and the Heavens
when all can be so painful that
the heart bleeds and burns

Josephine summoned us to the table. When she brought the large golden turkey with all the trimmings, I thought how lucky we were to share Christmas with such lovely people. After coffee, Josephine suggested that she and I walk in the garden. On the way, she told me about her marriage crisis. James often flew on business to Bangkok, and she suspected him of having affairs with Thai girls. James had talked about his trips earlier on. He even showed us the gold silk V-neck dress he had bought for Josephine. I saw the look on her face, which seemed to say, 'Does he want me to recreate the intimate moments he had shared with his mistresses in Bangkok?'

'We've agreed to have counselling sessions,' Josephine confided. I didn't tell her what Peter and I were going through. After all, she and James had invited us to cheer them up. When we kissed each other goodbye, everyone responded warmly, including James, confirming that we had fulfilled our harmonising mission on this special day of Christmas.

After the festivities, we attended another of Arthur's services and met the Americans again. We learned Vern was on a two-year contract with Airbus Industry. His family had emigrated to America from Ireland between the two World Wars, and Marian's parents had left Holland around the same time. They had never lived away from home and missed their daughters and grandchildren in America, so they adopted us. We were wined and dined at their flat on the outskirts of Toulouse. They loved old musicals, and we brushed up on *Oklahoma*. Vern said: 'We don't watch anything we wouldn't allow to happen in our own home.' I sobbed to *The Sound of Music.*

The Canal du Midi reopened the first week of January. Meanwhile, Peter had found work as a shipwright for an English company, Blue Line, near Béziers. Our good fortune seemed to have started the day we visited the pregnant social worker. By now, she would have given birth, maybe to twins! As if all these gestures of kindness weren't enough, Marian and Vern's gift enabled us to stock up on food and fuel during our four-day journey down the Canal du Midi to Béziers. I thought of the Reverend Arthur Harvey's sermon when he said, 'Receiving graciously can be as godly as giving.' Peter was right, too, when he kept saying it would all work out.

Before leaving St Sauveur (St Saviour), we swept a generous layer of powdery snow off the deck. We could have built a snowman. The sun was breaking through a dark sky, lighting the way like a biblical scene. I could hear the Angels singing *Ave Maria* by Franz Schubert and thought we had experienced a Christmas miracle.

17. Stranger than Fiction

'Are we going to survive this?' I cried.

'Don't be silly, we'll be alright, sleeping close to the heater,' Peter insisted.

I could hear the ice cracking around *Capricorn's* hull and felt like somebody was scraping on a tile. I thought of the *Titanic*. What if the ice around us broke our boat, and we sank in our sleep, still tied to a wooden pontoon?

Thankfully, we awoke to another day. But seeing the inside of our hatches covered in ice wasn't reassuring. On the other side of the canal, white horses were grazing in the frosted fields. How resilient these equines were in temperatures plummeting to minus twenty degrees centigrade during the night. Not far away, in the Camargue region, local firefighters had tried to rescue flamingos trapped in the frozen waters where they stood. The men couldn't save them, even when they melted the ice around their legs. What a tragedy for those splendid crimson and white feathered birds who visited the salt marshes every year, never to soar into foreign skies again.

Capricorn was ice-bound for two weeks. When the weather improved, our American friends Vern and Marian came to stay with us at Port Cassafière. He had steered *Capricorn* two miles up to the Herbettes Aqueduct, where the canal straddles a four-lane highway. He found it unbelievable vessels could float above a motorway. It was a unique experience, hardly relatable to their Arizona home turf.

Spending time with people in a restricted space can be intense. Peter and I were anxious to meet our friends' expectations, not that we knew what they were. At least we all shared an adventurous spirit. So, in this nowhere place surrounded by arable fields as far as the eyes could see, we offered them a piece of my homeland, eating fondue and listening to traditional Swiss folk music. I even wore my costume to complete the theme. Would Marian and Vern remember being on a British ocean yacht, celebrating Swiss culture in southwest France?

The English company Blue Line, for whom Peter was now working, owned more than a hundred boats from the Norfolk Broads, which were moored inside an artificial lagoon close to where we were tied in the canal. Lewis, an ex-bobby in his forties, thin with a weathered face, oversaw the repair and maintenance of these boats in readiness for the summer season. Rented mainly to inexperienced British holidaymakers, the hired boats were used and abused, banging into banks and locks like bumper cars at a fairground. Peter was employed as a shipwright to fix them.

Lewis told us that he and his girlfriend, Anna, had sailed their 28-foot yacht, *Fairwind,* from England through the canals to the Med with another boat. In the Gulf of Lion, the two vessels were caught in savage seas and torrential rain. With no visibility, they lost contact with each other. Anna and Lewis had no idea where they were themselves either. They could only guess that land lay somewhere to the west. By then, the pair were far too exhausted to fight against the storm, so they decided to drive their yacht ashore, even though they knew they would be shipwrecked.

As they crashed through the surf, preparing for the inevitable, they suddenly realised the waves were moderating, but the visibility was still abysmal. The next thing they knew, they ran aground on a sandbank. By then, the rain had eased just enough to make out the shape of a jetty a few yards ahead. Lewis prepared a rope to take ashore, but Anna feared *Fairwind* might drift off the sandbank, leaving her unable to cope with the boat alone. So Lewis tied a rope around her waist, and Anna lowered herself over the side, waist-deep into the water. Halfway to the jetty, she disappeared. Lewis cursed himself for letting her go. He began to fear the worst until her head suddenly popped up like a cork. He yelled across: 'Are you alright?'

'I fell into a hole but managed to swim underwater and touch the jetty,' she shouted. After Anna had secured the rope to the wooden structure, she pulled herself back to *Fairwind*. Then, when the tide came in, they hauled the yacht alongside.

Such a miraculous escape is comparable to being blindfolded, trying to hit the bull's eye on a dartboard while somebody spins you around. As for their friends, the sea granted them no mercy. They were lost without a trace in the Gulf of Lion. Devastated and bereft, Lewis and Anna sold their boat. She returned to England, and he found the position of manager for Blue Line.

Popeye-lookalike Frank and the romance writer Eric arrived in Port Cassafières at the beginning of April. They tied up next to our pontoon for a quick catchup. They were heading for Santa Margherita Marina in the Costa Brava, where boats could moor for free until the local council had dealt with the developers' liquidation.

Eric loathed cruising on the Canal du Midi. With a 1.63-metre draft, his yacht practically dredged the canal from Toulouse. Furthermore, travelling with Frank was an absolute nightmare. Every time he entered a lock, his catamaran would drift sideways. It was hard enough for Eric to manoeuvre his heavy concrete yacht, let alone handle Frank's catamaran simultaneously. Their boats were battered even though they had covered the sides with fenders and tyres. Frank's hulls looked partially damaged. When they left Port Cassafières, we thought it might be weeks before we re-encountered the comic duo.

Surprisingly, we were soon hot on their transoms. Peter's diligence had worked him out of a job. Lewis was sorry to see him go. As a bonus for his hard work, he filled our empty fuel tanks. Had he known we could cruise several hundred miles on two full tanks, I doubted he would have made such a generous offer.

Aigues-Morte was out of our way to the Med, but our friends Jean-Philippe and Véronique, whom we had met in Toulouse, insisted we visit them. They owned a barge moored outside the city walls in a small canal lay-by where we tied up amongst several other foreign vessels. Some of them looked as if their journeys had ended there. It was the weekend, and Véronique had arranged an evening meal with their friend George, who owned an apartment in the upcoming resort of La Grande-Motte and a wood factory in Nigeria.

As our hosts had an aversion to washing up, they served us a three-course meal on the same paper plates. Then, we were spitting out pieces of paper when we ate our desserts. Later, I sang for my supper to an attentive audience. Then Jean-Philippe mentioned their cat Minette, who had been missing for several days after he let her go ashore to relieve herself.

'While I am on the subject,' he said: 'If anyone needs a pee, do it overboard or in nature, but make sure you don't get lost like Minette. We've spent enough time looking for her.'

They had a toilet on board, but pumping the barge's sewage tanks out was expensive. The French have strange ideas about relieving themselves. I once sailed on a French yacht, and while underway, they asked me to relieve myself over the side, all because the chemical loo was strictly for 'number two.' I had to perform acrobatics to avoid falling overboard.

Peter chose the bushes, and he didn't get lost. Luckily, it was a beautiful, starry night without a whisper of wind. When rejoining the party, he told our hosts he'd heard the faint sound of a cat meowing and traced it to their forward locker. Everybody rushed on deck to go and look. Jean-Philipe prised the forward hatch open, and a very frightened Minette jumped up at him, clinging to his jacket with her claws. That night, Minette resumed her position in their double bunk between Jean-Philippe and Véronique. They woke up before sunrise in soaked pyjamas and bedcovers and accused each other of forgetting themselves. Then, when Véronique turned her bedside light on, she saw that Minette had given birth to three kittens.

We could have stayed longer in Aigues-Mortes for all the applause I received when I busked in the medieval square. People said they heard my voice bouncing against the city walls like a siren call. But the world was beckoning us.

Before we left, Peter had to lower the mast with 'block and tackle' to forty-five degrees from the deck so we could get under the high-tension cables that straddled the canal a mile away. Otherwise, it could have been an electrifying experience indeed!

Sailing through the resort of La Grande-Motte shook our senses after the quaint villages with medieval stone bridges we had enjoyed seeing along the canal. The holiday resort was built between 1960 and 1975 on pristine beachfront dunes, artificially irrigated to create a green environment. Architect Jean Balladur drew his inspiration from the pre-Columbian Teotihuacan Pyramids. The buildings resembled giant ant hills where swarms of people carrying their shopping home looked like scurrying insects returning to their mounds.

Finally, we reached the Mediterranean and hoisted sails, racing through the water with the wind on our beam. The Gulf of Lion was granting us a smooth passage across an emerald sea. It was such a liberating feeling to be in open waters after the constraints of bridges and locks on the canals. We hugged the coast of the Languedoc region for a couple of hours without a boat in sight until a menacing French Customs patrol vessel approached from astern.

'We're going to be rammed,' I shouted to Peter. 'Why are they chasing us?'

Peter yelled and waved his arms at the boat, signalling they should back off.

The vessel's flared prow was now towering over *Capricorn's* cockpit. On their decks were two customs officers standing with machine guns strapped across their backs. Over the tannoy, the captain ordered us to hand the crew our passports and ship's papers. How did he expect us to do this with both vessels tossing in a swell at different intervals? Furthermore, a rating would need to reach down from the bow and grab our documents from Peter as he stood on the aft handrails displaying acrobatic prowess, not to fall in the water, so I informed the captain on Channel 16 that we weren't prepared to take the risk.

There was a pause in the proceedings. Then, a crew member rushed up on deck with a net on a long pole. He lowered it, and the captain ordered us to drop our documents inside. Then, they bore away, requesting that we follow the vessel to Port La Nouvelle.

Once up the river, one of the crew pointed us to a concrete jetty with the sign *'Réservé pour la Douane.'* 'Reserved for Customs.' What a coincidence to be intercepted by officials in the same river where 'ex-bobby' Lewis and his girlfriend Anna were saved from the jaws of the Gulf of Lion. Although we were spared a rough passage, dealing with Customs was a worrying prospect. We had heard so many stories of yachts being pulled apart as officers searched for drugs, leaving the owners to repair the damage and pay the cost themselves.

When two officers boarded our yacht later, they asked to see the ship's logbook. It soon transpired they couldn't read English. They tossed the book back on the chart table and quickly glanced around. One of them said before they left, *'Si vous êtes en règle, vos documents vous seront restitués à notre convenance.'* 'If everything is in order, we will return your documents at our earliest convenience.'

It was too late to set off when Customs returned our papers. So we remained tied against the concrete jetty, unable to sleep with a dredger working non-stop through the night. At times, it came so close that we feared it might suck us up and then dump us out at sea without a trace.

Santa Margherita had a network of canals throughout the resort, but it didn't possess the wow factor of Venice. Getting around in a dinghy was fun, though. Every night, Peter rowed through the maze of canals to deliver me to my singing venue. Meanwhile, Big Eric could always tell by Peter's singing when he had visited the bodega and sampled too many wines before buying.

My employer was a petite blonde with blue eyes called Brigitta. Although she ran a thriving restaurant alone, she didn't seem happy. One night, I found out the reason why. She and her former chef and four staff had been in a syndicate playing the lottery. They won 100,000 pesetas, representing a great deal of money in the 1980s. However,

Brigitta didn't see a *peseta* from their winnings because the chef cashed the ticket and ran away. She told me never to sing *The Gambler* by Kenny Rogers.

Humphrey and Gladys's cabin cruiser, *Sweet Breeze,* was moored at the far end of the marina. The craft would have looked more in place on the Norfolk Broads than the Costa Brava. (I thought they were brave, maybe a tad foolish, to cruise with such a flimsy craft at sea.) The couple invited us aboard one afternoon after Frank, *the lookalike Popeye,* introduced them to us, declaring, 'If you need anything like a winch or a spanner, Humphrey is your man.'

Upon boarding *Sweet Breeze*, I noticed the jumble of nautical paraphernalia randomly secured on the coach roof and side rails. Not yet retired, the wheeler-dealer picked up work on yachts during the summer. Short and thin, the few grey hairs combed over his bald head seemed to stray rebelliously, while his wife, Gladys, was a tall and heavily built bleached blonde in her early fifties.

The only unencumbered area on the boat was the afterdeck, where we sat under a parasol to escape the beating sun. Humphrey offered us a beer. He returned with a few chilled bottles, handed us one each, and then flopped into his threadbare deckchair.

When boat owners from all over the world get together, they usually share their nightmarish stories at sea. We all had at least one. Humphrey was keen to talk about their recent ordeal.

'Gladys and I usually make short passages along the coast,' he explained, his voice quivering. 'We prefer to cruise in calm weather as *Sweet Breeze* isn't an ocean-going boat. The sea was like a pond. Gladys had been at the helm for a while when she shouted, "I can see something floating in the water straight ahead. It looks like a dead dolphin."

She eased back the throttle and let the boat glide up to the creature, then, with a touch of reverse, Gladys brought the vessel dead in the water next to it while I scrambled onto the forward deck and yelled to her, "It's someone in a wet suit face down with a neoprene hood on."

I pulled the person closer to the hull with the boat hook, half-expecting the snorkeller to shout at me. At that point, the body rolled over, and a woman's face, with lipstick and heavy makeup, stared at me with dead eyes. I freaked out. We were having a quiet cruise in the blue Mediterranean, and this had to happen to us. Taking a closer look, I noticed she had no snorkelling mask, was barefoot, and had a gold chain around her ankle. What were we to do with her body now? We couldn't leave it at the mercy of the sea.

I put a ladder over the side, climbed down, and got a rope under the woman's arms with a makeshift lasso while Gladys, lying on her stomach on deck, reached over and hung onto my lifejacket. The woman had diamond rings on her fingers, which matched her earrings, and we saw a gold necklace through her partially unzipped wet suit. Had we been tempted, we could have bought a brand new boat with all that jewellery. It was spine-chilling to see her blonde hair protruding from her hood, wafting in the water like seagrass. Her eyes will haunt me forever.'

'What did you do next?' I asked.

'We tried to lift the body out of the water, but with our boat's high sides, neither of us could lift it on board. We were less than a mile from our destination, so we towed it unceremoniously from the stern. After all, the poor thing was dead. I radioed the marina ahead, and they, in turn, alerted the police.

When we approached the harbour entrance, someone directed us to the visitor's pontoon. Two police officers, with guns in hand, clambered on board before we could make fast. A couple of firemen retrieved the body, and the standby ambulance crew took it away on a stretcher. By then, a big crowd had gathered. The police arrested us as prime suspects for the woman's murder. At the station, several officers interrogated us for days. They kept us in separate cells, and I had no idea how Gladys was coping. It was terrifying.

The Mayor, a yachtsman himself, finally stepped in. He had heard our saga and told the police to release us immediately because it was highly improbable we would have committed the murder and then delivered the victim to the police in person. He stated the officer in charge of the arrest should have commended us. Instead, they treated us like criminals. The Mayor's intervention allowed us to return to our boat, but our passports were seized, and our engine immobilised.

A few weeks went by before the inquest. The police checked if a woman in her early forties, possibly affluent, had been reported missing, but no match was ever found. Forensics later confirmed she hadn't been in the water long before we picked her up, and no visible signs of foul play could be identified.'

'What would you have done in our place?' Humphrey asked Peter, though he didn't wait for an answer.

Santa Margherita Marina was a magnet for characters like those one reads about in novels. That afternoon, we were in for a surprise when we heard successive thuds vibrating over the water and through our chests. Moments later, we saw a tall chimney belching out black smoke and a vessel approaching us through the canal system. With its massive propellor churning the water into a Niagara Falls, the tug boat entered the marina like an orca swimming into a goldfish pond. We thought the iron-clad riveted vessel must be an escapee from a maritime museum. There was no doubt about her nationality, with her red, white and blue horizontal striped flag the size of three bedsheets sewn together. The tug approached the quayside. *This thing is about to rip Capricorn open like a ring-pull sardine can.*

Peter swiftly grasped the rope and made fast to a bollard. Then, the tall, athletic blond captain brought his steel monster alongside the quay like a toy boat at the end of a string, leaving just a metre between our bow and the stern of the yacht in front. The man thanked Peter and then introduced himself and his wife, Bertha. She was skinny and had striking jet-black hair down to her waist.

'My 70-foot long, 70-ton tug has been our whole life for thirty years,' Harmen explained. 'My vessel has a soul.

If we hadn't brought her to the Med, her last voyage would have been to the scrapyard. I couldn't live with that.'

The couple had worked the tug on the Esselmere Inland Sea, moving cargo-laden barges all over Holland. With the advent of containers and road transport, *Ria* became redundant. Using Harmen's early pension, they decided to retire to the Med. They left Amsterdam and cruised through the Rhône River to Sète and the Costa Brava.

'People haven't been kind to us,' Harmen lamented. 'Customs gave us a hard time. They questioned why a Dutch tug was travelling to the Mediterranean. They thought we were drug runners.'

He described his tug punching into the waves like a submarine coming to the surface. (The vessel had heavy watertight hatches.) They couldn't store anything on deck as it would be washed away. He also needed to manually lubricate the old engine tappets with an oil can every hour. Bertha always stays in her bunk on passages,' Harmen explained. 'She gets seasick and scared watching *Ria's* low free-board constantly awash, looking as if she is about to sink.'

It wasn't long before a large black truck with *Aduanas* written on the front and a flashing blue light pulled up on the quayside, followed by two Land Rovers. Half a dozen men with guns poured out from the back of the truck. A handler and his Alsatian sniffer dog were in one of the vehicles; the officer in charge was in another. He stepped aboard the tug, pistol in hand with the dog handler in tow while the men stood in line on the quayside, machine guns at the ready, pointing at Harmen and Bertha. They didn't flinch. Could they be rehearsing for a new James Bond movie?

Luckily, the officer spoke good English. Bertha offered to make coffee, but he declined. Once inside the tug, the dog sniffed around while another two ratings searched through every locker and drawer in the restricted living area. The engine room took up two-thirds of the vessel.

After a chaotic rummage throughout, they found nothing. But the officer wasn't satisfied. He demanded Harmen discharge his diesel tanks into the canal. as he suspected he might have been hiding drugs there.

'Are you aware of the damage two tonnes of diesel could cause?' Harmen said brazenly. 'It would be an ecological disaster, destroying all wildlife and tourism. I swear there are no drugs aboard, and you'll find nothing if I empty my tanks. But should you insist, I'd like your request to be put in writing first.'

Harmen's warning made the stony-faced officer turn on his heels. He climbed on the tug's deck, waved his gun, and shouted to his men, '*Vamos.*' They proceeded in the same cinematographic style as when they arrived, with their engines screaming, wheels spinning, and dust kicking up. The tug was kept under surveillance day and night after that.

As for us, our eyes were decisively pointing towards America. I thought of Salvador Dali's paintings in the Figueras Museum, which had propelled us through a world of absurdity. By contrast, ours was a boat that liberated us from mundane restrictions and constraints as we opened ourselves to the elements to achieve a semblance of freedom. Our tomorrows could be sunny or stormy, depending on Neptune and Poseidon, but we were the masters of our own destiny. At least, we thought as much.

18. Reading the Signs

A narrow shaft of light pierced through a brooding sky. The sea surged and shone like somebody had poured oil on the surface. The level dropped a metre, then rose alarmingly. Tides in the Balearics are usually insignificant. The forecast didn't mention gales, but these signs had the foreboding element of a storm.

Peter tied extra lines to the quay and secured steel shutters to protect our forward glass wheelhouse windows. He had never felt the need to do this before, yet there was still no weather warning. We saw holidaymakers strolling happily up and down the jetty, watching the flotilla of boats moored to the harbour wall, surging in the swell like puppets on a string.

The wind increased. We could hear it whistling through the rigging. Halyards began to drum against masts like Royal Marines calling Nelson's Navy to 'action stations.' The sky looked ready to tumble down on this October day. It appeared as if the weather was declaring war on the quaint Mallorcan fishing village of Puerto Andraixt. We stepped ashore, looked over the parapet wall, and saw marching waves heading for the bay.

'We should get back,' Peter said as we hurried along the quayside against the wind-driven spray. 'If we don't, we'll have to leave *Capricorn* to her own devices.'

Peter walked across the wobbly gangplank and got on board safely. I followed him, but he had to clutch my wrist to stop me from falling into the water. I shuddered at the thought that I could have been squashed between boats or hung by the neck amongst all the mooring ropes.

Below deck, my home rocked and pitched like a wild beast. Undeterred, I removed my wet weather gear and prepared a stew on the diesel heater. It had a hot plate with a round fiddle that secured our kettle and pans. We had never used the heater in such conditions before. Danish fishermen praised these stoves when fishing in rough weather.

The fragrance of *Herbes de Provence* wafting across the saloon soon conferred the semblance of a cosy night in, but what was shaping up looked far from reassuring. As dusk fell, the wind howled. Standing on deck, we saw waves tearing through the marina's flotilla. Only the stone wharf stood as a bastion between the onslaught and us. Every gust sounded like an express train travelling through wayside stations at full speed. In the lulls, the ghostly silence felt even more threatening.

Why didn't I book a room in a hotel?

Peter was up and down the decks, checking for chafe on the lines. Each time he heard a gust approaching, he had to wrap his arms around the mast to stop the squall from sweeping him away like yesterday's newspaper. When he returned to the warmth inside, he looked like he had been playing under a giant waterfall. He removed his sodden, wet weather gear and hung them in the shower cabin to drip dry.

'Surely, this can't get worse,' I said as we peered through the galley window, watching palm trees bending double, masts gyrating like demented pendulums and waves pounding against the harbour wall. When vast plumes of spray hammered onto her decks, *Capricorn* shuddered under the weight. Luckily, our storm shutters bore the brunt of the assault, but the cockpit drain struggled to clear the heavy volume of water. And what if our ropes and the two anchors laid out astern no longer held? There were other boats to worry about as well. If they dragged their anchors, they could break loose and collide with us in an entanglement of masts, ropes and anchor chains.

'I'll make a cup of tea,' I offered as a diversion. As I filled the kettle, I heard Peter shout: 'There's a yacht drifting from the outer anchorage with no sign of anyone on board.'

The boat was ploughing its anchor along the seabed, catching anything in its way. If it snagged ours, the surge could push us onto the stone wall, and if we tried to avoid it by turning our engine on, ropes might become knotted around our propellor. We were in the hands of fate, and we could do nothing to help ourselves but hope. Then, all of a sudden, a savage gust blew the *Marie Celeste* off *Capricorn*. She veered away before careering towards a cluster of yachts in the anchorage behind us. We knew the family of New Zealanders on the large yacht, *Freebooter,* anchored ahead of the flotilla. Peter called the skipper over the emergency channel 16 to warn him of a boat drifting down his way. There was no reply, but deck lights were switched on, and someone was fending off the *Mary Celeste.* She floated away to her doom and finished her journey on boulders by the promenade.

Freebooter and her crew were thankfully spared. If they had failed to part the two yachts, their anchor couldn't have borne the weight of both vessels, and they would have been shipwrecked, too.

Our stew simmering on the stove seemed as unreal as a cat smoking a pipe. Despite the inviting aromas, neither Peter nor I felt hungry. Dawn was still a long way off. I picked up a book and started to read but stumbled over the same lines. The silence inside my head was deafening. Could our home be wrecked against the wall?

Then, all of a sudden, amidst the fracas, we heard a bang on the coach roof and footsteps resonating through our steel hull. Peter and I looked at each other, wondering if the monster from the deep had crashed down on our foredeck. I doubted anyone in their right mind would pay us a social visit on such a hellish night.

Peter opened the wheelhouse door. Two people were standing in the cockpit like drowned corpses. How did they get here, and what did they want? Then Peter recognised the man from the 'once-new yellow winter jacket' he had lent Guido at the airport. The Dutchman owned the motorsailer moored next to us. He was an artist paid by the government to produce eight paintings a year, and Maggie, his girlfriend, worked as a civil servant in London. The woman was like a firecracker, ready to go off anytime.

I remembered the day Guido had asked Peter if he would drive him to the airport in Maggie's car because he was sure the woman had a death wish.

We met at the harbour car park and were surprised to see Maggie. The pair stepped into the back seat, and as soon as we drove off, the pair began shouting at each other. They never stopped for the whole fifty-minute journey to the airport.

When we entered the terminal building, Peter and I waited beside the checking-in desk. Would they notice Guido was using somebody else's return flight ticket he had bought cheaply? We could see the airline staff handing out boarding passes without checking the passengers' passports against their flight tickets. Fingers crossed, for Guido's sake, he might get away with it. But the couple's constant arguing disturbed everybody in the hall, so he was asked for his passport. Seeing the name didn't match the flight ticket, the airline staff shook her head, returned his papers, and waved him away.

Depleted, we returned to the car with them still quarrelling. A mile down the road, Maggie had an idea. 'Guido, you could try to check in again, this time in disguise. Peter could lend you his bright yellow jacket. Just turn the collar up and wear a pair of sunglasses; then, by the time we drop you back at the airport, you might be waved through without checks, given it would be the last boarding call.'

Her plan worked. Guido was quickly ushered through but didn't have time to return Peter's beautiful jacket. Maggie then took the wheel, and we gripped onto our seats back to Puerto Andraixt. Guido had said, 'She drives like a demon stock-car racer.' The vehicle's many dents reflected that, too. Later, she returned to London in her car. We could imagine her bouncing off lamp-posts, signs and other vehicles like in the old flickering movies, where one saw the Keystone Cops chasing Charlie Chaplin.

Guido had reappeared in our lives in the middle of the storm, but this time, he was with another woman. Surely, he hadn't just come to return Peter's jacket? His companion looked pitiful, hair hanging down her face like wet seaweed over a mermaid's forehead.

'Can we come inside?' Guido asked, with eyes like a sad puppy. 'We've just got back from Amsterdam. We've neither heating nor food.'

How could we say, 'There's no room at the Inn.'

They stepped into the wheelhouse and removed their sodden, wet weather gear and wellies, leaving a puddle on the cabin sole. Peter's once-new yellow jacket looked like a floor cloth someone would use for mopping up. Guido introduced Anna. She sat on the saloon settee while Guido rubbed his purple hands over the stove, looking relieved. I dished out two bowls of stew but didn't have time to bring them to the table when I saw Anna's face turning white. I rushed to fetch a bucket and got there just in time before she threw up.

This didn't stop Guido from shovelling a bowlful of stew down him like a stoker feeding the boilers on the *Titanic.* Then he left us to go and light the diesel heater on his boat. Anna stayed, keeping the bucket on her lap.

Peter remained on watch through the night, checking the ropes and looking for signs of any anchor dragging. Neither Anna nor I got any sleep rocked about in this cradle of hell. At daybreak, the wind eased into a force eight gale, which felt like a breeze given the night's battering we had endured. Our decks were a tangled mess of seaweed and flotsam.

The wind had abated in the late afternoon. Guido came to collect Anna. She followed him like a zombie and left us to empty the bucket. By then, we couldn't wait to stretch our legs. Once again, we had to watch our step and gauge our timing across the gangplank onto the jetty because of the surge.

Further down the quayside, we met a French couple in their Renault 4. They had stayed all night in their vehicle, watching their boat pitching and rearing in the swell. The pair had been too afraid to return aboard but worried about being swept over the jetty by torrents of seawater hitting the car's roof.

On the pier, large concrete blocks with rings had been ripped out of place by the yanking of several vessels. The ferryboat got stranded on one of the beaches and would have been smashed against the rocks had it not been built out of steel. Instead, the hull was pummelled like a Jamaican steel pan drum.

Thirty-nine boats were wrecked that night, with many reduced to no more than fragments of wood or fibreglass. The marina resembled a graveyard, with stumps of aluminium masts protruding from the water like gravestones. Some yachts had broken away from their moorings; others had dragged their anchors and drifted onto rocks. We saw boat owners trying to salvage winches and odd removable deck fittings.

The beach was littered with personal belongings, fenders, and mangled boat pieces. It was a bounty for looters eager to scavenge what they could.

We met the crew on *Freebooter*. Samuel thanked us for our warning over the VHF radio. He said it gave him just enough time to start the engine, swing his boat on her anchor chain, and push the *Mary Celeste* away. Then, they spent the night with the engine ticking over in forward gear, taking the strain off the anchor chain during the gusts.

No one had known that an impending cyclone had been heading our way. A weather warning from the mainland marina office had been faxed to the Harbour Master in Las Palmas, but nobody was there to acknowledge it. Only those who read the signs of an approaching storm were prepared.

That night, we opened a bottle of wine to celebrate our survival and finished the stew. In a day or two, we would set off to Almerimar, in the Province of Andalucia, to haul out and remodel *Capricorn*. It might be thought relatively easy to alter a steel yacht. Some people would consider having an extension built on their house difficult enough, but adding a metre to a boat was drastic, and we would still be living aboard.

As we lifted anchor, leaving the aftermath of the cyclone behind, I thought of the lyrics in one of my songs:

'And my love for you is stronger than my fears of stormy weather. As long as you are near, we'll brave it together.'

Puerto Andraixt will forever be etched in our memories, for safety in a harbour that night had proved as hazardous as riding a storm out at sea!

19. The Ugly Duckling

It was *mer belle,* 'the calm after the storm,' when we headed for the southeast coast of the Iberian Peninsula. With barely a breeze to fill the sails, let alone blow the lettuce off our plates, we glided through the tranquil blue Mediterranean towards our next destination.

Once in Almeria's yacht harbour, we dropped anchor. We ate the last of the Quiche Lorraine I made on the way, and then we walked to the commercial dock to stretch our legs. The port wasn't exactly what you would see in glossy magazines, enticing the rich to adopt a new paradise for their superyachts. It was like a graveyard of rusty old trawlers, working ships, and many deemed obsolete. Here and there, a shrub or a flower growing through the cracks and crannies of disused dockside cranes livened the bleakness of what must once have been a thriving enterprise. As we wandered on that late afternoon, I pondered the next stage of our journey to the shipyard in Almerimar. I didn't relish our home undergoing such radical reconstruction and wondered how I would cope.

Peter interrupted my thoughts when he pointed toward the Dutch tug *Ria* tied against the hulk of a trawler. The vessel stood out with her repaint, but what was she doing here?' Had Spanish Customs impounded her?

Peter hailed: 'Ahoy, *Bertha*.'

Harmen emerged from the engine room, his hands covered with thick yellow grease. 'Are we disturbing you?' Peter quizzed. 'Maybe you're in the middle of something.'

'Come aboard,' Harmen replied chirpily. 'Bertha will be pleased with your impromptu visit.'

Oddly, he didn't seem that surprised to see us.

Bertha came up the companionway, a cigarette dangling from her mouth. The skin of her index fingers and thumbs appeared yellower than when I last saw her. She also looked frighteningly thinner. Cruising in the Mediterranean on a tug only meant for the Dutch inland sea, including canals, must have taken its tow. Over a beer, Harmen complained about his vessel arousing continuous suspicion as a drug-running operation. It must have been hard to cope with all the Customs searches every time they docked in a harbour. The conversation moved to big Eric, the romance writer on his yacht, *Second Wind*.

'You know, after you left Santa Marguerita, my mother had an affair with Eric,' Bertha said with a tinge of anger in her voice. 'She was just a plaything for him. He broke her heart,'

Knowing Eric was married, what could I say about his transgression? Peter took up the story.

'We've unsettling news for him. Has he ever mentioned his French legionnaire friend, Louis? He dreamed of sailing away with his girlfriend once he retired. One night, he threw a party in his honour to thank Eric for his help while fitting out his new fibreglass hull. Impressed by the people he met, Eric, in turn, organised a party on his boat. As you know, he likes taking pictures of anyone who visits him. Do you remember, we all got the third degree about our lives before signing his visitor's book?'

'It'll be a shock when he hears the sad news,' Peter continued. 'Louis is now in prison. We learned about it from our friends Véronique and Jean-Philippe. They sent us a newspaper cutting from the Toulouse Gazette while we were still in Puerto Andraixt. What a shock it was to read the headlines,' *"Legionnaire strangled his unfaithful girlfriend in a jealous rage."* Because it was a *crime of passion,* he was given a seven-year sentence.'

Bertha's suntanned face had turned grey. She looked at Harmen for reassurance, but he seemed just as stunned as we were. He paused, then said, 'Eric and I used to give each other feedback on our writing. I remember his story about a French foreign legionnaire whose girlfriend had an affair while he was posted away. He found out while he was on leave and, in a rage, stabbed her to death. I was shocked and asked him what prompted him to write about the murder of a couple who were his friends?'

I felt as if somebody had just slipped ice down the back of my neck. 'Did Eric have a premonition?' I quizzed. In his story, it was a premeditated murder, using a knife as a weapon. How spooky!'

'What will Eric think when he hears about his friend Louis strangling his girlfriend? Peter remarked.

'We're still in touch with each other, 'Harmen declared. 'I'll have to tell him.'

'It makes me wonder if Eric has written about Harmen and me.' Bertha continued.

'What about us? Would he tell a story about me pushing Peter over the side in mid-Atlantic after an argument?'

There was a painful silence before Frank, the Popeye lookalike, sprang into another conversation.

'Is he still cruising?' Peter asked.

'Frank should never have been allowed to sail alone,' Harmen declared. 'Something was bound to happen sooner or later. As he headed along the coast from Gibraltar to Cadiz one day, he suddenly noticed he was getting too close to the shore, so he hit the auto-pilot button and altered his course by twenty degrees to port. Then, he went down below to make himself a drink. The next thing Frank knew, he was thrown off his seat, the coffee flew across the galley, and the catamaran came to a grinding halt. Frank had mistakenly punched the auto-pilot button twenty degrees to starboard towards the shore, ultimately putting him on the rocks.

The catamaran was now impaled but in no danger of sinking. Thankfully, the sea was calm, so Frank sent a *'textbook Mayday'* on the emergency channel. After all his years in the Navy, he was a stickler for the correct procedure. Didn't he tell you he was one of the survivors of a torpedo attack in WWII? So it wasn't his first shipwreck.'

Bertha took up the story. 'Only one of the hulls got damaged when the catamaran hit the rocks. The Spanish lifeboat came to Frank's rescue and wanted to salvage the vessel, but he refused. He had had enough of sailing, and the seaman's mission took him under their wing. The lifeboat returned to his yacht later, stripped her bare, auctioned the bounty off, and gave him all the proceeds. Frank even made the headline in the local newspaper:

'Wartime hero wrecked on rocks ten miles south of Cadiz in a storm.'

He had become a local hero, and the Citizens of Cadiz looked after him with honour. He could now retire from sailing with pride and not because he was getting too old. Then, when bad weather came a week later, the yacht broke up. Frank didn't seem concerned even though he wasn't the sole owner of the 38-foot wooden catamaran. There were three other shareholders. When Frank broke the news to them, he said, 'When you give a toy to a child, what do you expect?'

The shoreline looked as if the fields and hillsides were covered in snow from a distance. But as we approached the entrance of Almerimar Marina, we suddenly realised what we saw were flat-topped polytunnels stretching for miles. The land had once belonged to goat herders who lived below the poverty line. Then, when a Dutch company discovered water in vast quantities beneath the ground, they bought the land off and made those herders overnight millionaires. A few miles away from the marina was Ejido, which was still under construction. Some houses were only partly built with steel reinforcing bars sprouting from their ground floors. The main street remained unsurfaced and looked like a Western film set. The only thing missing was Clint Eastwood riding on his horse. Apart from a few banks and jewellery shops, there wasn't much else. The hospital, supermarket, and school were far from complete. In contrast, the marina was almost finished, except for the waterside apartments and hotels. Within this construction frenzy, *Capricorn* would undergo a total makeover and much more.

From the start, *Capricorn's* stern had never looked right. Apart from its square appearance, the transom came down at a steep angle, thirty centimetres below the waterline, causing a tremendous drag. As a result, the self-steering servo-paddle never worked efficiently because it sat in the back eddy. Peter had no desire to tow half the Atlantic behind us to America. He had lived with Bruce Roberts's design long enough to be ready to alter it. Little Joe, Roy's youngest son, who was seven at the time, had said when we launched *Capricorn*, 'I like your boat, Pete, but the stern is ugly.'

So it was back to the drawing board, the sound of the grinder, the hammering on the steel, and the fumes from the welding rods. At least, this time, it would be happening in a warm climate over a relatively short period of four to six weeks, according to Peter's estimation. He said casually, 'I'll just need to cut off the old transom and weld the new one up.' He made it sound as easy as Noah nailing a box to the stern of his Ark to accommodate a pair of hedgehogs!

Moreover, Peter reassured me that life inside wouldn't change much. The alteration would occur outside, some three metres above the ground. I was accustomed to ascending and descending vertical ladders with six-metre tides while we were anchored in Scarborough Harbour, where getting it wrong meant either a mud bath or a splash into freezing waters. This time, however, I could get a serious headache falling on concrete.

With our boat hauled out, I could still cook and wash up because the waste would be siphoned through a pipe and into a drain below. And yes, the toilet would have to be the bucket or a fast run to the shower block. Our aft sleeping quarters would remain untouched, as the transom extension would only affect the stern locker.

Peter made a scale model before he began *Capricorn's* initial reconstruction, which proved particularly helpful. He even tested it in the bath to see where the waterline would reach. Then, before building the new transom, he altered the model by adding a few centimetres to the size and adapted his calculations to full scale.

Capricorn was now a building site with scaffolding all around the stern. It was a dramatic moment when Peter made the first incision with the grinder, extracting a large piece off the old stern. Everyone in the marina came to look, thinking the man must have lost his mind.

Next, we drove to a merchant in Ejido to buy steel for Peter to start building the tubular framework that would form the skeleton for our new transom. When we arrived, there was only one person in the workshop. As Peter's translator, I told him what we needed, and he pointed towards the steel rack so we could help ourselves.

After welding the transom frame, Peter made plywood patterns, which he would use to cut the steel to the correct size. We revisited the workshop to buy two sheets of three-millimetre steel plate. When I asked the worker how much it would cost him to cut the steel from our patterns, he grunted something in Spanish, which translated as 'I'm too busy. The guillotine is over there.'

Peter didn't flinch. Health and safety never crossed his mind. I was glad I never saw him carrying an oxyacetylene cutter across an eighteen-inch-wide girder fifty feet above the ground when he helped dismantle Scarborough gasworks.

Watching him at the guillotine was nail-biting. I counted his fingers every time the lethal blade came down with a thud, and it wasn't a minute too soon when he finished. Then we loaded our bounty into the open boot but had to leave it ajar. On the way back to the marina, I asked about the car making a scraping noise. 'There's nothing to worry about,' Peter said. 'It's just the tyres rubbing on top of the wheel-arches.

The welding went splendidly well until forty knots of wind blew from the Sierra Nevada. Peter should have waited until the gale abated, but we had just learned that the travel lift would soon be out of commission for a few months, which was terrible news if we wanted to cross the Atlantic Ocean to the Caribbean this year, so he carried on.

20. Sonar or Sauna?

One might say it was a fluke when a fierce gust suddenly blew from nowhere, and a spark bounced inside Peter's welding mask and into his right eye. 'You'll need medical attention,' I said, hearing him complain about the discomfort and noticing his eyes constantly watering.

'It may work itself out,' he replied. 'I don't like the idea of Spanish hospitals. I'd rather fly back to England if I have to.'

Our Norwegian friend Arno and his wife were expecting us for dinner that evening. I had met him when he dropped by to answer my advertisement posted at the marina office, calling 'all musicians and singers for a musical jam session.' He was a medical doctor who enjoyed playing his guitar. He and his wife were on sabbatical leave with their young son and daughter. They also had a yacht in the boatyard near us.

Our friend was surprised to see us so early when we called on him. Peter explained he had caught a piece of molten metal in his right eye. Arno looked at it and said, 'I can sort you out. I've done this procedure before, which would be the same as if you went to a hospital. At least I could save you the trip to El Ejido. But first, I'll have to buy some anaesthetic drops and sterilised needles from the local chemist. Let me have some money to cover the cost of these and can you be back in an hour with a good torch. Monique, you'll need to hold it for me.'

We returned to Arno's apartment an hour later, nervous and apprehensive. He led us into the lounge and asked Peter to sit in an armchair and tilt his head back while I pointed the torch into his eye. I noticed Peter's face contorting when Arno administered the eye drops.

While we waited for the liquid to take effect, our friend distracted our attention by talking about his sailing adventures; then, once he felt sure Peter's eye was fully anaesthetised, he pulled a sterilised needle from a sealed pouch. I saw Peter gripping the upholstered arms of his chair as Arno, with remarkable precision, removed the piece of metal from his eye. The procedure only took seconds, but it felt as if the world had momentarily stopped, only to restart when Arno said to Peter, 'I'd need to scrape some burnt tissue off the surface of your eyeball next.' It was like hearing the executioner telling the prisoner, 'Don't worry about shaving; I'll do it after I have chopped your head off.'

We postponed the evening meal and music session and arranged a time to reconvene the following day.

We arrived at his flat promptly as scheduled. I thought Peter looked relatively calm, but how was he truly feeling?

Unlike me, he didn't wear his heart on his sleeve. Arno asked him to settle into the armchair and underwent the same procedure until Peter's eye was sufficiently numb for our friend to begin the delicate operation. I continued shining the torch into his eye, watching Arno scrape off the burnt tissue with a needle while steadily holding Peter's chin with his other hand. It was so surreal that I thought I must be watching a horror movie, assisting a psycho. But Arno was a doctor. Still, if he jerked slightly, it could jeopardise Peter's eyesight forever. After an agonising moment, Arno finally announced, 'I've done all that's needed.'

His words hung in the air like muffled notes on a piano. He covered the eye with a patch and told Peter to keep it in place overnight. His face regained some colour when he lifted himself off the armchair. He thanked Arno with a voice that seemed to echo from afar.

As we returned to our boat, I felt like a frontline nurse leading a wounded soldier off the battlefield. Over a cup of tea, Peter described how his vision would shift each time Arno removed another piece of burnt tissue from his eyeball. I couldn't imagine how frightening this must have been for him.

Thankfully, his eye healed, and the swelling disappeared. After that day, the saying 'eyeball navigation' would never be the same for Peter and me.

A black cat we named *Blackie* visited us every morning. He liked to stay lying on the concrete all day, watching Peter welding. His miaowing was a lively conversational piece, and although unrehearsed in cat language, we felt as if we understood each other. Then one day, as Peter lifted his visor to pick up another rod before continuing welding, he noticed *Blackie* staring directly at the arc. He chased him away, concerned about his eyes. Arc-eye is a painful condition that causes blisters on the eyeball if someone looks at arc welding at close range.

Blackie developed the condition, and there was nothing we could do to help but wait until the swelling reduced. Meanwhile, Peter laboured on, tackling every piece of steel he had cut with the guillotine, then tacking each section in place before welding them up.

Once he finished, he trimmed down pieces of the original transom to complete the conversion. After grinding the welds off, he painted the stern. Then, he played a game with passers-by, asking them to spot the join. Nobody could see it, including us.

Without a doubt, *Capricorn* was a recycling flagship. We had scanned numerous boat jumbles around England for deck fittings, anchors, rigging, and bottle screws and had even bought an obsolete mast extrusion from Kemps as well as secondhand sails and charts. The only items purchased new were ropes and anchor chains. We could have called *Capricorn Second Hand Rose* (the song Barbara Streisand made famous) and painted her hull pink, but Peter wouldn't have it. Come to think of it, I was his 'secondhand wife,' too!

My skipper was incredibly inventive, practical, and able to manipulate several materials. In contrast, my tools were words captured in songs, stories, and poetry. Unless supervised, I was dangerous with a hammer, but I could serenade my beloved and make perfect Swiss Rösti. Most of all, I could keep a steady course at the tiller.

One day, while checking for mail at the marina office, I met a tall man with jet-black hair and vivid blue eyes. He said hello and asked the usual question: which boat was I on? I told him I was on *Capricorn*, on the hard standing, having a new facelift.

'I have a Nicholson 42. I'll soon be sailing non-stop to Panama.'

He made it sound as if he was only hopping down the coast.

'I'm a retired airline pilot and have been everywhere.' A female companion for the voyage would be great, but I can't find anyone willing to sail on long passages.'

Was he chatting me up? I introduced myself and said: 'I'm sure my husband would love to meet an intrepid yachtsman like you. He was dismasted alone in the deep Atlantic. I feel you both have a lot to talk about single-handed sailing. Come for dinner when you are free.'

Trevor called round in the afternoon, suggesting we eat on his boat instead. (He could see we had a lot to do).

'Are you free tonight? I'll cook a chicken curry if you like?'

'It would be lovely,' we answered.

'Then I'll see you both at 7 pm.'

Peter finished work early, and we cycled to Trevor's boat. It wasn't difficult to spot the navy blue Nicholson with *Treasure* written in white across her blue mainsail cover. Peter knocked on the teak deck, and Trevor called out from the companionway, 'Come aboard.'

The accommodation below was roomy with a galley, navigation area and saloon where we sat comfortably on settees around a drop-leaf table. Trevor asked if we drank wine. Peter said, 'If it's made from grapes, then yes.'

Trevor served us from a large plastic container. 'I've got this red wine from the bodega in Ejido,' he explained.

Does he want to get us drunk?

'Your curry smells wonderful,' I commented before the conversation turned to nautical affairs.

'Do you see a nasty dent on the ceiling?' Trevor asked us, pointing upwards. 'It happened when I capsized in the roaring 40s, and the fridge hit the roof. Silly me, I'd sailed too far south.'

'Did it spill the bottle of wine?' Peter jested.

Trevor grinned.

'I wrote to Nicholson's representative about my capsize, and he said,' "Our yachts were never built for those conditions!" One time, I was so exhausted while sailing in the Red Sea in a storm that I fell asleep. Fortunately, I woke up seconds before being wrecked on a coral reef. These things happen.'

Trevor said it casually, as if he had forgotten to put the bins out.

'Doesn't it get lonely sometimes?' I ventured.

'I never feel alone at sea. My boat keeps me company. I'm always well-stocked up, and that includes cigarettes.'

The subject moved to his first aid kit. I was surprised when he showed us a small box with plasters, bandages, and aspirins. Noticing my scepticism, he remarked, 'If you set off in good shape, you're unlikely to fall ill at sea. There are no viruses out there.'

Most yacht owners tell stories about storms, boat damage, broken limbs, and crew overboard. Trevor made it sound so easy to sail around the world that our impending voyage across the Atlantic Ocean to America no longer felt such a big deal.

The following evening, I picked up my guitar and poured Trevor's story into a song. I renamed him 'Peter' as 'Trevor' felt like a tongue-twister. The lyrics practically wrote themselves.

My friend Peter sails around the world
He says his boat keeps him company
From the Straits of Gibraltar
All the way to Panama
Navigating with the sun and stars
He doesn't like to stop anywhere
'Cause he's happy out there
Doesn't like the hassle with the officials…

It was bitterly cold when we were hauled back into the water, having just met the deadline before the travel lift underwent its yearly maintenance. I wouldn't miss the hammer chipping off the weld slags or the teeth-on-edge sound of the grinding. However, there was still a lot to do before casting off.

Every morning at the same time, we would see a bulky six-foot-tall blond chap walking past our boat on his way to the shower block. He greeted us with 'Hyvää huomenta.' We hoped it was 'Good Morning' in his language. On the third day, the giant introduced himself and asked: 'Do you like *saun-aor*?'

Peter felt confused. Did he mean sonar? The man repeated the question, and Peter answered 'Yes' nervously, still perplexed. I was washing up and could hear the conversation from the galley.

'Then you and your wife will *saun-aor* with us,' he said. 'Come at 7 pm tonight and bring a towel each,' he continued before striding away.

'I'm not sure I understood what the man meant when he said, "Do you like sonar?" Peter remarked. Does he live in a submarine, and why bring towels? Are we likely to get wet when the sub is submerged?'

We set off at seven, armed with two towels and the customary bottle of wine, in search of a submarine. Had we taken the man too literally, or was it lost in translation when we came across a sleek-looking sailing yacht with a Finnish flag?

Peter knocked on the hull, and we waited for the skipper's answer. The six-foot-tall blond welcomed us inside his warm and spacious saloon and introduced his petite, fair-haired wife, Vilia. She was holding a baby in her arms while it sucked eagerly at her breast. Borg invited us to sit at their lounge table and offered us beer and caviar. I sat next to the mother and baby.

Then, Borg announced in a sergeant major's voice, the '*saun-aor* is ready. Us two men will *saun-aor* first.'

He led Peter to the forepeak. Vilia explained that in Finland, people sauna every day. 'So this is how you keep your glowing skin,' I remarked.

She grinned with delight. For twenty minutes, the men ran a sweat. Then it was our turn. Villa opened the fully insulated wooden door with a double-glazed porthole, which led into a pine-clad two-seater sauna. Inside was a three-kilowatt heater. Borg had built a generator in the engine room, powerful enough to run it. He couldn't rely on marina electrics, which often tripped out even when switching the kettle on.

Vilia took the half-full can of beer Borg had left for us and poured it into the sauna heater. It hissed like chips in hot oil, raising the temperature and making the place smell like a bakery. Outside the sauna was a large hatch. Vilia mentioned Borg usually pulls himself through onto the deck in the nude. With the absence of snow, it was his way of cooling off. I wondered what the watchman thought when he was doing his rounds, dressed in a heavy winter coat with the collar turned up. Was he shocked to see the muscular man sitting on the forepeak of his boat, letting the ice-capped Sierra Nevada wind whistle around his private parts while drinking a cold beer?

We missed our furry friend and didn't expect to see him again. Then, one late morning, as Peter was working on the bench he had set up on the quayside, Blackie suddenly reappeared. He miaowed loudly. Maybe he was saying,

'You can't go without me.' How did he trace us from the shipyard, half a mile away? Was this a sign we should adopt him for good? Judging by his shiny black fur and calm disposition, he enjoyed a comfortable life. Would we be cruel to steal him away? He might get seasick. The hygiene side was also a consideration, especially in a confined space. A Belgian couple we met on their boat had a cat who learned to use the seat of their sea toilet. Could Blackie be taught too?

He was sunning himself on the foredeck when Peter decided to do a final wash-down. Blackie caught a splash and quickly retreated to the shore, then sat close to *Capricorn* on the quay. Peter threw some breadcrumbs over the side and scooped up a netful of tiny fish. The cat was delighted with this unexpected feast and swallowed them whole, one after the other. Then he took a nap. He looked snug and content, so Peter and I made a pact. If Blackie didn't wake up before we slipped the shorelines, we would just cast off.

We gently motored away, but he never raised his head. I felt a pang in my heart. Maybe he wasn't meant to come with us, but would he have made a ship's cat? I mulled over the question on our way to Gibraltar. I guess we'll never know.

21. The Graveyard of Dreams

We knew the Levante could lay a boat over when entering the Straits of Gibraltar. I heard Peter yell, 'Keep pulling on the tiller.'

'She's heavy on the helm.'

'You're doing great.'

'I didn't hear the starting gun,' I shouted back. Had my skipper forgotten *Capricorn* was our home and not a racing machine? With a lee-deck awash, we had never pushed her that hard before and achieved such a speed. It was exhilarating, though. The new transom was a triumph of engineering. If little Joe (Roy's younger son) saw our new stern now, he would say, 'Pete, you've turned the ugly duckling into a swan.'

As we approached the entrance of Sheppards Marina, I headed the bow into the wind, and Peter dropped the sails; I turned the engine on and gently took *Capricorn* in. The wind made it awkward to tie up to a pontoon. While we secured the lines, two young Customs officers jumped aboard like pirates. Did they think we were smugglers?

All nationalities and creeds live in the 6.8 square kilometres of British territory. The Indians run electronic shops, the Jews handle banking and shipping, and the Arabs manage the open market. However, the Army, the Navy, and the RAF set the stage, not forgetting the famous apes that roam the Rock. The British believed that if these primates were to disappear, Britain would lose her sovereignty over Gibraltar. That might explain why a specially selected army sergeant was feeding and defending a group of apes as a reserve in a secluded compound.

New banks, bars, and restaurants were opening everywhere like a gold rush, while Sheppards Marina looked like a graveyard of broken dreams. It seemed many boat owners were suffering from harbour fever, unable to embark on a new sailing adventure.

Our neighbour, a tall, lanky twenty-something with spiky ginger hair, owned a pristine, luxurious yacht. We thought he might be a smuggler to own such a vessel. He walked with a swagger and looked like someone worldly beyond his years. He lived with a curvaceous blonde, a movie buff would describe as a gangster's moll. Caution dictated we shouldn't get involved, but it was hard not to, with the couple's wild parties where guests threw their joints over the side onto our decks. The man usually got up at lunchtime, zombified.

As a man of action, Peter, in retaliation, set his radio alarm clock full blast at seven every morning. With *Capricorn's* metal hull, the sound vibrated through like a live steel band. After a few days of taxing everybody's ears, our neighbour finally asked: 'Do you need to turn your radio alarm up at such high decibels?'

'Maybe we can strike a deal,' Peter suggested. 'I could turn it down if you tell your guests to stop littering our decks with their joints.'

The man agreed. I wondered if Peter was pushing his luck, squaring up to a mean drug dealer. Later, we asked Sheppards Marina Office if we could move to another berth. Were we jumping from the frying pan into the fire?

Several semi-rigid inflatables with massive outboard engines were moored near us. Gibraltar Parliament had just passed a new law restricting them to a maximum of 150 hp to appease Spanish Customs' endless complaints, curb the contraband activities, and facilitate the capture of those culprits. To circumvent this latest rule, the smugglers bought wholesale engines from the manufacturers on the understanding that they supplied them with 250 hp but with a 150 hp logo labelled on the engine cowls. Unashamedly, mechanics worked simultaneously on the police patrol boats and the contrabandists' inflatables tied alongside. One of them openly advertised his activities by naming his boat *Twice Nightly*. And that was what he did, bringing illicit merchandise from Morocco to Spain twice during the night. These men didn't worry about what people thought. It wasn't hard to spot them in their Lamborghinis or Ferraris. Some even rolled up in them to collect their unemployment benefits. However, they could only drive around the Rock. They would be arrested if they attempted to cross the border to Spain.

One afternoon, after nipping sharply across the road to avoid being run over by a Maserati, I said to Peter jokingly, 'Do we want to stay on the straight and narrow? If we became smugglers, it would be a quick way to build up the cruising kitty.' (Our dream was on hold as we ran out of money after re-modelling and re-equipping our boat).

'But I don't have a parrot on my shoulder and a wooden leg,' Peter replied with an *Aharr.* He was looking at a prominent billboard advertising air-conditioning. 'Maybe this is the answer,' he announced. 'I'll call the firm on the off-chance of a job that doesn't require a cutlass and two flintlock pistols tucked into my belt!'

'I presume you didn't like my suggestion,' I chirped. 'Remember, you have no experience in air conditioning.'

It was no use telling him that. It hadn't stopped him before when his friend Eddie, a welder working for a company fabricating steelwork for skyscrapers and jumbo jet hangars, said to him one day, 'I can get you a job welding.'

'But I can't weld,' Peter replied.

Another friend barged in, 'Don't worry, Pete. I'll show you how before you go for the interview.' After practising for twenty minutes and with some exaggeration, Peter was hired.

This time, he didn't have a crash course in air conditioning before the interview, but the company offered him a job. Being a master at turning his hand to most things, Peter was later made a foreman of a big project in the dockyard, installing a massive air conditioning system in a paint-spraying workshop.

It was now my turn to find work. I had heard of a new nightclub opening on Devil's Tower Road, so I called the manager. He invited me to audition the following day. When I arrived, dressed for the stage, a local five-piece band was playing.

I was next and gave my whole to Stevie Wonder's latest hit, *I've Just Called to Say I Love You.* Nobody clapped when I finished. Had I lost my touch? Surely, it couldn't have been the house PA system. When I did a sound check, it was perfect.

My second number was a lively country song - the third *Evergreen* by Barbara Streisand. I was gutted by the time I finished my 30-minute stint. Then, I found out why the audience hadn't responded. The band leader had deliberately turned the sound down so no one could hear me properly. The man had sabotaged my performance so his group could be hired instead of me. However, management offered me a regular spot at their piano bar. I gave up after a month. My boss wanted me to flirt with the customers. It wasn't my style. I didn't dress like Madonna or play my guitar in frilly underwear. I tried the Holiday Inn next. When I saw the manager in her office, she said: 'We're looking for a pianist at the owner's request, but he never comes to the hotel. Anyway, what's your repertoire?'

'Everything from country and western to French and Spanish songs, especially evergreen love songs.'

'You'll go down a treat with all those lonely men,' she enthused. 'Let's see how you get on.' I wondered why the owner wanted a pianist. I never saw one anywhere in the hotel.

And so I gave my all, six nights a week from seven till eleven. It was a musical marathon. Sometimes, I wondered what men thought when they heard the petite, slim brunette with elegant flowing outfits singing:

I am a woman in love and do anything to get you into my world.'
The International International Manager from Barclay's

Bank, a distinguished grey-haired man wearing an expensive suit, requested this song every night. He would stare at me, checking my emotions like figures on his bank spreadsheets.

'Pearl the Singer,' by Elkie Brook, with the words *All those dreams that never come true,* resonated with me. In the song, Pearl wanted to be Greta Garbo. I never yearned to be anyone else but the best I could be and projected my musical dream higher than those airline pilots I met at the bar, drinking their gin and tonic hours away from flying a plane. There were surgeons, too, enjoying alcoholic beverages. Sometimes, one would hear a bleeper calling them to attend an emergency.

Then there was Brian, a muscly dark-haired Brit who served as a chef on a submarine. He was staying in the hotel for a few days with the rest of the crew. Brian never asked me to sing, 'We all live in a yellow submarine.' He was a fan of Janis Joplin. Bobby McGee was his favourite. When I sang it, I questioned if freedom in Peter's life and mine was *just another word for nothing else to lose.* I had fled my homeland, keen to re-invent myself. My father's damning comments would persist like an itchy rash when he said, 'You'll never amount to anything.' Had he heard this degrading remark from one of the Catholic nuns in the orphanage where he grew up? His cynicism must have emerged from freezing nights in the boy's dormitory. Moreover, I doubted he would ever forgive me for leaving such a perfect country as Switzerland.

And there we were at this aquatic crossroads between the Mediterranean and the Atlantic Ocean, forever prepared for the unexpected. Meeting Brian brought an element of surprise to our lives when he offered us a guided tour of his vessel. His invitation felt as exotic as hopping onto a rocket heading for the moon. We arranged to meet at the main gate of the naval dockyard one afternoon. I asked him if we needed to dress in combat clothes. 'Just snorkelling masks and flippers!' he answered.

I didn't know what to expect when we stepped down through the conning tower into the bowels of the submarine. The inside looked like a giant tube with pipes and valves strewn everywhere, including overhead cable trays and boxes with buttons and dials. Like some overheated car engines, an overpowering smell of oil soured the air. Brian must have guessed my discomfort and said, 'We don't notice it anymore, but for fresh air to circulate when the vessel is submerged, we still use oxygen candles like they did in WWII.'

Although Brian worked as a chef, he was fully conversant with damage control in every part of the vessel. He told us he could never serve on a nuclear submarine and doubted any submariners from a conventional sub would either. Nuclear submarines were too noisy, with the pumps permanently running to cool the reactors. On a traditional sub, in quiet mode, the crew could hear a pin drop.

After several exhaustive explanations on torpedos and engines, some of which were lost on me, I asked Brian what he cooked for the men?'

'The usual English breakfast, meat and two veggies,' he replied. 'I tried a pasta dish once, but the crew turned their noses up and whined. "What's this." So I yelled, 'It's lasagne, and it won't bite you!'

I thought I would use his humour if someone made a face at my table.

'What about washing machines?' I asked.

'They're here,' Brian exclaimed, pointing at the buckets in the engine room. 'When we finish rubbing and rinsing, we drape our clothes over the cylinder heads. I can guess what you're thinking,' he said, glancing at me. 'Don't imagine frilly knickers or bras. Women aren't allowed to serve on submarines yet.'

Then came 'la piece de résistance,' a visit to the periscope platform. (Brian had received the captain's permission). Alas, the myth of a crew handling the scope in a hat with the peak facing the back of his head was forever dispelled that day when Brian told us, 'Nobody wears hats in a sub when called to action stations. It only happens in the movies.'

Another day, Ludwich, whom I had also met at the Holiday Inn, gave us the grand tour of his tank-landing ship. It had a submersible stern, forming a mini-harbour for loading tanks onto landing craft. He showed us the loading area, which looked like a multi-storey car park for military vehicles. Between them, the Royal Marines had set up a makeshift gymnasium where they exercised. The men had more muscles than *Popeye* and *Bluto* combined.

Then, we saw the kitchens. All the walls and units were shiny stainless steel. Did the chefs have to wear sunglasses to work there? We never visited the bows as they were strictly reserved for the Chinese civilians who ran the laundry. This conjured up movie images of men in dark rooms, smoking opium.

After the visit, our host suggested we go to the petty officer's mess, but he warned us we might encounter an objectionable character there. Ludwich asked us what we wanted to drink. Peter said, 'I'll have a half, please.' Then, before I could tell him my tipple, the petty officer propped up at the bar and declared loudly, 'Only *poofters* drink halves.'

'Then I'll have a pint,' Peter retorted in the most resounding male voice he could muster. Ludwich told us that the ship's bilges had hundreds of barrels of beer in their inventory. After I had taken a large sip from my glass of shandy, I said, 'It would take more than one horse and dray to supply all the grog!'

From the Spanish Coast of the Mediterranean, the Rock of Gibraltar looked like a giant crouching lion. People from around the world converge on this aquatic crossroads before setting sail to the Canary Islands, Brazil, or the Caribbean. While our dream of crossing an ocean to the tropics remained on hold, we sampled the jewel of this British territory, 'The Mediterranean Steps.' From the eastern side to the summit, the climb is vertiginous and narrow in places where one has to squeeze between boulders and twisting steps (some are even carved into the Rock). After a dizzying ascent, one reaches the top, graced by the most phenomenal view over the Straits of Gibraltar, the Atlas Mountains of Morocco and Tarifa on the Atlantic Coast. Along Spain's Mediterranean shore is El Costa Del Sol. We felt as if we could spread our wings and fly. This stretch of water is the only natural link between the Atlantic Ocean and the Mediterranean Sea, one of the busiest waterways in the world.

The Rock of Gibraltar and Mount Jebel Musa in Morocco are known as the Pillars of Hercules. According to Greek mythology, Hercules crossed Mount Atlas to steal the herd of cattle from the giant Geryon. But with his superhuman strength, he broke through the mountain and thus created the Straits of Gibraltar. Below us, the agglomeration looked functional, with warehouses and docks scattered randomly. Multi-storey dwellings seemed to cling onto the lower slopes, huddled together as if trying to keep each other standing. The steep cobbled street steps where loaded donkeys once carried goods had ramps to allow small vehicles access. Then, there were high-rise buildings on reclaimed land, which used to be part of the harbour anchorage for the British Grand Fleet. During WWII, they strung heavy wire mesh across the bay as anti-submarine defences. It is still being utilised over vulnerable cliff faces to stop rockfalls.

Our unique lifestyle helped break barriers among people from all walks of life. One day, we saw a notice at the local health food store window advertising workshops on co-counselling, 'Heal the Child Within.' I called the number and arranged for Peter and me to attend Heather's course the following Monday. She and her husband, a high-ranking army officer, lived at the military barracks near the airport.

On meeting day, we crossed the runway to their place. It was surprisingly warm for March, especially walking on the asphalt for over a kilometre. We were sweating when we approached the barracks gates, where we saw two burly military MPs standing to attention. They wore peaked caps pulled down over their eyes with their heads tilted back. The way they looked down at us made us feel nervous. We told them the reason for our visit, and one of the MPs rang to confer with Heather. They searched my handbag and then asked us to open our coats to ensure we didn't have a bomb strapped to our torsos.

Once satisfied we weren't about to blow up the army barracks, the MPs ordered two armed soldiers to let us through. They directed us towards a two-storey detached house on one side of the barrack square. We knocked on the door. An army sergeant answered. He was wearing a khaki uniform with three stripes on his upper arm. He politely ushered us in. As we entered the small lounge, Heather came to greet us. She must have seen the puzzlement on our faces. She quickly said, 'That was our batman, Henry. He is such a darling. He cooks, does laundry, and all the housework.'

Heather was in her late forties, slim, with short, mousy hair and a commanding voice. She harboured a certain mannerism probably adopted from her husband's rank. She pointed us to some chairs. Once everyone had settled down, she soon mellowed. Heather spoke of her co-counselling charity, which originated in America and operates worldwide voluntarily. When her short presentation finished, she invited each attendee to stand up and talk about themselves, allowing us two minutes each.

Nick volunteered to go first. Short and slim, with close-set brown eyes, he took a stance as if he was about to report to his superior. Nick was the Chief Provost Marshal in charge of the naval police in Gibraltar. He explained he had worked his way up 'through the decks' but never felt fully acknowledged amongst men trained through the naval academy. 'As long as I can remember,' he confessed, looking embarrassed and confused, 'I've never cried in my whole life.'

Tears were rolling down his cheeks. For him, the floodgates opened that day.

His son Shaun was next. The young man, twenty-something, was tall, dark-haired and athletic. He needed a listening ear to unload the recurrence of his psychedelic dreams of dinosaurs and monsters. He felt he was going mad, convinced those creatures wanted to punish him. Shaun had colon cancer and had undergone two serious operations. 'God is taking me back bit by bit,' he lamented.

When his two minutes had elapsed, his mother, Beth (Nick's wife), introduced herself. The attractive, curly blonde complained she felt rejected when the officers' wives organised events. She thought they should work as a team, but these women adopted their husbands' ranks, alienating her from their hierarchy system. Beth said she suffered from low self-esteem and felt her mother never really cared for her.

'Then came my turn. I was used to being on stage, yet I was nervous and shaky. I couldn't hide behind a song and a guitar and just burst into tears. 'I never feel good enough,' I confessed. My father told me I wasn't sufficiently intelligent to go to university. Swiss schooling was the death of me. It seemed all I learned in my earlier education was to knit baby clothes and cook while I yearned to attend music school and become an opera singer.'

Peter seemed more relaxed when he spoke of his Dickensian childhood. As a five-year-old, he was made to work at his mother's boarding house, plucking chickens and washing up piles of plates and cutlery as he stood on a stool to reach the sink. His passion for the sea helped to save him from earlier dramatic events, including a near-death experience in the operating theatre. Peter was thirty-six and I twenty-seven when our two ships met in Los Cristianos.

Once we had finished introducing ourselves, Heather set a couple of chairs in the centre of the circle and asked two participants to sit facing each other. She gave them core tools to learn how to co-counsel each other. The session entailed participants taking turns, pairing up for an hour each during which the listener was only allowed to interrupt with encouragement.

Heather mentioned yawning was part of a release technique. I noticed her mouth opening wide a few times without restraint. 'Talking about yawning,' she said, 'one can come unstuck in a certain milieu like my husband experienced one day. While entertaining a visiting commander of an Indian Navy Covert in his office, he suddenly yawned but did not try to suppress it. The following day, the Indian Commander complained to the Governor General of Gibraltar about the top-ranking army officer's total disregard when he yawned in his presence.'

We took a break when the Batman brought coffee and homemade biscuits. Then Heather paired us up: Peter with Shaun, me with Beth and her with Nick. We disappeared into different rooms with boxes of Kleenex. 'I think you'll need them,' Heather intimated.

After a counselling session with young Shaun, Peter suggested he might try painting the monsters hunting his dreams on large canvasses and forget his auntie's words when she told his mother, Beth, 'The devil possesses your son.' At sixteen, Shaun had designed his first computer game, earning him £20,000, a fortune in the late 1980s. With the money, he bought a secondhand Ferrari even though he was underage to drive. His father was more than happy to be his chauffeur. Then people started to gossip, wondering how a Chief Provost Marshal could afford a Ferrari on his salary. They thought he must be taking bribes. In the end, Nick asked his son to sell the car.

Another time, I teamed up with Heather in a one-to-one session. She explained how her father, once a medical surgeon, used physical force to scold her and her brother when they were children. 'I got into co-counselling because I used to smack my three boys whenever they were naughty. It frightened me to see how easily I resorted to physical punishment. I was repeating the pattern and needed to break the mould.'

Heather was shocked to learn of the neglect and abandonment I suffered in my childhood. As a teenager, I often contemplated suicide. 'I knew the river close to our house could offer me a way out of this world,' I said, almost choking. 'But a voice deep inside thankfully stopped me.'

Peter and I attended these sessions to help heal the child within. Given our forthcoming Atlantic crossing, they revealed more to us than we could cope with, but surely unshackling all that burden beforehand could help to open up a new rite of passage to the 'Big Blue.'

Once again, after one final session at Heather's, we walked across the runway back to Sheppard's Marina, feeling more numb and heavy-headed, as if our emotions had been through the mixed fabric setting on a washing machine. Everywhere seemed unusually quiet, even when we passed the filling station. It was always busy with Spanish motorists driving over the border to buy fuel at subsidised prices. Was something amiss? We suddenly had a foreboding feeling of being in danger, so we pressed on.

The next day, we read about the shooting in the Gibraltar Chronicle. We realised if we had walked past the filling station five minutes earlier that afternoon, March 1988, we could have been killed by stray bullets in the crossfire of Operation Flavius, where three members of a Provisional Irish Republican Army (IRA) cell were shot dead by undercover members of the British Special Air

Service. These deaths were the first in a chain of violent events over fourteen days. The Army believed the IRA were about to blow up the Governor's residence.

Reflecting upon all these events, it seemed a pattern had established itself from the time we visited the submarine, the tank-landing ship, and the army barracks where Heather, the high-ranking officer and the Chief Provost Marshal in charge of the naval police in Gibraltar, were stationed. Over dinner one evening at Nick and Beth's house, he told us of an incident when the Army decided to deploy a mock battle between the *Blues* and the *Reds.*

'Through the night, soldiers, black-faced, ran through the streets of Gibraltar, carrying weapons loaded with blank ammunition. When *The Reds* began to suspect the *Blues,* they tried to outflank them by positioning a few combatants on a secluded beach by boat and setting up an ambush. Tension increased when two blacked-out inflatables carrying several men in balaclavas landed on the beach. *The Reds* watched the men dragging their boats up before flooding them with powerful searchlights. More *Reds* in balaclavas closed in, screaming and pointing their machine guns, ordering the men to remove their disguises and raise their hands. Then, one of the squaddies started to yell, "Bloody Hell, Sarg, they're not the *Blues;* they're smugglers."

The *Reds* had caught the villains red-handed. They corralled them to a corner of the beach and called the police. The smugglers didn't try to flee because they didn't realise the Army had no jurisdiction to make an arrest and believed the machine guns pointing at them were loaded with live ammunition. When the police vans arrived, they arrested them. Had these thugs realised the local garrison played soldiers with blanks, they might have tried to escape.'

'What a story,' we said to Nick. 'At least justice was served that day.'

He grinned.

Gibraltar was a mini Miami Vice. Helicopters often hovered over the smugglers' boats to assist the police patrol vessel with their chase. One day, 'things got ugly,' so the rumour goes when the police intercepted an inflatable. As an officer was about to board the craft, the smugglers took off. The man fell into the water, and the villains made a U-turn and then tried to run him down. From that point on, the police patrol was out to get them for attempted murder. Until now, the authorities and the Gibraltarian police had been half-hearted in trying to arrest these contrabandists. Everyone seemed so closely related to a brother, an uncle or a cousin. Then it all came to a head when ten thousand demonstrators, mostly mothers and fathers, marched along the streets of Gibraltar holding banners with: "We don't want our children to become smugglers." They were shaming the government for ignoring those criminal activities.

At last, we were about to cast off on our voyage to America. Gibraltar's marina was now bustling with new arrivals. We saw people pushing supermarket trolleys full of victuals through the streets and queuing at marina chandlers to buy last-minute equipment before the crossing. Our friends Harvey and Lilian were ready to set off to Brazil on their Westerly 36, *Crosswind.* It was Harvey's ultimate dream. Lilian didn't like sailing. 'I usually knit on passages to alleviate the boredom when I'm not terrified or seasick,' she told me in passing. Would Lilian have enough wool left before they got to Brazil? When I told her that I had once hitched a lift from Tenerife on a yacht to the Caribbean, she thought I was crazy.

But Lilian couldn't face the long days across an ocean and decided to let Harvey follow his dream, although it broke her heart to leave him. Hers was to live in the country somewhere in the north of England. Their love story inspired me to write, 'Two Ships Passing.'

I'm caught between my fears
of the deep blue sea
and the future for you and me,
You've made up your mind,
You're leaving me behind.
I don't want to sail to Brazil,
Your dream is an ocean crossing,
When we say goodbye,
We'll be two ships sailing in the night.
In a crosswind from the start,
We slowly drifted apart
I want to live in the country,
You prefer the sea.
You never made it to Brazil

You were weather-bound
in some Spanish island
There you met somebody new
I wished I'd sailed along with you.

Unlike Lilian, the inspiration for such a unique and adventurous lifestyle wouldn't steer me away despite my fears of the many dangers looming ahead. My love for Peter was as vast as the ocean and stronger than my fears of stormy weather.

22. Friday the 13th

Peter flicked the rope with his wrist, and the bowline loop recoiled from the bollard back to him like a striking cobra. The time had come to sever Gibraltar's grip and make the giant leap, leaving the Mediterranean Sea for the Atlantic Ocean. I thought of words for a new song.

Many long-distance sailors
driven by the call of the sea,
braving wind and weather
for the love of adventure.
The Ocean Blue is waiting for you,
put some miles under the keel
and follow your dream.

The forecast was NE wind, force 5 to 6 for the Straits of Gibraltar, which suggested a lumpy ride off Tarifa, given the funnelling effect through the Pillars of Hercules. Fortunately, this should be brief. When Peter sailed across the mouth of the Straits to Morocco on his boat *Ellis,* he only had time to yell out to his nephew Bruce, 'For God's sake, hang on' before a rogue wave savagely threw the yacht on her beam-ends. The top of the mast hit the water, and within a split second, the crew went from reclining to standing on the side of the cockpit locker, clinging for dear life to the guardrail. For us, it was *mer belle,* with the blue sea and the sky blending splendidly into one.

The wind died down at dawn, sixty miles out of the Straits. I read somewhere that bygone sailors believed throwing an old broom overboard would bring fair passage. I had such an item in one of the lockers as a backup in case we got caught in the doldrums, but I didn't tell the skipper.

In the evening, the wind increased. Peter reduced canvas and fully reefed our brand-new mainsail. With our working jib still boomed out, we maintained a regular 6.5 knots, which was very good for an 11-metre yacht weighing ten tons and carrying one hundred and seventy gallons of water, one hundred gallons of diesel and enough food for at least five months. 'I should have painted the waterline higher,' Peter said.

If only I hadn't bought so many toilet rolls!

The weather remained steady for the whole day. I warmed a tin of stew, harnessed to the galley to avoid being thrown across the wheelhouse cabin like a ping-pong ball. When the wind picked up, we hoisted more sails. Then it died altogether, only to blow again, this time from the west, just before midnight. Peter started the engine. There were still two hundred and eighty-eight miles to go. Our progress was still impressive, with our course set at 260 degrees, boat speed 5 knots, and a westerly Force 3.

Then the wind veered, and we ploughed into a head sea, with the swell converging from two directions. It was like being in a cocktail shaker. Surprisingly, I didn't feel seasick. As I stepped on deck, I ensured my Sou'wester was fastened tightly under the chin because, according to myths, losing a hat overboard could mean a long, uncomfortable passage.

Later, the barometer plummeted, drifting clouds darkened the sky, and lightning appeared on the horizon. Were we in for a bumpy ride? I suspected Peter must have realised it was Friday the 13th when he logged our position. In the past, sailors thought women on a ship brought misfortune because they distracted the crew and angered the sea, which caused treacherous conditions as an act of revenge. On the other hand, women in the nude, as figureheads embodying the vessel's spirit, were believed to offer protection to the crew on their journey. I told Peter, 'Don't even think of lashing me down to the bowsprit topless!' But why worry about our survival with Peter's teddy bear tied to the mast, guarding us?

As a boy, Peter had piano lessons at home with Mrs Johnson. Sometimes, she brought her daughter Fleur along. While he sat at the piano, Fleur would play with his teddy. One day, with crocodile tears streaming down her face, she yelled, 'I want to take Teddy home.' Peter couldn't bear seeing her so distraught that he gave his teddy to her. Surprisingly, a few years later, Fleur, now a grown woman, came to the Wellington pub where Peter's parents were tenants to return it. Peter never had the chance to be reunited with his childhood friend because his mother raffled his teddy off for the dart team's fund. She thought her son was too old for one.

Maybe she was trying to redeem herself when she bought him a brand new one as a mascot at the launch of *Ellis of Tamar*. He tied it to the mast for good luck. That bear saw Peter through a collision, a storm in the deep Atlantic, and much more. Teddy would hopefully continue to keep a protective watch on our way across the Big Pond.

The wind shifted again. I might try to whistle to encourage it to blow us in the right direction, but I had to stop myself, remembering the old sailor's tale that it was bad luck. Moving inside or on deck was like trying to keep one's foothold on a rock scree upon the Jungfrau Mountain. If Peter or I lost our balance and broke a leg at sea, we couldn't call 999. Also, our first aid kit was limited, but it had more than just aspirins and Elastoplast. Stuart, a military paramedic in Gibraltar, had shown us how to make a splint for a leg or arm, using one of us as guinea pigs. 'You need to be inventive and make do with whatever is at hand, such as a sail batten,' he emphasised.

Darkness had fallen, and I barely had time to imagine what might yet happen (it was still Friday the 13th) when the sound of a shotgun shook me to the core. My heart jumped. Were pirates about to board us? Then, I heard Peter shout, 'A shackle on the sheet block has just snapped. I should have changed the genoa earlier!' The thrashing foresail was flapping around and sounding like the cracking of a bullwhip. Dropping it down would be akin to catching a tiger's tail. A wrong move could knock Peter out.

He turned the spreader lights on to illuminate the deck and made his way to the mast with his harness clipped onto the lifeline. Although this restricted his movement, the alternative could have been an unwanted dip in the deep Atlantic. Thankfully, the sail came down when he released the halyard that was holding it up. He replaced the shackle and changed the genoa for a working jib. Until then, the decks had remained dry, but suddenly, out of nowhere, a breaking wave submerged the starboard bow, and Peter got thoroughly drenched. Undeterred, he quickly added another reef to the mainsail. From inside the wheelhouse, I caught the look of horror on his face.

What now? I wondered.

When Peter returned to the warmth of our cabin, I heard him mutter, 'Why am I doing this?' Then he explained: 'The sail has a chafe through one of the batten pockets.'

It wasn't the time to mention the leaking fore-hatch, but I just had to. I stayed on watch while Peter rushed to the saloon to fetch an old towel from one of the lockers. It was next to a beautiful blue glass oil lampshade that had been carefully stowed away. Alas, Peter clumsily picked the towel up and broke one of our most precious possessions. I was peeved but said: 'It's only a lamp. Worse things happen at sea.'

I don't think Peter heard me. He was soaked and in a bad mood. He quickly changed into dry clothes and then joined me on my watch. I had been watching the distant lights of a ship ahead.

'I never expected any shipping in this area at all,' Peter exclaimed.

Were dark forces playing against us?

He swiftly switched our spreader lights back on, thinking *Capricorn* would be more visible with a powerful beam illuminating our sails as the ship drew closer. We could see her green light to starboard. The two masthead lights growing apart indicated she would pass safely behind us. Then, as we checked again, to our dismay, the ship had changed direction, and it looked as if we were now on a collision course.

'We're going to be run down,' I yelled.

'No, we won't be.' Peter retorted as he quickly activated the autohelm's tacking mode to turn *Capricorn* 100 degrees to starboard. He completed the manoeuvre, and the vessel passed close enough for us to recognise the outline of a Russian fishing boat. It was well-known that they used this type of vessel to spy on NATO naval exercises.

Our suspicions were confirmed when we saw the aerials, antennas, and radars on her superstructure. The ship was well outside the shipping lanes.

'Peter, they could have collided with us if you hadn't altered course. They might have sunk us.'

'She wouldn't have gone down, being steel, but *Capricorn* could have been seriously damaged.'

I took his word for it! Peter was angry at the captain's behaviour. He picked up the ship's radio mike and shouted over channel 16, 'You should have given us more sea room.'

'But we've passed you now!' the captain answered with a heavy Russian accent. Had he been playing chicken with us to alleviate his boredom at sea? Then, as if to redeem himself, he asked, 'Is there anything you need?'

I wanted to shout back, 'Don't try to ram us down next time.' Peter didn't wish to argue and just requested a weather report. We saw lights coming on in the ship's wheelhouse, then heard the captain over the VHF radio, forecasting NW 5 to 6, becoming westerly, which confirmed our fears.

We were now hard on the wind as it veered from northwest to west, doing as little as three knots. *Capricorn* bounced about awkwardly between the troughs, falling short of our desired course. All the signs indicated we would be in for a turbulent passage to Madeira. Neither the skipper nor I enjoy sailing to windward for long periods. Peter asked if I wanted to see the island badly enough to risk breaking things on board and how I would fancy Lanzarote instead. Then, before I could answer him, he had already set our new course of 194° into the autohelm.

The motion and the wind immediately eased. Peter unfolded the reef in the mainsail and found a few squids which had landed in the fold after being washed on deck by one of the waves. Amazingly, these creatures hadn't squirted ink on our new mainsail, which would have permanently ruined its look. Our speed soon increased to six knots without having to boom out the foresail. Then, when I looked at my watch, it was 00.05 on Saturday, October 14th.

Steady winds stayed with us, more or less, for the next four hundred and twelve miles to Lanzarote, and we only motored the last few hours when the wind died altogether. We made for a tranquil bay south of the island of *La Graciosa,* off the Northern tip of Lanzarote, dropping anchor in five metres of clear turquoise water close to a deserted sandy beach. It seemed the perfect oasis.

'It's beautiful here but a bit eerie,' I remarked. 'Why are there no other boats?'

'If the wind picks up during the night, there could be a funnelling effect between the mainland of Lanzarote and La Graciosa. Maybe this is why we are the only yacht here.'

Peter quickly plotted an escape route for us to follow in the dark in case we had to leave in a hurry. There were no navigation lights or habitation to gauge our exact position to avoid rocks while exiting the anchorage.

After lunch, we went exploring. When we landed ashore with the dinghy, we still felt the motion of the

Atlantic Ocean. Terra firma was moving under our feet, and it was no wonder, given we had been vertically challenged for almost six days.

At first glance, the island of La Graciosa seemed uninhabited. There was no defined path or track, so we had to weave through the scrubland to reach the summit of a small volcano. From there, we caught a stunning view of the partially inhospitable island. Sadly, our visit was brief, but being the only people there made us feel like true explorers.

Later, as we sat in the cockpit, watching a blood-red sunset with *Capricorn* lulling on the calm waters, I asked Peter, 'Do you think our remaining passage was trouble-free because we altered course for Lanzarote, or was it that Friday the 13th had passed?'

'I don't believe in fighting against the weather. It was the right choice,' he replied.

For me, it felt more profane and something of a miracle that we hadn't been rammed down by the Russian fishing vessel on that ominous night. As for Peter's sense of humour, I was pleased to note it had resurfaced when he acknowledged my earlier remark, 'Worse things happen at sea.'

23. Estonian Rose

Santa Cruz of Tenerife looked as bright from a distance as Blackpool illuminations. Even with powerful binoculars, Peter couldn't identify the 'port and starboard' of the harbour's outer mole lights. He was blinded by neon signs, street lighting and vehicle brake lights flashing on and off. After an anxious moment, he finally guessed where the entrance might be, and to our relief, the lights and the silhouette of a fishing boat indicated the way in.

We motored in, creeping past two large Russian fishing trawlers. Upon the third one, we noticed a few men on the foredeck, leaning over the rail, looking at us curiously. One shouted and beckoned, 'English, come and tie up to us.' Peter cut the engine and let *Capricorn* drift, then gestured to me. 'Should we?' I responded with pursed lips. The rusty old ship wasn't an enticing place to be, but it was night, and we still had a quarter of a mile to go to the end of the harbour, where there might not be anywhere to moor. With that, Peter made a U-turn.

When we came alongside, I threw the stern rope to one crew member and the bow rope to another. Once we finished tying up, the men invited us aboard. To get onto the trawler, we had to stand on our side rails, and then some hefty hands lifted us to their deck. From the wheelhouse top, the lights beaming down could have lit Wembley Arena.

One of the crew, a young, short, and athletic man, introduced himself as Kalev. He spoke little English, enough to invite us to sit at a large table made of fish boxes, including the seats. Someone brought two paper cups, a bottle of vodka and lemonade, and another, some biscuits, a tin of sardines, and a bag of boiled sweets. All this promised to be a memorable feast.

Then, someone called Adrus asked where we were sailing to, and Kalev translated our answer. The young or old crew were lean and athletic, with rugged faces and shortly-cropped hair. Only Ramus, the cook whom Kalev introduced us to, carried a bit of a tummy. Peter whispered, 'If I had walked into a bar where these men were drinking, I would have backed out slowly. Don't worry; we'll find a berth further down the harbour tomorrow.'

'How unreassuring,' I remarked. 'Do you think these men were press-ganged?'

'Maybe they had no choice if they wanted to feed their families.'

We finished the fish and biscuits and slowly drank their vodka with lemonade. Although the crew seemed excited about our company, plucking words from a dictionary proved laborious. To ease the atmosphere, I proposed to sing. Peter went to fetch my guitar. All eyes and ears were on me as I bellowed 'La Vie en Rose,' losing myself in the magic of Edith Piaf's song. One crew brought his radio cassette and recorded my performance. After my impromptu concert, we bid the Estonians goodnight. By then, we had learned to say thank you and goodnight - *spacibo* and *pokoynoy nochi*.

The following day, we woke up expecting the throbbing of generators, hammers chipping at steel and loud voices. Instead, we heard the sound of my last night's performance through the ship's tannoy. To be praised for my singing by some rugged Estonian fishermen hit something deep in me. I thought of my mother. She would ask me to sing whenever we had guests and cried each time.

My reverie was sharply interrupted by the sound of rattling on the rigging. Was the crew coming to tell us they were leaving? Peter rushed on deck. I followed. Then, out of thin air, we saw someone bent over the side, holding two plates while waiting to pass them down to us. On the menu were poached eggs on toast and a tomato cut into the shape of a rose. What had we done to deserve such kindness?

We returned our plates to the cook later and thanked him for the lovely food. Kalev was on deck, and we told him we were going out. Would the ship be leaving that afternoon? We didn't want to be cast off like a discarded toy. But Kalev said, 'We'll look after your boat while you're out.' Peter had left the sliding hatch open. He was more trusting than me. Then, he asked Kalev if he could secure our rope ladder to the side of the trawler so we could hop over from our boat more easily.

Kalev nodded.

Santa Cruz harbour was long and narrow and must have been a hub of activity in the past. At the far end, a few yachts were tightly moored astern to the quay. The only other place available was amongst three further vessels, tied up against the abandoned fish processing factory ship, *El Caribe*, the height of a four-storey block of flats, with a large aperture near the waterline of her slab-sided hull.

We returned to the ship after midday and met Adrus and Kalev on the foredeck. They seemed agitated. They handed us our shopping once we boarded *Capricorn.* As we stored the food away, we heard the rigging rattling again. Peter rushed on deck, and once again, two plates appeared, and a crew passed them down. We said *spacibo*, feeling overwhelmed. The two young fishermen smiled. On the lunch menu was some stew served with a chunk of bread and a tomato, again cut into the shape of a rose. What a romantic gesture from the cook. I wondered if he treated his wife the same at home. The crew were at sea, fishing for six months, never seeing land, just the mother ship collecting the fish they caught each day. Being away from their wives and children for so long must have been very challenging for them.

We sat in the cockpit and finished our plates. The evening meal followed the same ritual. Two of the crew watched us approvingly, eating their food in our cockpit, and Peter gave them the thumbs up. Then, he returned the plates to the cook with one of my cassette albums, *'Ma Passion.'* I had recorded the songs with some talented musician friends in a professional studio before setting off.

Until then, the Estonians were playing my last night's poorly recorded performance, but it wasn't long before we heard my album over the tannoy. 'I bet the cassette will be worn out if we don't leave soon,' Peter chuckled. I thought of the lonely souls I had serenaded at the Holiday Inn in Gibraltar, and now I was the sweetheart of some rugged fishermen sailing on an ocean trawler. Despite their appearance, these men had gentle souls, not forgetting they were somebody's son, brother, husband, or even grandfather.

Kalev solemnly announced an impromptu invitation to the captain's quarters the following day. 'Captain Aleksander is expecting you at 5 pm.'

On the hour, Kalev marched us to the upper deck and almost to attention, he knocked on the captain's cabin door. An answer bellowed back in Russian. Kalev opened the door, motioned us in, and then closed it after him, leaving us to face Captain Aleksander. He shook our hands, smiled, and invited us to sit down. Apart from his high cheekbones, the Estonian bore a similar stature to Admiral Nelson. He wore a blue cashmere jumper and navy blue press-creased trousers. I thought he looked young to be a captain.

His quarters, however, were decayed opulence. The wall panels cried for a lick of varnish; the top of his wooden desk looked marked and worn, and his couch close to the wheelhouse was threadbare. We never saw his sleeping cabin, which had an en suite and a sauna.

Captain Aleksander served us some Scotch Whisky and opened a tin with the attached key. 'These pilchards are from England,' he said in perfect English.

We politely ate the fish with the ship's biscuits, trying hard not to pull a face as we swallowed. Although he was extending his kindness by offering us the use of his sauna until the ship set sail, we felt we had been under interrogation. Once our audience with him was over, and he seemed satisfied we weren't spies or MI5 agents, we thanked him for his hospitality and took our leave.

The crew invited us to their mess for burgers and chips in the evening. I noticed their plates with half a cucumber and a couple of tomatoes slapped on as if served from a field canteen. Ours had the customary cucumber and tomato shaped like a rose. After our meal, we watched an American beach party movie dubbed in German with Russian subtitles. How odd. Then Kalev suggested we play a game of dominoes. Ramus filled our glasses with more vodka and lemonade. After this, one of the crew asked me if he could read my palm. I said, 'Yes.' Maybe I should have declined.

When Kalev translated, 'You'll live to the age of sixty-six,' I thought maybe he got it wrong. But if it were true, I would at least be granted another thirty years!

That night, the crew announced they were leaving the following day after 1 pm. It was sad news because we felt we had met real comrades of the sea. Kalev mentioned that while everyone was excited to see their family again, they dreaded crossing the Bay of Biscay in December in such an old trawler and wondered if she would complete her last voyage.

We passed the galley on our way back to *Capricorn* and saw Ramus kneading the next day's bread, thoroughly unconcerned about cockroaches scurrying across the shelves. It was just as well we hadn't seen them before.

In the morning, some of the crew signed our visitor's book; a few wrote their addresses down and gave us some family photographs, even a few roubles to remember them by. Such spontaneous friendship and kindness would live in our hearts forever, especially when Kalev told us they had never had interactions outside their fellow citizens before now and could only use the duty-free shop strictly reserved for the crew of foreign national fishing boats, provided they paid in roubles. He also said that a party member on board monitored all conversations between them. The cook had a going-away present. He brought us half a sack of potatoes but said apologetically, 'There might be a few bad ones.' He also gave us six frozen chickens and a family-sized loaf of freshly baked bread. He hadn't seen our tiny fridge that could only fit one bird at a squeeze. But how could we refuse such kindness?

As the ship prepared to cast off, the engineer gave Peter a miniature socket set, another crew presented us with a wooden African mask, and someone else, an elephant, beautifully carved in wood. We waved the men off, and there were tears on both sides. Then Captain Aleksander kicked the ship's stern out, and just as he reversed, Kalev ran up to the bow. With seconds to spare before the vessel was out of reach, he handed Peter something wrapped in a Russian newspaper. Then, the trawler headed out of the harbour, and we waved the crew goodbye. It felt like we were leaving bosom friends, knowing we would never see each other again, and it hurt. Later, when we unfolded the wrapping, we found the set of dominos we had been playing with the night before.

Another ship was on standby, ready to adopt us, but how could we spoil the experience and betray these amazingly generous Estonians? However, there was still no room at the far end of the port, so we decided to join the three yachts moored against the derelict *El Caribe.* The owners insisted we tie up against the factory ship upon our approach. *Capricorn* had a steel hull, while theirs were fibreglass. Our boat would be a floating pontoon for them, not that they said as much.

Boarding *El Caribe* was like entering a multi-story factory, reminiscent of a 007 film set where the villain kept his secret headquarters in the vessel's bowels. Everything on her had been stripped off, including the upper deck cut away to remove the engine and other machinery. To get ashore, one needed strong nerves to climb through an aperture in the ship's side, a metre and a half above the waterline, then walk across some planks placed there to spare anyone from falling through the rotting steel deck, three storeys down to the hole below. There was rainwater seeping through the corroded steel. Who would know if there were a skeleton below, maybe a villain pushed over the edge from the top deck by 007? There were warning signs in Spanish, 'Danger, Do Not Enter.' We soon discovered why when we pushed through a watertight door onto a deck at the quayside level and had to negotiate several flights of iron stairs with some missing. Carrying a torch with us was vital when returning in the dark. I felt Indiana Jones' exploits were like a walk in a park compared to these hazards and fatal traps. At least nobody would dare come to collect harbour dues. Meanwhile, we ran around the harbour like headless chickens, desperate to find some takers for five frozen birds.

We soon grew tired of being used as a giant fender, with our neighbours tramping over our foredecks like marauding pirates in old-fashioned divers' boots. Besides, someone told us a yacht at the far end of the harbour was leaving, so we untangled our ropes from El Caribe and departed. The crew were casting off when we approached, so we motored into the berth like a nautical game of musical chairs before anyone realised the music had stopped.

And now, we had a goose to contend with. It guarded the German yacht next to us as tenaciously as an angry bulldog. When we stepped onto our boat, the goose would honk at us as it ran across the decks, thrusting forward a defiant neck with its wings spread out. I wondered if the bird was the reincarnation of Audrey's pet (our former landlady). Was it here to exact revenge on us for banishing it from our paddock and causing its tragic end when a fox caught it?

As we prepared for our Atlantic crossing, Peter asked, 'Are you trying to sink *Capricorn*?' We had enough victuals to cross the Atlantic and back again. Our plimsoll line was already submerged. What was my buying frenzy about? The lockers bulged with cans of cured meat, tins of vegetables and fruit, pasta, rice and long-life loaves of bread. We had even stored the sack of potatoes the Estonians gave us in the forward locker amongst the sails. In the wheelhouse, tucked securely in a corner with bungee cord, was a large bucket with a few dozen eggs wrapped in newspaper, whilst an orchard of large apples and half a banana tree hung along the passageway to the aft cabin. We bought fresh food from the trader's market in Santa Cruz. Peter searched inside the banana bunch, looking for a possible black tarantula. He was relieved he didn't find one. We sang Harry Belafonte's Banana Boat song anyway.

A beautiful bunch of ripe banana
Daylight comes, and we want to go home
Hide the deadly black tarantula
Daylight comes, and we want to go home

Our friend Patrick, who had seen *Capricorn* taking shape, suggested we put a chicken coop over the stern for our daily supply of eggs. Was he serious? Our once beloved pet hen, Marie-Allen, would have flown out of her grave had we followed his advice. Then, when Peter noticed the number of toilet rolls stored away, he said: 'Do you intend to use them as a paper trail across the Atlantic so we can find our way back?'

'We can never have too many,' I replied like a child scolded for eating too many sweets. Someone lent us an old Renault 4 with a 'push me pull me gear change' to transport over one hundred forty gallons of spring water collected in plastic containers from the Santa Cruz Mountains to fill our water tanks, as tap water was heavily chlorinated. Then, our boat insurance company informed us they would only cover our Atlantic crossing provided we had one extra crew.

Finding someone seemed relatively easy. We saw a few hopefuls walking up and down the jetty, asking boat owners for a passage. José, an Aztec-looking Spanish student, had already approached us. He wanted to sail to Brazil and tried to persuade us to change our destination to accommodate him. The following evening, he knocked on our hull and announced he had decided to compromise and would sail with us to the Caribbean instead. We never saw him again. Then came Harry, a stocky middle-aged chap dressed in a blue-knitted Guernsey, shorts and deck shoes. He had flown on a cheap ticket from Gatwick for a bit of a holiday adventure and was looking for a passage to the West Indies. He mentioned having crossed the Atlantic in a Canadian yacht two years earlier. He carried his safety harness and wet weather gear in his backpack. We wondered if he was a schemer planning to throw us overboard halfway across and steal our yacht.

Sharing a limited space could be a floating hell with the wrong crew. We concluded that taking a chance on a total stranger was high risk. So Peter called our friend Roy. His younger son Tom had sailed with us before. He jumped at the offer but wanted his eldest brother, Philip, to come along. So, the two young men flew to Santa Cruz a week later to join us on our epic voyage to the Caribbean. Although we all liked each other a lot, I hoped there wouldn't be a mutiny aboard the 'good ship *Capricorn*' while sailing across the Atlantic to the Caribbean.

24. In Search of the Trade Winds

The island of Tenerife was fast fading away, with the peak of Mount Teide merging into a distant cloud. My heart felt full as I sat in the cockpit, staring at the boundless horizon. It was too incredible to contemplate pitting ourselves against the mighty sea. I thought of my father. What would he have said if he were alive? He had seen *Capricorn* under construction and couldn't fathom the concept of boat-building, let alone one that could sail oceans. Papa was afraid of water. I had seen him once or twice paddling on Lake Neuchâtel up to his knees - not that being good swimmers in the Atlantic, a thousand miles from the nearest land would help anyone. If we were becalmed, we certainly wouldn't take a dip over the side, unlike a young couple Peter had read about, who did just that. They never tethered themselves to their boat with a rope, and when a breeze picked up, the pair watched their yacht sail away like the Mary Celeste. What a heart-wrenching tragedy, picturing them adrift in the deep ocean until they exhausted all strength and hope of rescue, only to kiss each other goodbye before sinking into their watery grave. When the coastguard found their boat adrift later, they read the couple's last entry in the logbook: 'Becalmed, going for a dip to cool off.'

Capricorn ploughed through the Atlantic swell under full sail. By then, we had been at sea for a few hours, and I had exhausted all possible scenarios, including how we might survive a capsize.

'It's time you took a rest before your watch,' Peter said, interrupting my rambling thoughts. I left him and the boys to take over. Once in my quarters, I climbed into our double bunk, barricaded myself with four pillows, and tucked the duvet along my hips so I wouldn't roll out onto the cabin sole. Then I dozed off.

I woke up, feeling Peter's salty kiss on my cheek. 'Don't rush,' he said. I could hear the wind whistling in the rigging and saw a grey dawn filtering overhead. I grabbed my tracksuit, held tight to the pole by the bed, and sat on the locker seat to lace up my deck shoes. Then, like a sleepwalker, I staggered through the narrow passage to the wheelhouse.

'I've got tea brewing,' Peter whispered to avoid waking Philip and Tom, who were sleeping in the forward saloon. I could only just make out their faces behind the beige lee cloths that stretched across the full length of their berths. The two brothers looked like babies tucked inside their cots. Peter showed me our estimated position on the chart. He noted the time and miles with a pencil, then headed for the aft-cabin to catch some sleep in the warm bed I had reluctantly left.

'I poured tea into a mug just as the boat lurched in the swell, spilling half of its contents down the sink. I could have scalded myself, but I withdrew my hand in time. I remembered what paramedic Stuart, serving in the Military in Gibraltar, told Peter and me. 'In an emergency, if you have nothing else to hand for a burn, wrap the wound in cling film to keep it airtight.'

I had met Stuart at the Holiday Inn one night during a break from my singing and mentioned our pending voyage to the Caribbean. 'My skipper and I wish to learn more about first aid,' I explained.

'There won't be any backup in the deep Atlantic,' he exclaimed. 'You'll need to improvise like we do on a battlefield.'

Stuart was intrigued about our forthcoming Atlantic crossing to America, so much so that he offered to teach us First Aid for free.

Peter ferried him to our boat in our dinghy on the day while Stuart clutched a large suitcase on his lap. Inside was 'resuscitating Annie' - a full-size folded dummy, which bore a woman's body shape when he laid her down on our deck. We took turns giving Annie CPR and mouth-to-mouth resuscitation (other boat owners were also attending Stuart's course), and I wondered if people in their balcony flats overlooking the anchorage and watching us thought of calling the police or the ambulance. Thankfully, we never heard an approaching siren. Once satisfied we all understood the procedure, Stuart folded Annie back in her suitcase, which could have given onlookers the idea we had failed to revive the woman and were planning to get rid of her body.

I laughed at the memory of that quirky event, which was a pleasing distraction. I stepped on deck to scan the horizon for shipping, checked the compass and looked at the sails in case they needed trimming. I could hear whispering sounds in the bow wave. Were these the voices of bygone sailors who had crossed this ocean for thousands of years before us? Sometimes, in the creak of the rigging, I could almost hear someone calling my name, yet I could see nothing but blackness and drift of bioluminescence. These tiny shimmering organisms live in the sea and appear like flashes of bluish-green lights when the water is disturbed. Their glowing felt like divine messages from the deep. It was mesmerising. Yet, I was foxed when I tried to relate the Atlantic Ocean to a sea chart. Peter took sun-sights twice a day. For the best chance of an accurate reading, he would tie himself to the foot of the mast and choose a lull in the mountainous swell. Only then did he point his sextant in the direction of the sun. This device was once as vital to a sailor as the stethoscope to a doctor. The GPS, a satellite and computer system that calculates latitude and longitude, tracing a boat's progress over electronic maps, has since replaced it.

Peter began his sailing with just a sextant and a radio-direction finder and had learned to recognise which transmitter he would be pointing the RDF at by reading its call sign in Morse code. Then, he could assume his position where the lines crossed by taking compass bearings of at least two different transmitters and plotting them on his chart. The more stations he picked up at different angles, the greater the accuracy. Despite using a GPS, Peter was relying on his navigational knowledge. What if all electronic devices suddenly ceased? Salt air and electronics make for a bad marriage. What would a sailor do if his only knowledge of navigation was pressing buttons on a GPS that suddenly failed? I often watched Peter take sun-sights and then return to the cockpit, unhooking and re-locking himself to the lifeline. In our sailing courses, we learned about 'man overboard' rescue, then practised it by throwing a buoy into the sea and retrieving it. However, we had a strict rule - nobody was allowed to fall over the side, and the crew on deck would always be tied up to *Capricorn* when alone on watch, even in calm seas. If Peter fell overboard, would I have the swift reaction required to throw the lifebuoy over the side, start the engine, turn the boat around and steer *Capricorn* onto the opposite compass course to track our way back? I would need to hold my nerves amidst the flapping and cracking of the sails to find Peter drifting in the big ocean and rescue him back on board. I reassured myself it couldn't happen because everyone wore a harness, and the safety line that stretched the full length down the centre of *Capricorn* would prevent the crew from going over the side as they would be hooked on.

The days merged between our watches. Peter and I were like two ships passing in the night. We slept, ate and occasionally read. The motion sapped all energy out of us. I found it hard to stay awake during watches. Philip and Tom were taking *Surgeon* tablets for seasickness, which made them drowsy. I should have listened to my acupuncturist friend Derek when I showed him a pressure point wristband to avoid *le mal de mer*. 'This is the wrong pressure point, he said. 'It is likely to make you seasick.'

Lying down seemed to soothe the symptoms until one had to get up for the next watch.

One morning, we were all wedged in the cockpit in T-shirts, enjoying the first rays of sunshine since casting off. The swell had subsided, but *Capricorn* was still bouncing and pitching about. Below deck, my stew was steaming in the pressure cooker, clamped to the stove to stop the pan from sliding. To prepare the meal, I had to brace myself, strapped to the galley frame with two leashes fastened to my webbing harness so I wouldn't find myself at the other end of the pilot house. Philip always queried the menu. Pleasing him with my cooking seasoned with herbs, garlic, spices, and a little salt was hard. He was used to heavily processed food. Tom had a more pliable disposition and fell in with everything. While he had a slim frame, Philip was stocky and broad-shouldered. He had big blue eyes like his brother, but his hair was straight, while Tom's was curly. Philip was only twenty-four and appeared to have lived a lifetime. He often moved about on deck, without a harness, as if the Atlantic Ocean was as safe as his front room. 'Philip, you cannot be on deck without your harness clicked on,' Peter would yell. 'If you fall overboard in these twenty-foot waves, you'll be lost.' But Philip loved a thrill, and I wondered how far he would go to get his next adrenalin fix.

He told us one day what fun he had when a few friends gave him a lift across Scarborough Bay in their fast rib. As he sat on the side of the inflatable with them and three girls, he decided to liven up the ride by falling off the boat backwards, hoping he might get the kiss of life from the girls. When they fished him out of the water, Philip thought his friends would thank him for the rescue practice opportunity, but they weren't amused, and Philip never got a date with the girl he fancied.

Sitting in *Capricorn's* cockpit after lunch another day, with a heaving deck and the backdrop of big rollers, Philip proposed a game of cards. This was far removed from playing 'Rummy' on a garden patio. He shuffled the cards at the speed of light, then fanned them adroitly across the cockpit table. Playing poker with him could be disastrous, seeing how fast he ran the whole deck of cards down his forearm like falling dominoes. Philip had been a croupier in Amsterdam, where his last job was at a Chinese illegal gambling joint. He told us that he once witnessed a fight to the death between two opposing gang leaders. Maybe he was desperate to flee from a fast and furious gangster milieu. Crossing an ocean on our boat would certainly provide him with a new horizon.

Philip won each game and got bored with us. However, he wasn't so great at fishing.

'It is hard to keep a kipper up one's sleeve.' So far, he had lost all the plastic lures bought in Santa Cruz because he would forget to tend the line. He and his brother became bored of constantly having to pull it in. 'We must have caught some big ones,' Philip would say, 'but they broke the line and got away.'

Undeterred, he made his own bait by cutting a piece out of a sardine can and shaping it like a small fish. Then, he attached it to the line and twisted its tail to make the lure spin in the water. It was a work of art, and I admired his inventiveness. However, despite his efforts, there was never any fish for dinner. Peter said laughingly, 'I made a pact with sea creatures - I won't eat them if they don't eat me.

The fair weather with blue skies suddenly turned into menacing clouds, the wind shifted direction, and the sails flapped like thunder. Peter was soaked when he went to do a sail change despite his fully rainproof jacket. He was up a few times during the night, and by morning, I took his watch. The barometer had steadily plummeted. Thankfully, the rain stopped, and the sun started to peer through the clouds, then suddenly, the wind died altogether. What a cocktail of weather and sea conditions to contend with. Now we were becalmed. How long would this last? Drifting on the ocean for days would be an eerie prospect, so Peter switched the engine on to counteract our angst.

When the wind returned, we set the sails like angel wings, poling out the big genoa and reefing and booming out the main on the opposite side to maximise the pull of the two jibs. The waves were now massive. 'The further west we sail, the kinder the waves will be,' the skipper told us! His optimism did nothing to reassure me. By then, it was a mountaineering feat cooking a meal in this cross swell. We moved cautiously inside the boat, choosing our time to avoid breaking a limb in the process. But we had to eat regardless of the sea conditions. The motion was unbearable at times. If only I could have got off. I told

Peter, 'I'll see you in Antigua.' Sailing on *Aubade* had been an easy ride compared to what we were experiencing now.

We had been at sea for days and never saw a ship until today. It was about two miles away, and sharing this gigantic highway at such close quarters felt amazing and strangely comforting.

When Philip woke up to take his watch, we had eggs with soldiers for breakfast. He said, 'You've cooked my egg perfectly.' Was he being sarcastic?

Later, the wind died, so the engine was switched on again. 'Time to try the spinnaker,' Peter announced. Our dentist in Scarborough had offered it to us after he sold his boat. Maybe it was his way of relieving our pain when settling his fees.

Three pairs of hands prepared the sail, which Peter had tied up in a sail bag like a giant sausage. We released the ropes, and the spinnaker ballooned out with a crack. Although it was an impressive sail, white with a large blue cross in the middle, I felt sure it would all end in 'tears,' if not 'tears.'

Then I heard the skipper urgently shouting to Tom, 'Pull in the sheet,' but he was too late. The self-steering gear couldn't handle the power of the sail; *Capricorn*'s bow veered off to one side, and the wind got behind half of the spinnaker, which then wrapped itself around the forestay. We sailed on like that until Peter had figured out what to do. He disengaged the tiller from the self-steering gear and circled the boat clockwise, hoping the spinnaker would untwist itself. It didn't work, so he tried turning anti-clockwise, to no avail.

Next, he attached a bosun's chair to a rope from the top of our 52-foot mast, and Tom winched him up a metre from the deck. I was horrified when I saw Peter swinging like Tarzan in a one-tree forest, with only water and sharks on either side, where he might fall if something broke. He was now two metres beyond the side rails. With a grin, he said: 'It's an exciting view of *Capricorn* from out here.'

My pulse juddered.

When the skipper careered to the opposite side, I had had enough and yelled to Tom and Philip like an Admiral giving orders against a howling gale: 'For God's sake, get him down.' The boys knew how to react to such a command. While Philip and I grabbed Peter's legs, Tom released the rope from the winch, and then we all fell in a tangled heap on the deck, still attached to our lifelines. I wanted to scream at Peter and the boys. They treated the spinnaker incident lightly as if they had been playing volleyball and the net needed adjusting.

'Think of your safety,' I cried out. 'It's no use trying to save the sail.'

As a last resort, Peter extended the aluminium boat hook, which he tied to our scrubbing brush handle, to untangle the spinnaker and force it down. But after clawing at it long enough and ripping it to pieces, the spinnaker came down, never to fly again. Then, when Philip took the rope halyard off the winch, it ran out of control through his grip, causing him 'rope burns' while the shredded sail disappeared up the mast again because Peter and Tom had pulled it down too enthusiastically. The rope came through the pulley from the top of the mast and landed on deck. I rushed down to fetch some ice from our fridge and the rescue cream for burns from our first aid kit. Philip soon forgot the incident. As they say, worse things happen at sea!

During the night, the wind increased, and the crew on watch reefed down. I heard the big jib falling with a bang onto the deck. When I took my watch, Peter told me we had lost another halyard. We only had the boom halyard left as a spare to hoist the sails.

'I could try going up the mast during a quiet spell,' he suggested. Tom quickly said: 'Peter won't be dangling back and forth on a halyard; he will be firmly up the mast.'

'Alternatively, we could stop in Cape Verde,' Peter responded. It's not much out of our way.'

I wanted to use the skipper's favourite Yorkshire expression, 'I don't mind a circus, but bugger a pantomime,' but I wasn't laughing. Peter always maintained that he was the Captain on board but only with the Admiral's permission, that being me. In reality, though, Peter was well and truly in charge of most decision-making and just as well. However, I declared in a tone not to be challenged: 'We'll stop at Cape Verde, no discussion!'

On the way to São Vicente, Peter thought he would trim his beard. (I had never seen him without one.) Philip gave him a haircut. He looked so different, and I wasn't sure whether I had liked him better beforehand. Later, I tried using the sextant. With Peter's hand around the mast and the other holding on to me, I took a sun-sight and brought the sun's lower limb down to the horizon, which proved challenging with the swell. The boys had been taking readings and working them out with the timetable in Reeds Nautical Almanac. We compared our findings, which thankfully matched. Then, Peter made fresh coleslaw for lunch, and Tom washed up. All was well on board, a long way south of the Canary Islands.

After we had finished our salad, the skipper suggested we put a message in a bottle like famous French yachtsman Bernard Moitessier, renowned for his Golden Globe 'Round the World' voyage in 1969. On his passages, he would write his longitude and latitude on a piece of paper with his home address, lodge it in a bottle, and then commit it to the sea. Moitessier would have won the Golden Globe Race but opted out of 'the pomp and accolade' to continue sailing alone to his chosen destinations.

Capricorn wasn't in a race, and I doubted the crew enjoyed long-distance sailing that much. Later, Tom wrote a message with his name and address, put it in a bottle, and then committed it to the ocean. We watched it disappear, wondering if someone would find it washed ashore on a faraway beach.

When the auto-helm struggled to keep us on course with such huge waves, I could only grab the tiller to stop *Capricorn* from turning sideways against the swell. The big Genoa needed to come down. Peter and Philip spent half the morning re-adjusting the sails. Then, the pin holding the auto-helm broke. Philip offered to steer while the skipper looked for a replacement. I saw him losing our course and shouted, 'This isn't a game.' Maybe I was a bit hard on him. Being at sea does strange things to people.

Luckily, Peter was able to repair the self-steering. I wasn't enjoying life that day. 'Why did we have to choose the slowest mode of transport?' I grumbled to the crew. Tom suggested travelling by donkey might be slower. We could have debated the subject, but I was certain of one thing: sailing was a ruthless test of courage, and no one on board could hide their weaknesses. I felt the sea was like a mirror to the soul.

At dinner, Tom announced he was feeling itchy and hot, and we all noticed his red face and the spots on his chest and back. 'It's measles,' Philip said. 'You can forget about chasing girls when we arrive in Antigua.' Tom laughed, trying to cover his concern. He took two painkillers and hit his bunk. We all thought, 'Who will be next?'

The wind vane behaved well through the night, but the motion was so violent that I felt as if my head was about to explode when I took my watch. Philip had finished his and was talking to the captain of a bulk carrier on the ship's radio. He explained they had gone through a gale after leaving Cape Verde but reassured Philip we would find the swell easing off the nearer we got to land.

When Philip finished his conversation with the captain, he asked me, 'What's for lunch?'

'Spaghetti in a cheese sauce,' I told him.

'Can't we have bolognese sauce?'

'We can't just stop at the butcher on the way, Philip,' I snapped.

'Didn't you get a few tins in Gibraltar?'

I shrugged my shoulders in response.

The next day, Tom insisted on resuming his watch. He said he felt better. I wasn't convinced when I saw a nasty spot lodged at the corner of his right eye. During the night, the wind freshened, and *Capricorn* rolled in the mounting swell. Was it the motion or the fear that kept me awake? Peter noticed my despair when he called me for my watch. 'Shall we swap *Capricorn* for a mobile home?' he said.

'Don't talk like that,' I answered. Although crossing the ocean was proving an emotional rollercoaster, I knew I had signed up for an adventurous lifestyle when I left the paradise island of Martinique to fly into the arms of a man whose passion was sailing. I felt the sea had found me in Lanzarote the day I took the job as a cook on the luxury yacht *Spirit of Labrador*. Yet, it was a love-hate relationship.

The following day, Philip caught a large yellow-striped fish. After he cleaned and gutted it, he put it in the pressure cooker. 'It's a type of tuna fish. I'm not sure I want to eat it,' Peter said, remembering the story of his friend Arthur. His blood pressure rose alarmingly for twelve hours after eating tuna. Maybe he had left it on deck in the sun, and he and his crew got food poisoning?

Philip, undeterred, looked at my recipe books. Meanwhile, I made a sauce with lemon, olive oil and tarragon to accompany the fish. Philip was impressed. I was pleased he had appreciated my cooking, though I reminded him we weren't in the QE2.' I could have asked him about the crate of beer that had disappeared. Peter was easygoing - just as well. However, chocolate for him was sacrosanct. He had hidden his precious cargo somewhere nobody would stumble upon. Tom, meanwhile, was still suffering from measles and eating very little; Philip was dreaming of girls he would meet in Antigua; Peter was uncomfortable with sunburn, and I was feeling seasick. Thankfully, there was no sign of mutiny breaking out on the Good Ship *Capricorn* anytime soon.

As we approached land, we saw small flying fish appearing out of the water, skimming fifteen to twenty feet over the waves, then landing on our decks sadly to die. With three or four hours to go, we tried to slow *Capricorn* down to reach the Harbour of São Vicente by daylight, but we were still sailing too fast despite hoisting the smallest Genoa or even the storm jib. The wind seemed to be playing tricks on us, blowing harder and harder through the night. The waves increased and bashed us sideways. We had hoped to get a lee from the island of Santo Antão.

With a hazy dawn, we entered the Harbour of São Vicente, where we saw a curious display of old trawlers, tankers and warships. I wondered if the broad-shouldered blonde Arlette with glasses à la Nana Mouskouri, who insisted she could tell a man's character by hand-weighing his jewels, might be waiting on the quay to jump ship again. Surely not!

25. *The Higher the Adventure*

'Permission to come aboard,' the African customs officer asked with a Portuguese accent. He had arrived in an open boat accompanied by his minion, a muscular man who looked as if he did press-ups regularly. He remained in the launch, awaiting orders from his superior, who stomped aboard *Capricorn* with his heavy boots. We would have cringed if we had been yacht owners of a pristine teak deck. The officer entered the wheelhouse cabin and requested to see our ship's papers and passports. He scrutinised our documents, asked if we had anything to declare, and peeked around. The young man seemed tame enough, given that customs officers have sacrosanct authority at all times, whatever that meant in those parts of the world, with a reputation of being on the take. 'One has to oil the cogs to ease the bureaucracy machine,' the yachting fraternity maintains, but at what price?

The officer's eyes rested on our bulging fruit hammock hanging from the deckhead. 'Can I have two of your apples?' he asked. What a startling request from such a high authority, which sounded like some child pleading for sweets.

'Please help yourself,' Peter replied, flummoxed. Surely, the officer wouldn't stop at that. Yet, he seemed satisfied. Before he left, he instructed us to bring our ship's papers and passports to the police station for them to keep until our departure. We didn't have to oil the cogs after all.

There wasn't much to see in Mindelo other than a few official colonial-style buildings, a leftover heritage of the Portuguese occupation before the Ilha de São Vicente reclaimed its independence. The town was mostly made of wooden shacks, which were randomly built. Supplying fuel to aircraft and shipping was the island's primary income. On the outskirts, we stumbled across a walled open market and walked through the gates, where we saw people mostly dressed in Western clothes. Only a few women wore veils. Displayed on some stalls were tiny tomatoes, green and red wrinkled apples the size of golf balls, shrivelled-up cabbages, sweet potatoes, and dry vegetables covered with buzzing flies. No wonder our apples, the size of turnips, made the customs officer's eyes pop. We saw a tiny piglet on sale tied to the leg of a stall. I wanted to adopt it as a pet, although I thought the little 'wiggly-tailed cutie' might feel seasick on a boat bouncing in big seas.

In the afternoon, two fishermen rowed alongside in an open boat to sell us freshly caught lobsters. They wanted ten dollars for one, which seemed a lot. They must have mistaken us for wealthy Americans. As a gesture, Peter gave them a few coins, and they left.

Early the following morning, Tom and Philip decided to go ashore, but it wasn't long before they yelled to Peter, finishing his breakfast, 'The inflatable dinghy has gone. We'll buzz around the bay and see if we can find it.'

Philip was the perfect candidate for such a task. Still, I hoped he wouldn't be forced to use his fists to retrieve the tender. He revealed one day how he sorted out four thugs who attacked his policeman friend outside a Scarborough nightclub. Philip tackled the villains so effectively that he put them in hospital. Luckily, his friend only suffered minor injuries. The following day, a high-ranking officer visited Philip's father, Roy, and warned him unofficially that his son displayed high combat skills, and therefore, he considered him a dangerous weapon. Furthermore, while he appreciated that Philip had defended one of his young off-duty officers, he advised that he return to Amsterdam on the next plane and lie low for some time, as he suspected the troublemakers' families might press charges.

But back to the missing dinghy. Tom and Philip returned to *Capricorn* triumphant. They had found it tied to a ladder on the far side of one of the harbour walls. We'll never know whether the rope to the tender had become loose and a charitable soul decided to secure it to a ladder or if someone tried to steal it. We winched the craft up on deck in the evening after that episode.

When we felt the weather was right to leave, we informed the customs officer who had visited us on arrival. He returned our passports and ship documents and arranged for us to fill our water tanks from the ice house that generally dealt with fishing boats. It was apparent that we were the apple of the officer's eye.

A light wind was blowing across the bay when we slipped our lines. Poised at the tiller, steering *Capricorn* 275 degrees towards the open Atlantic while the men hoisted the sails, I pondered how life is a series of episodes that mark our memory like capes along coastlines. It wasn't every day one set off across an ocean where, at one point, we would be a thousand miles from the nearest land in any direction. If anything befell *Capricorn*, we had a life raft with emergency food that would at least keep us alive for a few days. We also had a panic bag with our passports and personal papers ready should we be forced to abandon ship. There were flares we could fire off, hoping to be rescued if shipping passed our way. As I continued in this vein, I heard the skipper shout, 'You're off course.'

'Whoops,' I replied, pushing the tiller hard over to bring us back on the correct heading. I couldn't imagine the crew trying to hand-steer our boat for 1,750 miles across to Antigua. Thankfully, the electronic auto-helm or the wind vane self-steering gear would manage the tiller twenty-four hours round the clock. After all, no one on board had been press-ganged!

It didn't take long for the wind to pick up. Surprisingly, it wasn't the trade wind we had expected, but north westerlies forward off the beam. During the night, the swell increased. I was seasick but determined to get some sleep no matter what. Earplugs worked wonders. At least I couldn't hear the full impact of the howling wind through the rigging.

The following day, Peter announced we had covered one hundred and thirty-nine miles in twenty-four hours. Riding into the troughs of the Atlantic waves felt like going down a bobsleigh run, sitting on a tin tea tray. It was hard to equate my 'sweet home' with *Capricorn* being bounced about in the monumental swell. None of us wanted to guess the height of the waves. By then, we had been at sea for seven days with nothing else but deserted horizons. Thankfully, the trade winds settled in and became well-established. Neither Peter nor I got more than four hours' rest in one stretch. We took turns to double up with the boys while in the shipping lanes. If we didn't keep a permanent watch, it would be as reckless as a mother pushing a pram along the central reservation of a motorway. One morning, we briefly saw a large bulk carrier astern of us. Fortunately, the wind and the swell had subsided.

Meanwhile, Philip caught one of his fingers in the sliding hatch to the cockpit and had a nasty bruise. I applied Arnica cream to it. Another day, the fish he caught nipped his finger. I had antiseptic cream for that, too. But Philip was a tough young man. Just as well, for he was accident-prone like Peter. I was in good company.

One afternoon, to alleviate the weariness of being at sea, I picked up the VHF mike and called for any ships within radio range. I didn't get a reply, so I tried again.

'This is yacht *Capricorn*, *Capricorn, Capricorn,* asking for a weather forecast, over.' I made my request sound like Mae West, a Hollywood sex goddess of the 1960s, famous for saying *'Come Up and See Me Sometime.'* in the Comedy Classic "*She Done Him Wrong*."

I didn't expect anyone to reply, and I went red in the face when I heard: '*Capricorn*, this is the vessel *Golden Ore*. What's your position?'

The radio was crackling, and the captain bore a heavy Portuguese accent. The way he responded, I wondered if he thought it was a telephone sex chatline!

There was a pause before he asked again: 'What's your position over?'

'Position 15°N 41°W,' I answered like a pro, forgetting my Mae West mimicry. 'Are you picking us up on your radar, Captain?'

'Wait a moment.'

Had he just switched it on?

'Yes, I can see you,' he confirmed.

It was a relief. Then he said, 'We are a bulk carrier, transporting iron ore from Brazil to Germany, two weeks there, two weeks back on a twenty-year contract.'

At this rate, I wondered if he had a wife in either port.

He asked: 'What's your destination and course, over?'

'Our heading is 275° making for Antigua,' I responded.

'I should be passing your stern, and if you can't see my ship just yet, you soon will because she's a quarter of a mile long. *Golden Ore*. Out.'

'Have a good trip, Captain. *Capricorn*. Out.'

We never got a weather report, but what difference would it have made? Rough seas would be like a mill pond for such a giant vessel. Peter and I watched the ship steaming past our stern like a floating island. *Golden Ore* was on her way to Brazil to pick up another cargo, which explained why she was high on her waterline.

'How far is the ship from us?'

'About two miles,' Peter said. 'It would take twice the distance for her to halt. As for us, we only need to turn *Capricorn* into the wind, and she'll stop within metres.'

Two days later, we saw another ship abeam. Peter thought it was a large freighter. He called on the VHF, and someone told him to go to channel 10. No one responded. Maybe a sexy voice would have sparked some interest.

I couldn't look at the waves today without feeling horrified. I was breaking up inside with the relentless motion and the wind roaring in the rigging. Fortunately, we had two naturals on board, Peter and Tom. They moved about on deck swiftly, attentive to the wind shift, fully aware of the slightest adjustment needed to the sails. I noticed Tom was moulding himself in Peter's image. This Atlantic crossing nurtured his dream of someday becoming a ship's captain. As for Philip, I pictured him in a tailored suit, shuffling cards in a game of Blackjack on a cruise ship. Then there was me, with burning ambitions of breaking into the music business. Our friend Derek, a Chinese acupuncturist who had owned a practice in Birmingham, once offered to help.

He arranged for me to meet Ken Roach, a former patient of his who was an actor and a wrestler. Derek thought he could point me in the right direction. I remember the day Ken picked me up at Birmingham Railway Station in his pale yellow Rolls-Royce. I was wearing a rainbow jacket to be identified easily. He shook my hand, and I winced. He had a grip like a nutcracker. I looked at his plush vehicle and pictured myself being driven in a Royce to music festivals as a headliner.

After we had left the station, I asked him to play my demo tape on his machine. He listened and told me I had a beautiful voice. Was his compliment a promise of great things to come? On the journey, he asked: 'Do you mind if we call at an auction? I want to look for another Rolls Royce.' His request felt as if the audience had gone home early. To cover my disappointment at this turn of events, I checked my hair in the vanity mirror on the back of the sun visor. What a shock when I saw a gun strapped to it there. Ken quickly pushed the visor back up and said impatiently, 'It's just a toy.'

We spent some time at the auction. While there, I wondered what I was doing with this giant of a man, ready to buy another Rolls-Royce. Later, Ken and I sat at a table drinking tea in the auction house canteen, and we discussed how he could advance my career.

'It's a bumpy road, show business,' he declared. 'You'll need a lot of help.' He gave me a hard stare, then said, 'Let me make a call.' He left the table and went outside. I watched him through the glass canteen door, seemingly engaged in an animated conversation. What was he scheming? When he returned to the table, he asked: 'Do you want to go to London and meet a music agent of mine? He has invited you to stay at his penthouse for the weekend. He'll be able to tell you how he can help promote your music.'

Did he think I would fall for that?

As we drove out of the auction gate, he asked: 'Do you like nightclubs and champagne?'

'It depends,' I mumbled. Then, out of the blue, Ken said: 'I'm inviting you to a party tonight. We'll have some drinks and a bit of fun. I can show you my wrestling trophies and scars later!'

'Ken, it's nice of you to ask me, but I must tell you, I'm happily married and don't have affairs.'

'How boring it would be for me always to have the same partner,' Ken retorted. 'If you want to get on in the music business, you'd need to party with the right people.'

A very uncomfortable silence ensued on the way back to the railway station. The next thing I knew, Ken dropped me there and wished me luck. It wasn't even midnight, and my carriage had already turned into a pumpkin. I felt like a discarded party popper with all my glitter scattered on the pavement.

The flashback was a welcome distraction on that raging night, sailing on a switchback sea. One minute, it felt like we had fallen into a deep valley; the next, we had ascended a hill. The waves must have been enormous - just as well, it was pitch dark.

As I tried to rest in the aft cabin, I suddenly heard Tom shouting, 'I've spotted a masthead light behind us.' I got up, eager to see for myself and caught a glimpse of it as we mounted the crest of another wave. Were we about to be run down?

'This is *Capricorn, Capricorn, Capricorn,'* Peter called on channel 16. We're a sailing boat on a heading of 275°. We have a masthead light astern. Would the vessel respond over?'

There was an anxious moment before the captain replied, 'Okay, *Capricorn*, no worries. We have you on our radar. We're an ocean-going tug bound for South America, having to slow down because the ship keeps burying her bow into these twenty-foot waves. Out.'

'Thank you. *Capricorn* out.'

'This was short and sweet,' I remarked. It seemed the captain was reluctant to give his vessel's name. Then, in the grey light of dawn, we gasped at what a twenty-foot Atlantic swell looked like, let alone how it felt below deck. Each time *Capricorn* gathered speed, she dipped down into a trough, where she momentarily lost the wind before rising to the top of the next roller, and it appeared we were climbing the wave at thirty degrees or more, making the following onslaught from behind us even more menacing. Everyone was quiet. Then, amidst this survival challenge, Peter said, 'Who is for tea, boiled eggs and biscuits?' What a way to re-introduce the mundane in such threatening conditions. Clamps were put into action around our pans on the stove, and the brew was made by pouring hot water into cups in the sink. With no steady surface, anything set down would slide violently in the swell, so we hung on tight to our mugs while leaning on the chart table or sitting on the companionway step, choosing our time to take a sip. Amazingly, we adapted our tea-drinking technique and felt comforted that *Capricorn* and the crew were still coping.

We never saw another sign of the mystery ship. As the day drew to dusk, the turbulent swell finally moderated.

Alleluia.

We were almost becalmed four days later and down to eighty miles when our best 'noon-to-noon' run had been one hundred and forty. At least we could now enjoy the deep Atlantic, for it felt like God had flattened it, and we were floating in a blue paradise. Peter relaxed the rules of being clipped on at all times, but only while we showered. We lathered ourselves using saltwater soap and deluged bucketfuls of cold Atlantic Ocean over each other, giggling at our contorted faces. Then we all indulged, rinsing our hair in fresh water.

Filling a bucket from the side while a boat is still moving is an acquired skill. Peter showed me how to drop it well forward, use the momentum, and swing it swiftly over the rail with the rope at its shortest. The first time I tried, I got the angle wrong, and the empty bucket floated past me. On my second attempt, the pail at least filled, but I nearly pulled my arm out of its socket because I was too late bringing it back on board. The third time, I mastered it!

'Bucket chucking' was another dying skill like 'keel-hauling.' The famous pirate Blackbeard underwent such torture when the crew pushed him over the vessel's port side with a rope around him, then pulled him under the keel and back up over the starboard quarter. Blackbeard suffered this torture twice. The second time, his body was so flailed after he had grazed against barnacles on the hull that the crew thought he had died until he coughed up water on deck. Blackbeard survived but later was beheaded in a battle in 1718. They placed his head on a pole overlooking the southern end of the Chesapeake Bay to deter other pirates. According to legend, his skull became a drinking vessel, and folks today are still looking for Blackbeard's treasure. I wondered if it crossed Peter's mind to keel-haul me when I complained about the weather too much!

While sailing in moderate seas, Peter decided to try the shotgun he had bought in Gibraltar from an Englishman living on his yacht. We had occasionally shared meals on each other's boats. One day, James had approached Peter, and while leaning forward, he whispered, 'Do you want to buy a gun?'

Surprised by James's offer, he asked: 'What is it?'

'It's an Italian eight-shot pump-action shotgun, with seven in the magazine and one in the chamber.'

Hesitant, Peter said, 'How much do you want for it?

'One hundred pounds, which includes a carrier bag full of ammunition. If you encounter pirates on your way, there's even a box of solid-lead spiralled bullets instead of shot that would go through a quarter-inch steel at short range.'

Peter paused. We had agonised over this for so long, wondering whether we should have a means of defending ourselves if attacked. He thought, 'This must be an omen.' He shook James's hand and declared: 'It's a deal.'

When carrying a weapon on a boat, the main consensus is to know how to use it and be prepared to do so if confronted with a life-threatening situation. While working at Dale's Electrics as a production control manager, Peter was once part of a rifle club. However, he had never used a shotgun, so now was the time to try it. I counted as he loaded seven cartridges in a magazine and one into the firing chamber before lifting the weapon to his shoulder. I saw the look of apprehension on his face as he pointed the gun at an imaginary target and then pulled the trigger to discharge the first cartridge. Was he worried about what recoil he would feel? Finally, he drew back the wooden handgrip, which reloaded the chamber and shot off seven rounds. It shook every bone in my body as the sound echoed eerily across the empty ocean. I needed time to familiarise myself with my new *Clint Eastwood* skipper.

Philip and Tom tried the shotgun next. Were the men picturing themselves on a Wells Fargo stagecoach being chased by Billy the Kid? Peter remarked, 'Imagine the consequences of such weapons ending up in the wrong hands.' Although he knew how to use the shotgun to defend our lives, he didn't like the adrenalin rush when he let off eight shots of rapid fire. I was relieved when he put the gun back in its blanket as carefully as one would tuck a baby in a cot. Then he locked it away in a hiding place with the ammunition elsewhere. Then, almost simultaneously, following the gun-shooting exercise, we heard two big bangs and wondered if it was a foreign navy counter-attacking with gunfire. The skipper and crew rushed on deck to scan the horizon for warships. By now, I suspected Peter must have been on high alert, for he was once in the firing line of a Spanish shore gun battery, which narrowly missed blowing his fibreglass yacht and him to smithereens.

Looking up, we all saw two long white contrails across the sky. Peter grabbed his binoculars and identified the culprit with its unmistakable swept-back wing profile. It was *Concorde* flying at over 2000km/h. The two bangs we heard were the sonic booms as they reached optimal speed. Peter returned to his chart and drew a line from London to Buenos Aires, which coincided with our position, so neither *Concorde* nor *Capricorn* were off-course. The supersonic bird wasn't the usual navigational fix, but the skipper was pleased using it.

We saw no sign of shipping for two days, and everyone thought something was brewing across this aquatic desert. We had porridge for breakfast in the cockpit, waiting for the sun to burn away the hazy clouds. Peter mentioned how strange it was that we hadn't seen any marine life so far.

'Maybe your twenty-four-gun salute to Neptune scared everything off,' I said. 'It isn't as though you shot an albatross, and we're suffering the consequences as the Ancient Mariner did.'

Peter grinned.

The conversation then veered to the subject of eggs. 'We need to ration ourselves,' I declared. Philip gave me a look that said: 'Why didn't you buy more in Mindelo.' I remembered Peter meeting a chef working on a US Nimitz class aircraft carrier who cooked over a thousand eggs a day for six thousand crew. At least, my cooking facilities had improved from a paraffin-wicked stove aboard *Ellis of Tamar* to a two-ring gas stove with an oven - *the things you do for love.*

While we chatted, we suddenly heard the unmistakable sound of a whale blowing out air. Everyone turned their heads to look over the stern and saw a dark shape with a small dorsal fin metres away. The mammal gradually swam towards us. It came so close that I could have thrown a deck mop at it. Its head and tail were submerged, but what became visible on the surface seemed as long as *Capricorn.* It showed no interest in us and disappeared into the deep without a ripple. We looked at each other to confirm it wasn't a mirage. Then, the sun pierced through the sky on cue and highlighted the next spectacle of more than ten dolphins, perfectly aligned, breaking out of a rolling wave. We all rushed to the forward rail, hoping they would play with our bow wave, but they vanished. Next, we saw several creatures at least fifteen feet long, with black and white patterns like those on Friesian cows. They swam under our keel from one side to the other without disturbing the surface. Ahead of us, the water was boiling like a vast cauldron. Was there an underwater volcano about to erupt? Then, as we drew closer, we saw hundreds of tuna breaking the surface and jumping high out of the sea. It was soon all over, and it felt as if somebody had turned off the heat under a pan of boiling water. Had it all been a dream? We spent hours staring at the horizon, hoping for a replay.

When Peter announced we should soon see land, I stood on the bowsprit rail like a figurehead scanning the horizon.

The reward came when I saw two pale grey smudges ahead. 'Land,' I announced, shouting so loudly that my lungs could have burst.

'You can see the outline of Guadeloupe on the port bow and Antigua on the starboard quarter,' Peter explained.

He couldn't have made a better landfall even if he'd tried.

The good ship *Capricorn* had proven her worth across the Atlantic Ocean, and our marriage was still afloat.

As we approached the island of Antigua, butterflies touched down on our decks as if they were greeting us. After days of being imbued in greys and blues, the cliffs and hills had such vivid colours. Like bees, intoxicated by the scent of pollen, we inhaled the fragrance of trees and vegetation wafting from the shore. We dropped anchor in the crystal clear waters of Falmouth Bay, where a new adventure was about to unfold.

26. To the New World

Antigua was a panoply of enhanced senses - hibiscus, frangipani, and bougainvillaea, brightening the greens of palm trees, acacias and mangroves. Across the water, one could hear Bob Marley's song 'Get Up Stand Up.' The tune was being played in all the bars in the resort. In Falmouth Bay, a flotilla of yachts littered its magnificence. These vessels had sailed across oceans to find tropical paradise - many costing as much as the most luxurious mansions on the island while local people still lived in tin shacks. I was lucky Peter's hard work and resilience in building *Capricorn* had got us here despite all the promises I made to keep him in the manner he wasn't accustomed to. (I must have gone blind, painting too many rainbows).

Antigua was a leveller for all walks of life. It wasn't unusual to find oneself at a bar sitting next to Mick Jagger, sipping his fruit juice, or to hear Eric Clapton jamming with local musicians. Surprisingly, it was easy for me to find singing work. I had asked the Copper and Lumber Hotel manager if he needed someone to perform in his lavish restaurant, and he said, 'Yes.' One night, a blonde woman offered me a drink during my break. 'I enjoyed your performance,' she remarked, 'but I didn't clap because I was too self-conscious, sitting at a table on my own.' When I asked the receptionist who the woman was, she said, 'She's Keith Richard's wife.'

At the Tropical Parrot restaurant, where I sang two nights a week, a man in his forties approached me and said, 'Next time you're in London, make sure you come and see me at Chrysalis Records.' Then he handed me his visiting card.

The good times in Antigua were marching on. With the hurricane season soon upon us, we feared becoming entrapped on the island like insects in a Venus flytrap. Meanwhile, Philip and Tom were wreaking havoc amongst the young women with their dancing blue eyes and golden hair. Our cruising money was keeping them fed. Together, they ate for four people. Peter painfully tackled the issue one day. 'If you want to complement meals with fresh chicken and other meat, we can no longer grubstake you.'

His talk to the boys triggered an instant reaction. We wouldn't see them for days, yet we felt they were still our responsibility. When they reappeared, we nudged and quizzed them about their plans. By then, we had been on the island for almost two months. Would Tom and Philip get Antigua out of their system and leave the nest like new fledglings? 'Time and tide wait for no man,' the saying goes. We didn't want to face the hurricane season. Still, it would be hard to leave this enchanting island, but as German writer Jean Paul wrote: 'Recollection is the only paradise where one cannot be turned away.'

While waiting for the boys to make their next move, we decided to visit the town of Saint John, an hour's ride away on the local bus. It proved a hair-raising experience. Each time the young and muscly chap with an Afro hairstyle drove around a bend, he made the rear wheels drift, peppering bystanders with flying grit. Maybe he was a rally driver in his spare time.

On the way, he picked up people and children from the side of the road. When he got to the school, he walked the little ones to the gates, holding their hands. The girls looked cute in their checkered blue and white dresses over white frilly blouses, whilst the boys appeared so grown up in navy shorts and white polo shirts.

Saint John was worth the visit, with its cluster of brightly painted two-storey buildings, its skyline dominated by the twin-towered Anglican Cathedral, and the bustling market with the women stallholders wearing flamboyant headdresses, bandana skirts and puffy tops. They reminded me of Gauguin's bold and vibrant paintings. As for the women's voices, they cut through the air like town criers.

As we rowed the dinghy back to *Capricorn* in the late afternoon, Peter exclaimed: 'At least we are still in one piece.' Having just recovered from a harrowing journey on the bus, we were ready for an aperitif on deck, but then when we stepped into our cockpit, we had another surprise. The boys had left the wheelhouse hatch open. 'Anyone could have got inside,' I yelled. But worse still, they had violated one of our three major safety rules on *Capricorn.*

Rule number 1 - Don't fall overboard. (They hadn't.)

Rule number 2 - Always turn the seacocks off. (Thankfully, they were closed. If not, the boat would have sunk.)

Rule number 3 - Always switch the gas off after cooking. (They hadn't.)

Maybe the boys were late for a romantic rendezvous, but leaving the gas burning was the cardinal sin. *Capricorn* was our home and the means of seeing the world. How could they be so careless? The wind, blowing through the open hatch, could have extinguished the flame, and the escaping gas filled the bilges without our knowledge. Our fate would have been sealed as soon as we lit the stove to put the kettle on, marking the end of *Capricorn* and us with a bang as loud as a twenty-one-gun salute. What a way to die in paradise!

The boys were a liability. Fortunately for us, Tom later announced he had found a boat to sail back to England on, and Philip sought somewhere temporary to stay until his new contract started as a croupier on a cruise ship. We were now free to lift anchor and pursue the American dream. I thought of one of Abba's songs:

I have a dream, a song to sing
to help me cope with anything.
If you see the wonder of a fairytale
You can see the future, even if you fail.

My musical dream seemed like a fairytale, but whilst rainbows lured me on in my quest for stardom, I felt caught in the middle, with his love for the sea and mine, the stage, and I wondered if my crystal chandelier would shatter when I confronted the reality of breaking into American showbiz.

Meanwhile, there were uninhabited islands in the Bahamas to visit on the way, with white sandy beaches and turquoise waters where the 'encores' would grace us with unforgettable sunsets.

27. The American Dream

'Steer three points to starboard; there's a coral reef ahead,' Peter shouted from the bow.

'For Christ's sake, why risk our safety to anchor in this lagoon,' I snapped. Peter was spellbound by magnificent clear crystal waters, with their full array of exotic fish and shrimps swimming in the shallows. Having sailed in the fathomless waters of the Atlantic for days, eyeball navigation to spot coral reefs felt as threatening to me as walking in an unexploded minefield. Ancient mariners used a lead line with knots and a hole filled with animal fat to measure the water depth and pick up sand, shell or mud to confirm their positions on their charts. An electronic depth sounder was significantly more straightforward, though I dreaded the transducer becoming fouled in the bottom of the boat because it would involve pulling the whole unit out of its skin-fitting. Then a jet of water would spout forth, enough to extinguish a forest fire or sink *Capricorn* if Peter didn't swiftly put the cap back on. Despite this alarming process, there was never more than a few cups of water to be emptied from the bilges, thanks to the skipper's calm disposition.

We checked in in Puerto Rico a few days later. It was our first port of entry into the USA. We didn't stay there and sailed south of the island to Isla Culebra. The place was known as the best hurricane hole in the Bahamas until a two-hundred-mile wind hit, wrecking more than three hundred boats in a few hours. Until then, we had envisaged leaving *Capricorn* there and returning to England to top up our kitty. Being aware that hurricanes can strike twice in the exact location prompted us to move on to the uninhabited island of Allans Cay next.

While there, we met the rare natives. People say they are pretty tame, but all the same, coming face-to-face with a five-foot rock iguana with yellowish-green scales and a ridge that ran from the top of the head to the tail was particularly unnerving. One daredevil approached us as if wanting to assert its territory. Peter crouched down, stretched his arm out, and, with an open palm, offered the iguana some bread. Its teeth, normally shearing vegetation, inadvertently caught his thumb.

'I wonder if it liked the taste of your flesh, Peter?

Undeterred, he let the reptile have another try, and it swiftly snapped the bread.

'Have you still got five fingers?' I asked.

It's only a nip.' he replied.

The following day, we anchored in Wells Bay on Crock Island and were welcomed by the sound of honking and chirping. Seeing hundreds of flamingos on the far shore was a delightful surprise. They appeared like ballerinas wearing crimson tutus, performing a routine 'en pointe.' What a spectacle of beauty, with the backdrop of white sandy beaches and brilliant turquoise waters.

Later, I suggested a swim, thinking it would be like bathing in heaven. 'I don't think it's a good idea,' Peter said. 'I read the Bahamas have more sharks than anywhere else.'

'They are seven hundred coral islands. Surely, they aren't all together in one place. We could take turns shark-spotting.'

'I've just seen one,' Peter exclaimed. 'Look at it, stirring up the shallows.'

By then, we had lost all desire to dive over the side; we didn't want to become another link in the food chain. So we sat in the cockpit, watching a glorious orange sunset dipping into the water. We were Adam and Eve in the Garden of Eden, where no serpent would tempt me to eat the forbidden fruit except for fallen coconuts at the foot of the palm trees. We lived the Eden illusion until the sound of an outboard engine jolted us out of our heavenly bliss. A tiny sailing yacht, flying the Canadian ensign, was entering the lagoon. The helmsman circled around us, looking for somewhere to moor. There wasn't enough deep water for both yachts to swing clear of each other at anchor, so Peter shouted to the man: 'Throw me a rope, and I'll tie you to our stern.'

White Pearl looked so small compared to *Capricorn.* The man turned his engine off and disappeared below deck, reappearing shortly after with three Budweiser cans. He handed us one each before jumping to our yacht as if she were a floating pontoon. He introduced himself, sat in the cockpit, and we toasted the meeting of free spirits.

Scott was short, in his fifties, and wore a 'Robinson Crusoe' beard. He had left his carpentry business back in Vancouver, tired of working all hours and paying bills. When we told him we were sailing to the States, he said, 'Why go to such an awful place.'

'It was one of my ambitions to cross an ocean and sail to America,' Peter said.

'I'm a singer-songwriter and want to experience the music business there.' I added.

'Good luck. I think you'll need plenty of it and a thick skin,' Scott remarked.

We invited him to dinner, and I asked if he liked bean curry.

'Great. I usually don't bother much with cooking.'

We ate in the saloon as mosquitoes would have bitten us alive if we had stayed on deck. *Something always seems to spoil perfection.*

Over dinner, Scott mentioned a messy divorce. I thought of the lone sailor Trevor, whom we had met in Spain. He, too, had suffered a heartbreak but later found peace, sailing around the world alone.

We cast *White Pearl* off in the morning, leaving Scott to enjoy this heavenly lagoon alone.

Before dusk, we anchored in Clarence Town Bay, halfway up Long Island. We ate in the cockpit and watched another blood-red sunset fading away. With the breeze, we were unhindered by mosquitoes. We could hear reggae music drifting across the water. 'Why don't we go ashore?' I suggested. 'It would be great to check out the local scene.' Peter did the dishes while I tidied up. Then, we rowed across the bay and moored our tender to a quay.

The main street was a short walk away with little to see, just a few shops no bigger than single-car garages. All shutters were drawn for the night. Amongst them was a similar-sized building with a sign, 'Barclay's Bank.' I wondered if the employees used coconut shells as money deposit boxes for their clients!

Further on was the town hall building, where we could hear reggae music through its front double door. We stopped to listen to the live band and watched the dancers swinging hips and bumping buttocks, which would have rivalled any pole-dancing moves, especially when they faced each other. Maybe 'Dirty Dancing' originated from here. We walked gingerly into the smoky, dimly-lit hall with a few fairy lights strung across the ceiling and joined in, giving it our best moves. We were the only white faces, and nobody seemed to care, being too busy gyrating, including us.

The water was shallow when we entered the creek leading to Cape Eleuthera Resort. Although the marina was shown on our chart, it had no customary port and starboard lights at the entrance. There were fixed wooden pontoons, which looked dilapidated. Once inside the marina, Peter hesitated; only six inches of water were beneath our keel. He still instructed me to head for the concrete wall, where I saw two mooring rings let into the side of the quay. Being far apart wasn't a problem; Peter had more ropes in the forward locker than the Women's Institute knitting groups had yarn. There were water and electricity points, but all had been stripped out. The place was deserted. We couldn't see a boat, vehicle, or even a marina office or hut nearby, just some bungalows in the distance.

Intrigued, we decided to explore. On the way, we noticed compounds with parked electric golf carts. Some were utterly buried in ivy. The buildings nearby were once part of a golf club complex. Further along, all patio doors to the bungalows were flung open, revealing fully carpeted floors; the only visitors inside were a large colony of land crabs scurrying around. Sensing somebody could be watching us and we might get into trouble for trespassing, we didn't venture in. Besides, if we were to trip, we could be swarmed by those pink crustaceans. I noticed one of their claws looked larger and more lethal than the other and pictured our flesh being stripped from our bones, the land version of piranhas. Although these land crabs were small, their sheer numbers were spine-chilling. Beyond was a concrete airfield runway where someone had ditched a big pile of rubble, which must have been there to stop planes from landing.

On our return to *Capricorn*, we walked through the remains of what might have once been a manicured garden. Only a few bits of scrub with bright red flowers had survived. Peter was strolling ahead when I noticed he had suddenly stopped and looked frozen. I couldn't understand why until I saw a hummingbird hovering inches from his nose. The feathered aerial acrobat had a long, thin beak like a rapier. Its wings of iridescent colours were beating so fast they were a blur. I stood in awe, watching the turbo-charged bird almost touching Peter's face. The two stared at each other for what seemed to be more than just a few seconds. Then, it flew off. Peter said with his usual sense of humour, 'I now understand the meaning of the country and western song I heard as a lad, *May the Bird of Paradise Fly up your Nose.*'

When we returned to our boat, we were surprised to see a tall, lanky black man in shorts standing on the quay, staring intently at *Capricorn.* He didn't look happy. 'You can't stay here,' he said. 'You've got to leave now.'

'It's getting late, and navigating in shallow waters at night is dangerous,' Peter pleaded. 'Can you please let us stay until daylight?'

'Okay, but you'll have to remain on the boat,' the man grunted.

We quizzed him about the resort. He explained it was once thriving until some Saudi Arabian businessmen bought it out, and through mismanagement, it became derelict.

'What about the airport runway? We saw a pile of rubble there,' Peter remarked.

'It's to stop smugglers landing.'

We wondered if the man was the custodian of the place, worried we might be running contraband and waiting for a boat to come in, or if he was simply up to it himself. Without another word, he left us. We watched him walk towards the bungalows, where he disappeared.

We were relieved to set off the following day.

The entrance to Nassau Port proved tricky with its shallows. We had radioed the authorities, who permitted us to enter the harbour and take fuel and water. Once inside, we docked at the commercial jetty and paid for two hours to fill up, stretch our legs and find a shop to buy vegetables. On the way, we strolled along wide boulevards lined with colourful residential houses, some charmingly rustic, others in a sorry state. Next, we came across a small market where we bought peppers, tomatoes, plantain, and mangoes.

When we returned to *Capricorn*, a cruise ship had just tied up, and it was a shock to see the skyline blotted out and watched in awe over a thousand or more tourists disembarking. Four young and well-built women approached us. They asked: 'Do you know where to find the nearest McDonald's?'

'Sorry,' we chorused. Was McDonald's renowned for its conch burgers? Cracked conch is a local shellfish delicacy. It is usually sliced, battered, and deep-fried to form golden, crispy strips of flesh, but one needs good teeth!

We left the four American women to their gourmet pursuits and anchored near a barrier of rocks, which offered protection from the cruise ships and the madding crowds.

The following day, we sailed to Bimini Island. The wind was strong, whipping up an awkward swell. At least, spring in the Bahamas was balmy. We anchored in crystal clear water, although it felt strange because no other boats were in this bay area. I put the kettle on to make tea. Then, as I poured the boiling contents into the teapot, we noticed a sudden heavy splash of water erupting near us. A passenger seaplane had just touched down. It came so close to *Capricorn* that if we had been in a Bond movie, my 'crackpot' skipper would have grabbed a rope and swung from the mast to land on one of the plane's wings. Joking apart, was it a telling-off from the pilot?

We didn't wait to find out and swiftly lifted anchor. Peter looked at the pilot book printed in the 1950s somebody had given us. It showed two sticks marking the narrow channel between reefs. And there they were, leading us to the next anchorage. Maybe they weren't the originals, but some things never change.

It had been over a month since we left Antigua for the Bahamas. By then, we had covered almost a thousand miles. Lulled by the slow pace of life, it was time to shake out the sails and embrace the winds of change. Fifty miles separated us from Fort Lauderdale, which seemed a world apart. The Gulf Stream, which finishes up in Scotland, flows between Bimini and Ft. Lauderdale with a current running up to four knots, the speed of *Capricorn* sailing in light winds. The shortest passage for us would be to motor over a shallow area of thirteen miles. An American sailor we had met mentioned he had made the journey numerous times and thought we would save a good few miles.

There was hardly any wind when we set off, which was ideal. We covered twelve miles and then started to navigate with only five to ten feet under the keel, me at the tiller and Peter at the bow, watching out for coral heads. Instead of walking on eggshells, we were floating over seashells. We wouldn't be clearing this dangerous area before dark at this cautious pace, so we found a sandy patch and dropped the hook in fifteen feet of water. Bimini was twenty miles behind us, and Ft. Lauderdale thirty ahead. Remote from anywhere, it was the most bizarre experience we had encountered on our journey from England; indeed not the place to be in a tropical storm. So, in no man's land, in the eerie stillness of this jet-black night, we waited with bated breath for dawn to release us from its treacherous grip.

We awoke to see another day and were graced by a pale crimson sky. We lifted anchor, hoisted the courtesy flag to the starboard cross tree and set off on course for the American dream. After an hour of Peter scanning the seabed while I steered *Capricorn,* the depth eventually increased, and not long after, the high-rise buildings of Miami and Ft. Lauderdale loomed on the hazy horizon.

Peter, who I consider my hero (he always tells me I'm looking at him through rose-tinted glasses), and I, his Swiss muse, would be reinventing ourselves in the land where the 'Wild West' was won with a gun and where the 'dollar is king.'

Ft. Lauderdale is the largest yachting centre in America. The city has over one hundred and seventy-five miles of canals, making it the Venice of the USA. As indicated in our pilot book, we tied up at a marina designated as a port of entry into the country, then walked down the quayside to a payphone directly connected to Customs. Peter punched various numbers through an automated service to get to the correct ethnic group. Eventually, he managed to speak to someone. The customs man took details of our boat and the number of crew, and then he asked if we had weapons and how much ammunition we carried. Peter informed him we had a shotgun and a small bag of cartridges. The man said, 'You'll need to check in at the airport with your passports to clear immigration.'

We walked to the marina office and inquired about the bus service to Ft. Lauderdale Airport. 'You'll have to catch a taxi,' the young brunette, sitting at the desk, suggested. She was talking to a man built like a wrestler. He must have overheard Peter's question when he said, 'I can give you a lift to the airport. I'm going that way.'

Doug was impressed when he learned we had sailed from England and across the Atlantic Ocean. 'I don't cruise further than the Florida Keys,' he declared.

'It's not how far one goes that counts,' Peter intimated. 'It is how much you enjoy the journey.'

Doug smiled. His willingness to help two strangers clashed with the soulless landscape of six-lane highways, drive-in banks, and liquor stores with barred windows we spotted en route.

Once at the airport, we followed the signs to the arrival lounge, which seemed large enough to accommodate the simultaneous arrival of several passenger planes. How odd it felt to be in a two-person queue, following the zigzagging barriers to the glass-fronted booths, where hundreds of passengers from different flights would normally check-in.

We waited over twenty minutes in the empty lobby before a black woman in a peaked cap, white shirt and black tie ushered us impatiently to a desk. Not that we had expected a brass band and the Mayor to greet us or the waving of the stars and stripes as if we were re-enacting the arrival of the pilgrim fathers. But, being addressed by a sergeant major of a woman handling us like raw recruits wasn't what we had anticipated.

It was evident that the customs officer didn't know what to do with two aliens who had entered America by sailboat and had no real idea how long they were planning to stay in the country. The official seemed annoyed and suspicious. For a minute or two, we thought, 'What do we do if she denies us entry?' Finally, she stamped our passports as brutally as if she had exterminated a cockroach on her desk, then dismissed us with a wave.

Welcome to America!

We left the airport hall and waited for a bus outside the entrance. Looking at the ugly warehouses and surroundings, I wondered how my musical dream would fit into all this. It was like arriving at a gig in a nightclub and pushing the garbage bins aside to get backstage. Peter didn't seem happy either. While trying to make sense of destinations and times, he said, 'The compass in my head is spinning. I've lost my sense of direction.'

I felt Peter was like a goldfish a child had won at a coconut shy and carried home in a clear plastic bag, which burst, leaving him floundering at the kerbside. Yet, we caught the right bus back to the marina by pure chance. Were we just two frightened rabbits eager to bolt home to our warren?

Back aboard *Capricorn*, I continued nurturing my musical dream, hoping the *Director of Serendipity* would snap the clapboard for the next movie scene where I'd win over the American public with my songs.

28. Isle of Hope

Were we not like frogspawn amongst caviar on a golden platter against all those glamorous yachts, opulent mansions and helicopters? All that decadence was like flipping through the pages of American lifestyle magazines as we glided through this labyrinth of canals.

Peter was unfazed and said, 'Let's explore and find somewhere to berth and swing the lead line to see what comes up.'

We set off and motored through a maze of waterways until we saw a sign, 'Berth for Rent.' Peter lined *Capricorn* up and slowly headed towards the dock. As he pulled the throttle into reverse to bring her to a halt, the lever broke off in his hand. He yelled, 'Grab the stern line quick. We're stuck in neutral.' (We always keep 'forward and stern' ropes ready to deploy.)

Spurred by the danger of our ten-ton *Capricorn* ramming the end of the dock, Peter jumped over the rails and on the shore like an Olympic hurdler. I threw him the aft mooring rope, and quick as a flash, he put a turn around a pontoon cleat, just enough to snub the line and bring *Capricorn* to a gentle halt while I ran forward and passed him the bow rope. When Peter turned the engine off, he cursed the second-hand gear lever he had bought at Beaulieu's boat jumble.

'Do you think this place will fit our budget?' I remarked, looking at the manicured lawn, palm trees, exotic-looking plants and the elegant two-storey condominium with colourful trailing flowers draping down from the balconies.

'There's no harm in checking prices,' Peter replied.

The reception was on the ground floor. A dark-haired woman in her thirties with large-rimmed glasses greeted us with a smile, then said, 'You've made a very slick manoeuvre to the dock.'

If only she knew!

'Thank you,' Peter replied with a grin. 'We'd like to rent a berth for the month. How much is it?'

When she quoted us $199 a month with water and electricity included, we found it hard to conceal our surprise. We filled out a form with *Capricorn's* details, presented our passports and paid a month in advance. The woman wasn't used to cash. She looked for her handbag, and Peter said, 'Never mind the change.'

Las Olas Boulevard's historical and upmarket district was a short walk away. The place had gondola rides on the canals, restaurants, art galleries, boutiques, and delis. With a country built for cars, it was remarkable to find horse-drawn carriages transporting tourists around, but seeing these horses wearing nappies astonished us the most. 'Do you think the London horse-guards parade might adopt this non-fouling method?' I remarked.

'They're robbing rose growers of their free fertiliser,' Peter chuckled.

Walking on, we came across an art gallery. Those establishments are magnets, especially for Peter. He had won a scholarship to attend Art School as a teenager, but his parents said, 'We're not keeping you till you're twenty-odd years old.' Peter's dream of becoming an artist or designer died that day.

We wandered around the exhibition, which featured significant works of Asian Art. A painting depicting religious scenes caught our attention. While we contemplated it, a very handsome young Asian Indian approached us and asked, 'Do you know what you're looking at?'

'Yes, scenes from *Bhagha Vita*,' I replied.

He looked impressed and inquired about what had brought us to Ft. Lauderdale. Peter explained we had sailed from England on a yacht he built himself.

'You're brave.' the man remarked.

'What about you?' I ventured.

'My parents emigrated to the States from India. My cousin is an Art dealer. I'm his American outlet.' The conversation was interrupted when a staff member called him. 'Will you excuse me for a minute,' the man said. 'Before you go, I've something for you.' He disappeared into the back of the gallery, then returned shortly after carrying a thick paperback of the *Bhagha Vita*. 'Take this with you on your travels with my blessings,' he declared. He shook our hands and bid us *Alavida*. The young man had parted with his precious copy, which looked as if it had been his companion for some time.

What an honour.

We continued our visit up the main street and noticed fireworks and a rock band advertised on a billboard for the coming Saturday evening. 'We know what to do tomorrow night,' I said. 'The concert is within walking distance of where we are.'

The band was playing *Key Largo* when we arrived. The song, written and sung by Bertie Higgins, was all the rave in the local radio stations. People were jiving on a dance floor deck laid out on the beach. Around the perimeter were beer tents and stands selling popcorn, hot dogs and ice creams. During the concert interval, we watched the most spectacular fireworks being launched from a barge anchored a short distance off the beach. We felt it heralded great beginnings ahead, and for the first time, we experienced a real buzz to be on American soil.

During the break, we found ourselves next to the group's drummer, a flamboyant character with a Mohican haircut. With his leather attire, he looked like a hell's angel. There were so many tattoos on his face and neck that, when our eyes met, he seemed to be staring out of a kaleidoscope of patterns.

How do you engage in a conversation with somebody like that?

'You've got a great sound,' I ventured, trying not to appear like a star-struck teenager. Despite his ragged edges, Clerk was eloquent and spoke about music at length. 'I'm hoping someone will be interested in my songs,' I mentioned. 'People say my style is 'Ethnic Pop,' whatever that means,'

'Our agent in Atlanta City might be able to help. You should go and see Eric. Tell him I recommended you.' He handed me his agent's visiting card and wished us good luck.

Was Clerk, the tattooed Oracle, showing us the direction we should aim for? Peter has an impetuous nature. Once we returned to *Capricorn,* he searched on a map for the nearest place to get to Atlanta by boat. 'We could journey up the eastern seaboard, using the Intracoastal Waterway to Savannah,' he suggested. 'From there, we could hire a car and drive the two hundred and forty-eight miles on Highway 75 to Atlanta City. To Americans, it's just a jaunt down the road.'

He made it sound so simple.

'The 3,000-mile Intracoastal Waterway stretches along the Atlantic seaboard, beginning in Massachusetts and continuing southwards to Florida, then up the Gulf Coast to Brownsville, Texas. Commercial barges and leisure boats use the waterway to avoid sailing offshore in unpredictable seas and shallows.'

Excited by this new venture, Peter and I cast off from Ft. Lauderdale bound for Savannah, Georgia. We sailed through picturesque neighbourhoods, waterfront mansions, and lush mangroves until we came to Palm Beach. The Southern Boulevard Bridge is one of three bascule bridges crossing the Intracoastal Waterway and Lake Worth Lagoon. Seeing all the glitzy estates and urbanisation wouldn't entice us to step ashore. With such a heavy spread of tourist industry, we couldn't differentiate one resort from another. So, we never touched land for three days, mesmerised by the ever-changing colours and patterns on the water and the variety of bird life. White Pelicans were a favourite. They looked majestic with their large wingspan and were swift at scooping fish up with their sizeable bill pouches.

In the evening, we stopped to anchor in shallow waters, away from the traffic. Then, when we approached the iconic Cape Canaveral, it was time to play at being tourists. We anchored in a lake near Titusville. From there, we could see the shuttle on its launching pad looming like a cathedral spire above the flat skyline. I thought of the lyrics in one of my songs 'Sail Away Today.'

Some people dream of flying to the moon,
others like to dream in their rooms,
but what I want to do is sail away with you.'

From there, we rowed ashore to the marina and asked somebody if there was a bus to Cape Canaveral. 'No,' the man said, 'But I'll take you myself.' He gave us a price, and we agreed. On the way, Frank told us he was stationed in England during the War, and his nickname was 'Frank the Yank.'

Once at the Kennedy Centre, we wandered around the exhibition. Peter and I tried to imagine what it must have been like for these astronauts to land on the moon. *The Dream is Alive* movie was being shown on a giant screen. We thought it was more like a Disneyland science fiction story than the genuine representation of an actual quest into space. Had the moon landing been just that - a Disneyland production? Speculation would never cease.

Cape Canaveral's further appeal extended to a vast sanctuary of alligators, manatees, armadillos, racoons, and hundreds of bird species, including the American bald eagle. The message throughout the exhibit echoed loud and clear: Technology and wildlife can coexist in perfect harmony. I wasn't convinced.

Our lives took a sudden turn a day away from Savannah, Georgia. One afternoon, under glorious sunshine and blue sky, we came across a superyacht powering on our side of the channel and heading straight for us. Maybe the skipper was too busy looking at his girlfriend in a bikini to notice us. He was contravening navigation rules, travelling two or three times over the speed limit about to cause a head-on collision.

What were we to do to avoid disaster? Regulations stipulate that the helmsman should turn to starboard to avoid a collision. This would mean us going aground. But if we turned to port and a collision occurred, we would be at fault. We were between the devil and the deep blue sea, and the only thing left to avoid twisted metal and shattered fibreglass was to ram our boat into the shallows.

With no time to spare, Peter shouted: 'Push the tiller hard over,' and I reared *Capricorn's* bow onto a sandbank. Then, just as she halted, the superyacht cut across our stern, still at full speed with no helmsman in view. We could only speculate that he had set his autopilot on without appreciating how quickly a boat or an obstacle could cross his way with him travelling so fast.

Although we had averted disaster, we weren't out of danger yet. Peter would need to get into the dinghy with an anchor and pull *Capricorn* off before the tide receded. A chap at the console of a ski boat motored alongside to offer assistance. Pasty-faced, wearing a baseball hat and shorts, he seemed to struggle to look cool. Peter extended a halyard from the top of the mast with another rope and asked him to secure the loose end to his craft. The man was foxed, especially when instructed to power off 90º from *Capricorn's* beam. 'Are you guys sure?' he probed.

'Yeh,' Peter answered. 'You'll cause us to lean over to port, reduce our draft, and we'll slide sideways off the sandbank.'

Although our rescuer was unconvinced, he pushed the throttle full ahead; the prop of his outboard engine thrashed away, and we gently eased into deeper water as smoothly as a duck sliding in the mud.

Our saviour was elated. We offered him a few cans of Budweiser to thank him, but he said, 'No, the story and the experience are all the thanks I need. They won't believe it when I tell the guys at the office that I rescued a 40-foot sailing yacht with my 40-hp ski boat.'

We licked our wounds in St. Augustine, where we dropped anchor near the marina. This historic city was a novelty with unusual Spanish architecture, including the Castle San Marcos.

In the evening, we shared a potluck with David, a woodcarver from England. He was sailing to North Carolina, where he planned to buy a property and settle down. But what he had seen made him question his intention to stay in America. It was a vast country with bold ideas and fast living. What a contrast to us travelling at the speed of a hurried walker. I read somewhere that one should not be afraid of moving slowly but only of standing still.

We spectacularly ran aground when we entered the tricky channel of Frederick River that joined the Intracoastal Waterway. The tide was falling fast. 'We just have to bear it,' Peter said. He set two anchors out. While we waited for the incoming tide, there was a violent thunderstorm, and we turned off all our electrical equipment on board, praying that it wouldn't strike our mast. The day's reward, however, was a secluded anchorage where we watched dolphins swimming with their young.

The following day, we arrived at the Isle of Hope, near Savannah, Georgia, where we moored on a horseshoe-shaped bend in the Skidaway River. Once *Capricorn* settled down with her anchor well dug in, we rowed ashore to the nearby marina and tied our dinghy to a pontoon.

'Are you the owners of the white sailboat anchored just off the marina?' the manager said cheerfully as we walked into the office. 'I saw the flag. Have you sailed from England to these backwaters?'

the full six-lane highway. *How does he think we got here?*

Peter mentioned we wanted to visit someone in Atlanta and thought the Isle of Hope was a good place to stop.

'Well, you guys are welcome here,' the manager said. 'If you are staying for a while, there is a charge of thirty dollars a month to land your dinghy. You can use the washing machine and dryer. It takes quarters. There is a supermarket down the road and a bus service to Savannah.

It is only nine miles away. We are a friendly community, but I warn you, the Isle of Hope is very quiet.'

'Wonderful,' I said. We thanked him and left to go and explore.

The island looked enchanting with its ancient oak tree avenue cloaked in Spanish moss. The waterfront, including colonial-style houses and white picket fences, has been used as a setting for several Civil War films. There was a large supermarket, a short bicycle ride away, called *Piggly Wiggly*. Its billboard, depicting an American Landrace pig with a curly tail bearing the motto, *pig out* at the *Piggly Wiggly,* fitted well with some nearby steak houses, where they offered customers free meals if they ate the restaurant's most enormous steak and trimmings in one sitting.

'I don't think a name like *Piggly Wiggly* for a supermarket would entice English people to shop there,' I said to Peter. Now that we had arrived, I was eager to pursue my musical dream, which pointed towards Eric, the agent who was the band drummer we met in Ft. Lauderdale, who suggested we should meet. I telephoned the office, and Eric offered me an appointment to see him. We rented a 'Japanese compact' and drove to Atlanta a few days later.

Naturally, we expected the drive on Highway 75 to be much more challenging than the MI, especially when reading signposts straddled the full six-lane highway, which proved almost impossible, even when Peter dropped his speed for us to concentrate on the signage. The traffic was intense, and as we continued this hellish drive, I heard Peter use the F-word, which surprised me as he doesn't usually swear. I understood why when I turned in my seat and saw three big *Mack* trucks approaching us as if the drivers were in a drag race. One vehicle passed us to the left, another to the right, and the one behind in our lane was about to squash and flatten us like in a Tom and Jerry cartoon. Our world went dark, sandwiched between the two trucks overtaking us. The driver in the same lane started blasting his siren. Peter shouted, 'I've nowhere to go.' I watched him stare at the *Mack* truck through the rearview mirror. Then, suddenly, the trucker shifted lanes and overtook us, a paint thickness away from the rear wing.

'We'll have to leave this interstate highway nightmare,' Peter announced. He took the next turnoff. Then, just when we thought we could be hopelessly lost in Atlanta City, we realised, by incredible fluke, we had taken the right exit. Maybe this was a sign of some good fortune to come.

We arrived at the agent well on time. Eric received us with genuine interest. He must have been intrigued by our adventure, sailing from Europe to America and landing in his office with a musical dream. I presented my demos to him, and he played them over a studio sound system. He looked genuinely impressed. *Symphony of Love* was one of my own favourites. Eric offered us coffee, talked briefly about the artists he managed, and then asked if we intended to settle in America. 'It depends on what the music business can offer me,' I replied. 'Do you think you could help?'

'I cannot give you an answer just now. I need to see where I can place you and your music. Let me have your details.'

I gave him Isle of Hope Marina's address and telephone number. We shook hands and left his office, feeling we had reached common ground. But how long would we need to wait for an answer? These things could take weeks. Meanwhile, we had made many friends and were even adopted by the Baptist Church, not that we wanted to be born again by submitting ourselves to full immersion. I had always hoped to rekindle my passion for choirs. As a little girl, I would attend two services on a Sunday to hear the singing. But such a big welcome into the church caused immediate jealousy among the American congregation, especially when Pastor Frank Johnson and his wife invited us to their home for dinner.

Upon arriving at their address, we were surprised to see it was a private estate with a lifting barrier. A policeman was manning the gate in his little glass hut. He stepped out and asked the purpose of our visit. 'We are coming to see Pastor Frank Johnson,' Peter explained. He made a phone call to check our story. Then, before the officer allowed us through, he requested we open the boot. Was the barrier to keep people in or out?

Pastor Johnson treated us like *his chosen ones*, and we felt overwhelmed by such reverence. We will never forget his words when he declared, 'The church is not a mausoleum for saints, but a sanatorium for sinners.'

One day, my friend Jane, a Hatha Yoga teacher, asked me to stand in for her while she was on a short yoga retreat. I took up the challenge to oblige. During one of my sessions at Jane's friend's converted barn, I met the Queen of Callanetics, Sallie Watson, whose book claims one can look ten years younger in ten hours. Sallie had taught various celebrities her unique set of exercises, which helped them shed all their extra weight. Sallie also introduced Callanetics to the Regiment of the Royal Marines. Surprisingly, she came to the class with a large beaker of Diet Coke with as much ice in it as an iceberg. She told Peter and me confidentially that she wouldn't allow people to cross her threshold unless they signed a disclaimer first.

Although we were having the time of our lives, playing the waiting game with agent Eric proved hard work. I called him several times, but he was out of the office. Then I tried again and finally spoke to him. I asked if he had made a decision about me, and he replied: 'I'm not one to be hassled. 'I've plenty of artists on my books; let's forget it.'

While deciding on our next move, Peter received an impromptu invitation from our new friend, Rob. 'My buddies and I are going for a shooting practice late afternoon. Bring your guns along,' he suggested.

Rob was a police photographer living in Nashville. The first time we met him at the marina, he asked, 'Are you the guys on the 'blow boat' anchored off?' This appellation was new to us. We shook hands, and he invited us to a coffee on his yacht, *Viewfinder.*

Peter was excited at the opportunity to improve his gun handling, and he jumped at the offer. He rowed ashore mid-afternoon with his shotgun and Very pistol to rendezvous with Rob and his mates on the trawler yacht moored at the marina. I stayed behind. It was a boy's game; mine was plucking the strings on my guitar and writing love songs, but I was curious and somewhat agitated. I had seen too many Western films where cowboys are killed like flies.

When Peter returned a few hours later, I bombarded him with endless questions, and he told me how the shooting went.

They had anchored off a remote island, carrying a sack of half-filled Coca-Cola cans they had dragged up to the top deck of the trawler yacht. (With water in a can, one can throw it further into the air.) Amongst the arsenal were a two-two rifle, a 44 Magnum (the type used by *Clint Eastwood* in the film*),* a Wyatt Earp's revolver, and what looked like a *GI* pistol used during WWII, Rob's short-barrelled pistol grip shotgun (he had a special licence for it), not forgetting Peter's Italian eight-shot pump action shotgun and a flare pistol. The number of guns between the six men could have started a revolution.

In Western films, Peter thought it was trick photography when a cowboy hit a can in the air and then put a second bullet in it before it hit the ground. He found out that afternoon that it was exactly what one of Rob's pals did, time after time.

Then, somebody rode ashore in the vessel's tender and lined up Coca-Cola cans on a large tree trunk on the bank. Peter had seen Bond movies where 007 defended himself with a Very pistol and knocked a villain off a bridge. There were discussions among the group regarding the effectiveness of using a flare pistol as a self-defence weapon. One theory claimed the flare would bounce off somebody, while others believed it might pierce through into an assailant's clothing and burn him to death because one cannot put out a flare by being submerged in water.

Peter said the men were very good marksmen, respectful of safety and gun etiquette. As for him, it was hard to miss targets, being able to let off eight rapid shots with his weapon.

Bizarrely, a new direction had presented itself from the improvised gun practice that day. Rob knew I was a singer-songwriter looking for an outlet, so he suggested to Peter, 'Why don't you sail to Nashville? My wife has a few contacts in the music business.'

'How the hell do I get there? *Capricorn* hasn't got wheels!' Peter chuckled.

Rob explained. 'Just nip down to Stuart on the Intracoastal Waterway, traverse Lake Okeechobee and make your way over the Gulf of Mexico to Mobile, Alabama. From there, it's 800 miles up rivers, lakes and canals to Nashville.'

Peter asked me what I thought about sailing there. 'It is an amazing idea,' I said.

However, there was one snag. Our visas were running out, and we needed to earn money to finance our next adventure. So, we decided to leave *Capricorn* in America while Peter and I returned to England to work. When we told Rob and his tobacco-chewing, gun-toting old boys we would be out of the country for a while, they said, 'Don't worry. We'll keep an eye on your boat until your return.'

29. The Green Marker

It must have been a blind leap of faith to leave *Capricorn* with all that we owned in an anchorage for three months on a river in Georgia, thousands of miles from England, but as the taxi pulled up at Isle of Hope Marina, she was there, tugging gently on her anchor chain. Peter's shooting buddy, Rob, was working on his boat. 'Hey, guys, I'm mighty glad to see you,' he said. 'I'm sure you need a ride back to your boat. We've kept an eye on her.'

Upon approaching *Capricorn*, we were shocked to see so much growth below her waterline, which looked like a new Garden of Babylon. We shouldn't have been surprised, given the water was the temperature of a warm bath. Later that day, Peter told Rob we needed somewhere to scrape off the hull. He mentioned careening posts a mile down the waterway.

When we cast off the next day, the tide was falling. Surprisingly, *Capricorn* could only manage 1.5 knots through the water, even when Peter opened the throttle to full revs.

We found the place Rob had described and lashed *Capricorn* to the stout-looking poles. There wouldn't be much time between tides to clean off the bottom of the hull, so Peter applied himself immediately while I held on to the rudder to steady the dinghy for him to reach below the waterline. It was hard to scrape off all that growth at such an awkward angle. With the tide fast receding, *Capricorn's* hull was now looming over us. Then, we saw the propellor. It was a ball of weeds. There was even a baby oyster, which had also established itself on the rudder. No wonder *Capricorn* was sluggish.

When I looked through the propellor's aperture, I saw a barge steaming toward us, with her bow pushing a wall of water. She wasn't the type one would see on the River Thames, being the size of a horizontal skyscraper. She was fully loaded and had a large accommodation area behind the wheelhouse, with the captain's car stowed on top of the cargo hatches.

I yelled to Peter, 'There's a barge coming. Will we be alright?'

'Sure, our keel is well and truly on the seabed.'

Suddenly, we heard a thud, and *Capricorn* started to rock violently. The next thing I knew, I was submerged in the darkness. I let go of the rudder, and when I put my arms above my head, all I could feel was the bottom of the hull. Still kneeling in the dinghy, my head broke the surface. I looked for Peter but could only see two hands pushing against the hull. Thankfully, the rest of him popped up a second later like somebody releasing a tennis ball from below the water. He started coughing, and I half-expected him to splutter a fish out of his mouth. Just as well, Peter had made our Puffin unsinkable. However, it was swamped, and we hung on to the side of the dinghy against the breaking waves while *Capricorn* was rolling like a drunken sailor.

When the wake subsided, we jumped from the dinghy into waist-high water and pulled it ashore to bail out. In shock, we sat on the beach for a while, feeling like we had been ducked like witches in the village pond. Why had *Capricorn* taken a sudden dive?

We remained there while the tide receded, too frightened to approach *Capricorn*. 'I warned you, Peter, the barge was coming. We could have been buried under our boat in a watery grave,' I said, trying to reconcile myself with the feeling of what another fine mess my skipper had got us into. As if this wasn't enough, we were being eaten alive by midges, locally known as *no-see-ums*.

When the tide finally revealed the keel, we realised what had happened. *Capricorn's* bow had been firmly resting on the sand, but the rudder support arm from the keel had landed on top of an old four-foot stump of a pole a foot wide. So when the wake hit us, *Capricorn* slipped off. It would have been impossible to place the boat like that had we tried it deliberately. Despite our narrow escape, we finished scraping the hull off and waited for the tide to re-float us. What a way to reconnect with *Capricorn* after our long absence. Then, just as I thought life was complicated enough, Tony, a young American who had arrived from Martha's Vineyard on a 19-foot sailing boat, asked Peter if he could tow him to St. Augustine Marina, where he hoped he would get his engine repaired and re-anti-foul the hull before heading for the Florida Keys. Tony was willing to share the cost of the diesel.

He ate on our boat most evenings, enjoying debating about the 'rights and wrongs' of the world over fruit juice. (Many Americans don't drink alcohol.) Then Tony met our friend Marian. She had been a ballerina and was now residing on the island. Her boyfriend Craig, a talented singer-songwriter, was living with her, keen to break into the music business. However, it was love at first sight for Marian and Tony when they set eyes on each other. Craig was heartbroken. He visited us, needing support. So Peter and I found ourselves caught in the middle. And so the song was born.

'What do I tell a man who comes to me with a broken heart?
What do I do to help when his world is falling apart?
He brings her a bouquet of roses as he comes to realise
that life is not as he chooses; it is a broken heart, or is it pride?

The waterway was quiet when we set off from the dreamy Isle of Hope, where we had spent meaningful time surrounded by people who became inspired by our lifestyle. I thought of Martha, a professional concert pianist and James, a pathologist. They had a full-size organ, a grand piano, and a harpsichord in the lounge, where they held meditation meetings with friends. Peter and I laughed when James said, 'I wish we could set off into the blue like you, but my two financial advisors told me I couldn't afford it.' And there we were, living a millionaire's lifestyle on a shoestring!

We had a 185-mile journey to St. Augustine but weren't in a hurry, especially with *Capricorn* towing Tony's boat. Marian had joined him for the journey. Along the way, we watched cormorants sitting on top of markers like cops checking traffic while carefree dolphins played in our bow wave. The swirling clouds with patches of blue in between looked as if an artist had dabbled them with a brush. I started to sing: '*With every brushstrokes like musical notes, the landscape is caught…*'

The towing went well. Although Tony's yacht was light, we could feel the weight on the tiller. We anchored in a creek for the night, and they tied the boat up to *Capricorn.* We ate sushi together. Though I still felt uneasy, I thought it wasn't such a bad idea after all to travel in company down the Intracoastal Waterway.

At the end of the following day, Marian was at the tiller. We slowed down so she could steer the boat alongside us for the night. But she hit us accidentally, and I shouted: 'Our boat isn't a buffer.'

'It's not Marian's fault,' Tony riposted. 'She has no experience.'

Seconds later, she hit us again. In a rage, I yelled, 'She needs to practise, but not on us.' (Was this the beginning of the end of our friendship?) I told Peter we should part and let Tony resolve his own problems. But we couldn't abandon him, knowing his engine was out of commission.

But 'Life is what happens to you while you are busy making other plans,' John Lennon said, borrowing journalist and cartoonist Allen Saunders's quote.

The following day, Tony and Marian were enjoying their honeymoon on the water, oblivious to everything else. Peter was in the wheelhouse with me, checking the chart. That was when we heard a bang from outside. Peter rushed on deck, and I followed, only to realise that our faithful electronic autohelm piloting the boat had developed a fault, and we had hit a heavy steel green marker. Meanwhile, Marian and Tony's amorous interlude was abruptly interrupted. He appeared on deck, scantily clad. He was too late to stop his boat from hitting the marker. Tony should have been at the tiller and not down below. We saw him frantically looking at the hull to see if the impact had pierced a hole. Thankfully, there wasn't one, but his boat looked partly shipwrecked with the stanchions and lines dangling over the side. *Capricorn,* too, suffered damage. The aft rail was buckled, and the hull looked badly scratched.

We continued motoring down the waterway until we found a creek on the edge of the channel. Before dark, Peter assessed Tony's boat's damage. What price would we have to pay for the unfortunate mishap? Of course, we should have learned by now not to trust electronics, but our autohelm had been so efficient until then, even in deep waves in the Atlantic.

We were four minutes late to catch the next opening bridge the following day. When Peter checked the engine, he had to make a minor repair. Then, he realised our batteries weren't charging. 'It is an alternator job, and I hate working with them,' he lamented. 'Everything seems to be stopping us from getting to Nashville,' he groaned with a furrowed brow.

By the time we get there, he will have completely rebuilt the marine engine with all these repairs.

When we arrived in St. Augustine, we dropped anchor outside the marina and, just on cue, watched the arrival of the replica of Sir Francis Drake's *The Golden Hinde*. Built in England in 1973, the 102-foot vessel first sailed to San Francisco before retracing Drake's route across the Pacific and Indian Ocean back to the British Isles to complete her circumnavigation of the world in 1980.

Just as we stepped onto the pontoon, the crew was coming ashore, all dressed in 15th-century costumes. We heard a woman speak with an English accent. Peter started a conversation, and she said she originated from Bristol. When he mentioned he was a *Scarborian*, she quipped, 'The engineer, Bob Grove, is also from Scarborough. I'll introduce you.'

At first, Peter didn't recognise Bob when he appeared on deck in his period costume with hair in a pigtail, but when he spoke, the memories of them working together as engineers at McCain's Chip Factory six years ago came flooding back.

'Good Heavens, fancy seeing you here,' Bob said.

'And you on *The Golden Hinde*,' Peter exclaimed.

'I saw an advertisement in a fishing magazine. *The Golden Hinde* was looking for an engineer, so I applied. It's a small world. I've often wondered about you and Monique and where you got to after setting off on your boat from Scarborough.'

We were hauled out at the Oasis shipyard one mile from St. Augustine. It wouldn't be a place of rest now that we had to do maintenance on *Capricorn* and repairs on Tony's boat. I felt he would be ruthless and probably take advantage of Peter's good nature, using his feelings of guilt to extract the maximum out of him. Tony wasn't practical and didn't like manual work. He started to blame me for causing his stomach ulcer to flare up.

In the morning, he came to ask Peter to help him drop his mast. We worked tirelessly on *Capricorn* over Easter and missed the fun in town watching the parade. Someone told us it was very patriotic. While at the shipyard one afternoon, we met André and Yonoko. They were enquiring about storing their boat there for a few months. Over a drink, we discovered they had tied up to the old fish factory El Caribe at Dãrsena Harbour in Santa Cruz, Tenerife, just as we did. To finance their sailing trip, they bought inexpensive reproductions in Paris and sold them on the open market in Japan. They shared a similar view of American life: fast and furious, where the dollar is king.

One night, I dreamed our boat had a yellow hull and deck. Yellow is Peter's favourite colour. The next day, he saw yellow paint at the chandler on sale at half-price. We felt as if our luck had changed. However, as Peter was grinding on deck later, he caught some grit in his eye and needed it removed at the local clinic, costing him $63.

After six solid days working on Tony's boat, Peter decided enough was enough and picked up his tools. Meanwhile, Tony and Marian had driven back to the Isle of Hope in a rented car. It was time to move, leaving them to buy wedding rings and baby clothes. At 36, Marian couldn't wait to embrace motherhood.

At least there was one consolation: Tony had introduced me to the outstanding American transcendentalist writer Henry David Thoreau, who famously said:

"The question is not what you look at, but what you see."

We cast off from the Oasis shipyard and anchored two and a half miles downstream. The following day, we set off for Daytona. The northwest wind was blowing strongly, and there was a violent thunderstorm. We turned off all our electrical equipment on board and disconnected the batteries.

It isn't always sunny in Florida.

We could have enjoyed some of the idyllic coves on the way, but they were often too shallow for *Capricorn*. Still, we contemplated life on the quiet waters until the day when I suddenly heard something snap below deck. Peter went to check the oil in the gearbox and found a problem with the pressure plate on the engine. Soon after, it stopped.

We were drifting with the current with a steady northwesterly wind when a large passenger ferry overtook us. The boat displayed a 20-foot banner along the side of the hull with 'Jesus Will Save You.' The captain slowed the engine down to keep pace with *Capricorn*. He left the wheelhouse, and from the wing bridge, three decks above us, he shouted, 'A lovely boat you've got there, skipper.'

'Thanks,' Peter replied, 'but we're having problems with the engine. We're making for Port Pierce. Is there any chance of a tow?'

'Hang on a minute,' the captain said before disappearing into his wheelhouse. He held station for a few minutes, then took off at speed without warning.

Jesus wasn't going to save us that day!

We had a bascule bridge to negotiate next with a strong wind astern, a following tide and no engine. With half a mile to go, Peter radioed the bridge office to say we were under sail and our engine had broken down. A female voice with a strong Southern accent replied, 'No problem, Captain. Keep "e coming" and I'll lift the bridge for you.'

Did the attendant appreciate our predicament? Our only means of stopping our boat would be to ram the bank. Getting so close to the bridge, we could see the drivers in passing cars. Peter called the bridge attendant again and asked, 'Are we still okay?'

The woman replied: 'I'll have the bridge open in time.'

Peter began looking for a place to run *Capricorn* aground. The clock was ticking. Then, we heard a bell ringing and a barrier dropping to halt the traffic. Peter yelled, 'The woman won't do it in time. I'll have to hit the bank.'

It was terrifying. Suddenly, the bascule bridge started to crack open, but it was agonisingly slow. 'I think we'll make it,' Peter said.

He had learned from his racing days to judge speed and distance. He computed the rate of the bridge opening and *Capricorn's* speed of approach. The gap increased as Peter lined *Capricorn,* and we shot through the middle, leaving us only two feet to spare on either side of the rigging. Then, as we swept miraculously past the bridge, a window on the corner of the control tower slid back, and the jolly round face of a black woman nonchalantly leaning on the sill hollowed out: 'Y'all, have a good day now.'

She couldn't have guessed what she put us through, but there was no time to waste because our ordeal wasn't over yet. We would have to enter an anchorage under full sail amongst other boats, then round *Capricorn*, up into the wind, and drop the hook at the last minute, all in one go. We had to.

'Good afternoon, Port Pierce!' I said as I put the kettle on, pretending nothing had happened. *Ah, the joy of sailing!*

When Peter built *Capricorn*, he made the cockpit floor directly above the engine room so that it could be removed easily, using block and tackle from the mainsail boom to lift the engine and disconnect the gearbox and bell housing. Upon checking the engine, he discovered the pressure plate was damaged, which explained why we couldn't engage the engine into gear. Later that day, I rowed him ashore to the repair shop at the marina. He had little confidence in getting the part at the Chandler and expected the staff to double up with laughter when he learned about our 1961 three-cylinder Perkins diesel engine. Meanwhile, I remained aboard guarding *Capricorn*.

Peter hailed me from the shore later, waving a flat cardboard box as proudly as if he had discovered gold. When I landed the dinghy, he said, 'You won't believe it; the man didn't laugh at me. He examined the pressure plate and declared, "It looks identical to a Volvo." Given they are Volvo agents, he had one on the shelf.'

Peter wasted no time and set about fitting the unit. When removing the cockpit floor, he needed to chisel off some bolts holding it down, but he believed he would easily find replacements at the Chandler. Unfortunately, they didn't have what Peter needed, so they suggested the hardware shop a mile away.

The following day, I rowed Peter and his bicycle ashore while I acted as 'the shotgun' on *Capricorn*. When I picked him up later in the dinghy, he looked out of puff. I asked him how it went, and he said, 'I'll tell you when we get back aboard.'

Over a cup of tea, he related his ordeal:

'I followed the directions from the Volvo mechanic, but what an eerie experience. The main street looked like it had once been a busy small town centre. There was no one within sight, not even a car. I saw billboards advertising various food stores and retail shops, but all were boarded up. I felt as if I had cycled into a disaster zone. I thought, did the locals get abducted by aliens or fall victim to some terrible disease? At any moment, I expected a creaking door to open from one of the dilapidated properties and someone to step out wearing a poncho and a dusty hat pulled over his eyes, smoking a cigar. The place was like a ghost town after an apocalypse. There wasn't even a stray dog, and I half-expected balls of tumbleweed rolling down the main street. A breeze was kicking up the dust which stuck to my sweating forehead. Then, I noticed a black guy with a straw hat sitting in a rocking chair, staring at me intently from his porch. Further on, I saw open double doors and a sign on the façade advertising Jo's hardware shop. I chained my bike to a metal rail, which must have been where they once hitched their horses. Parked outside was a pickup truck with guns on the rack behind the driver's seat. I could hear chatter and laughter as I walked into the store. Coming from the blazing sun outside, I struggled to focus. The place looked well-stocked but untidy. A man dressed in bib overalls was standing behind the counter, talking to three guys sitting on chairs. They looked like 'Red Necks'. The conversation abruptly stopped, and all eyes were on me. I asked timidly for stainless steel screws. My accent immediately broke the unease, and I was cross-examined. After giving an account of myself, the shopkeeper pulled a drawer from the cabinet behind him and asked me how many I wanted. I paid and left, feeling edgy.'

'What a place,' I remarked. 'Maybe I should have insisted on coming with you.'

We were relieved to lift anchor and head for the next bridge. On the way, Peter adjusted the cables to the gearbox and noticed they were worn. Still, we continued down the waterway to Stuart, hoping to buy new ones there.

When we approached the last lifting bridge, rain was pelting down like a monsoon, with thunder and lightning overhead. Peter slowed the boat, but the engine didn't respond. When he located the problem, he said, 'The cable for the throttle gear has snapped. You'll need to steer and find somewhere to anchor. I'll be down below while you shout when you want forward, reverse, or neutral because I can only do it manually on the engine.'

Are we meant to get to Nashville with all these mishaps?

I couldn't see where to drop the hook when we reached the anchorage. Many boats were swinging on ropes, which meant they used a wider arc. Peter had stressed, 'If you ram a boat, choose the least expensive one!' I struggled to see anything with the rain pounding and the wind howling. I continued steering between boats, terrified that our ten-ton *Capricorn* would bump into one. Finally, with wet hair dripping over my eyes, I found a spot and shouted to Peter over the thunder, 'Give me a burst of reverse. As soon as he had, he rushed on deck and dropped the anchor, which he had already prepared on the bow. He released what he thought was the right amount of chain and returned to the cockpit, looking as if he had just been for a swim fully clothed. 'We need a short burst of reverse to check if the anchor is well dug in,' he said. The next heavy gust did just that. Finally, we shut the engine off, looked at each other and smiled.

'You did great,' Peter commented. Being drenched, he couldn't have noticed my tears of relief. 'Time for pancakes and hot chocolate,' he suggested. Those were magical words to my ears.

30. Fairhope

We picked our way through a narrow channel of dense vegetation. Above us, a flock of white pelicans and eagles circled in a sapphire sky. A motionless heron suddenly darted its head into the water and retrieved a fish whilst exotic butterflies fluttered around in the warm, muggy morning air. We cut through a path of bright white lilies, which lifted gently in our wake. It felt like a cardinal sin to disturb such perfection. The mist rose from the water, spreading more magic to this enchanted scene. It was a lost paradise until we heard the hoot of a freight train in the distance, which abruptly broke the spell. We traversed central Florida by boat from east to west via the Okeechobee Lake.

We anchored amongst lilies for the night and watched a pink sunset sinking into the water like a big balloon. We could hear loud bellowing and hissing. During the alligator's breeding season, the male blows bubbles towards the female's belly to arouse her, and if she doesn't want to mate, she bites him before swimming away. Ten tons of steel separated us from these dangerous predators and their lethal teeth, eighty or more.

In the morning, we awoke to see cobwebs spread from stem to stern across our stanchions and lifelines. In the sunlight, the dew shone on them like multicoloured beads. We felt nature had cast a spell on us. Still, we left them undisturbed, hoping this might discourage swarms of mosquitoes from trying to fly in and devour us.

It was such a short crossing that we were reluctant to leave the beauty and solitude of the lake. There was a lock before La Belle called the 'City under the Oaks.' Cattle drovers and trappers straddling the banks of the Caloosahatchee River had brought fortune to the area. All we carried with us were our hopes and wishes aboard the yacht my skipper built. God took a rib from Adam and created Eve; Peter welded ribs from flat steel sheets and made *Capricorn*. Is it a coincidence that vessels are referred to as 'she?'

In La Belle, we tied up to a welcome pontoon, which offered water and electricity for all craft. The city was small and compact. Usually, when we arrive somewhere, we visit a bookshop first. This one was the size of an industrial warehouse. How could I resist buying another book, though I had so many already?

A tall, lanky chap with a bushy beard standing behind the counter looked at me with deep, penetrating blue eyes. I immediately knew we were kindred spirits. He commented about the amethyst stone pendant I was wearing. We introduced ourselves. He pointed to his partner Emma, who was tidying some shelves. The woman had long, dark hair down to her waist and wore a loose-flowing flower-patterned dress. We talked briefly about our journey to America, and then Jason invited us to visit them in the evening.

Over coffee, sitting in their private quarters, we related our adventures and explained how these had shaped our spiritual path. Then Jason told us about his abduction by Aliens. It certainly wasn't a normal conversation with somebody one had just met, but Emma and Jason seemed at ease with us. He showed us a scar on the back of his neck. As he couldn't remember his time on the Aliens' craft, he decided he would go under hypnosis. A hypnotherapist recorded the session, but the man never honoured the promise of letting him have the recording. He suspected the tape was handed to the CIA. From that time on, Jason felt as if people were watching him.

When we arrived in Fort Myer, I had high hopes of meeting singer-songwriter Michael Franks, a friend of our forensic photographer Rob, whom we had encountered on the Isle of Hope. When I called his agent, he told me Michael was on tour. Still, there was one consolation: we took advantage of being in the area to visit Edison's House Museum. Later, we telephoned Rob for a chat, as he had previously made that journey to Nashville on his boat. 'It's tricky navigation in the Gulf,' he stated. 'You need to be good at piloting. It's not like crossing the Atlantic.' He advised us to hug the coast of the Gulf of Mexico but warned us of its shallows, sudden wind changes and mounting swells.

'I wouldn't suggest Rob sail the coast of Brittany. It would freak him out if he had to deal with six-metre tides, eight knots of currents and rocks everywhere,' Peter said after talking to him. Although we had experienced 20-foot waves in the Atlantic, Rob still managed to scare me about sailing in the Gulf of Mexico.

We were hot and sticky, walking along a beautiful beach of fine golden sand, when we noticed a lagoon and thought we should have a dip to cool down. We sat on the edge and then lowered ourselves up to our waists. At least we wouldn't have to worry about sharks or the big surf rolling onto the shore beyond. We dipped in and spread-eagled; we savoured total bliss for a while.

Alas, the moment was short-lived when suddenly we saw a monster rising out of the water. Was it about to pounce on us and, with its jaw, swallow us whole? Then we recognised the huge creature was a manatee. These mammals can grow up to ten feet and are known to be curious and fearless, warm or indifferent to people. However, swimming with a manatee weighing over half a ton wasn't our idea of a relaxing time in a paradise lagoon. What if it wanted to play and, in the process, drown us unintentionally? We quickly leapt out of the water and scrambled onto a rock as if our lives depended on it. Perhaps it did!

Still shaken, we strolled along the beach and saw two fishermen struggling with their lines. 'That looks like a big catch,' I shouted. They didn't respond. The next thing we knew, they landed a huge stingray, which could have been over a hundred pounds.

We picked up some sand dollars on the way back to *Capricorn*. These are an absolute beauty. According to legend, the five slits represent the wounds of the body of Christ. There are pretty Easter Lily patterns on top, with five perfect miniature-like flying doves inside when broken open.

Don't they say politicians will promise you bridges when there isn't a river to cross? However, for us, it was always about clearance, which seemed to vary according to the height gauge accuracy on each bridge's pillars and the information gathered en route.

Our mast was 52 feet tall. I felt sure it could have made a wonderful comedy when we headed for St George Island with a 55-foot bridge to negotiate, only we weren't laughing. St George Bridge was a typical example of a skipper being left in limbo. As we passed a Marine Patrol Boat, we asked the crew if they could confirm the bridge's height clearance. 'Sorry,' they answered, 'The tidal gauge is too weathered and illegible.'

So we anchored near the bridge and visited the Marine Patrol Office. A helpful lady contacted some officials who confirmed the clearance was 55 feet. Peter decided we should attempt it. Otherwise, we would have to backtrack to the last outlet and head offshore. We favoured remaining in the Intracoastal Waterway as we could stop whenever we wanted and sail in relatively sheltered waters.

We returned to *Capricorn* and set off to St. George Bridge. The tide and wind were against us, so Peter could motor slowly without losing steerage. When we saw men working underneath the bridge, Peter shouted to them, 'Can we make it?' They ignored us. No wonder.

We moved at a snail's pace towards the edge of the highest part of the bridge, and Peter brought *Capricorn* to a standstill over the seabed (boats don't have breaks). It looked as if we were still moving because of the tide.

Then, Peter gave me the tiller while he went to the bow. 'Okay, ease slowly forward,' he instructed me.

If anything goes wrong, I will plead that I was following orders.

My heart was beating to the engine's rhythm as I increased the revs, and we cleared the bridge with only inches to spare. I told Peter, 'I've had enough of going under bridges. Let's take the next outlet to the sea and follow the coast?'

We had a rough passage along the open shore and were forced to batten down with sudden strong winds, monsoon rain and a violent thunderstorm. Still, it was the most spectacular natural pyrotechnics show ever seen. It was as if God Thor was blindfolded while still trying to hit us. Thankfully, his aim fell short, and it was a relief when we rejoined the Intracoastal Waterway and stopped at Pensacola Marina for some respite.

We anchored and went ashore to do some shopping. God only knew how far we would have to walk to a supermarket. In the marina, we met Charlie, who owned a motor yacht. He offered us a lift in his truck. Maybe we should have declined. He sipped beer on the way while we prayed for our safety.

After a bumpy ride there and back, Charlie invited us aboard his yacht, *Folly*. Then he hailed his neighbour Jack on his 17-foot plywood boat to join the party. During our conversation about mishaps at sea (we all have them), I mentioned that I believed in Guardian Angels. Charlie made a face. No amount of drink would alter his views on the existence of Angels.

However, Jack had a story to tell. We all took another slug from our beers, eager to hear what he had to say.

'It was one of these flash storms which came out of the blue,' Jack explained. 'The Gulf of Mexico has many shallows which can quickly whip up into confused seas. I tried hard to steer my boat to avoid a capsize, then suddenly, a breaking wave hit the stern, and the rudder jumped out of its pintles. When I tried to grab it, I was thrown overboard.

The next thing I knew, *Orion* was being pushed away by wind and sea faster than I could swim. I was now flotsam in a bubbling cauldron and felt my only hope of survival was to be picked up by another boat. But who would be out there in such stormy weather? And if one appeared on the horizon, would the crew be able to spot a head bobbing between the crests and troughs?

I fought hard to tread water and avoid swallowing the Gulf. I was getting more and more exhausted. It seemed such a hopeless situation, and I began to lose the will to live. So, I let myself gradually sink below the waves.

With my eyes still open, I waited for my life to flash in front of me. As I descended deeper into the abyss, the light became fainter, and air bubbles began to escape from my clothes. Then, I suddenly felt somebody urging me back to the surface. At that moment, I knew I didn't want to give up living.

Disorientated under the mass of water, I had no idea which way was up or down, but it dawned on me to follow the bubbles. I paddled for my life in their direction, praying I still had enough oxygen in my lungs to return to God's sweet air. I gulped for breath as I broke the surface. When I scanned the horizon, I saw a shrimp boat in the distance with her nets boomed out on either side.

I am saved. What a miracle! I gasped. But my hope of rescue was dashed when I realised the shrimp boat was sailing past me. I waved my arm and yelled, "HELP," in desperation. Then, when I saw the vessel turning and heading my way, I could hardly believe it.

The skipper slowed down upon approaching, and someone shouted, "We'll get you out of this. Just hang on, buddy." The man threw a lifebuoy, and I was dragged towards the shrimp boat, then hoisted aboard by the net winch like the prized catch of the day. I heard whoops of Alleluias from the skipper and his wife.

Once on deck, Marlin explained Scarlett had spotted my head in the water. At first, he didn't believe her. He thought it was a fishing buoy or something, but she insisted. They had been caught in the vicious line squall, too, and because they had had such a poor catch, they continued fishing to make up for it. But I guess they caught me instead!

"Why were you so far out to sea?" they asked. "Were you swimming from Pensacola to St Petersburg?" I told them what happened, and Marlin said, "We'd better chase after your boat." So we did, and would you believe it? As we followed the direction we thought the wind would have blown it, we picked up the rudder with their net and later came across *Orion.* Marlin took her in tow. This is why I now believe in Angels. They were watching over me!'

I had thought the afternoon would be boring, being the only woman drinking with Red Neck sailors, but I was wrong!

'Let's celebrate with another beer,' Charlie proposed. The can tabs were pulled, and we all toasted the Angels.

Moaning about monsoon rain and strong winds wasn't helpful when we made for English Navy Cove. How naive to think it was mostly sunny in Florida. We had taken so much battering with thunderstorms, strong winds, and rain until now. There was a force eight gale when we anchored, but fortunately, it passed quickly. We were keen to stretch our legs and see where we could get information about the Mobile River and the Tennessee-Tombigbee Waterway. Then, just as we were ready to go, someone in the anchorage radioed us. He introduced himself as Mr Dollivy, gave us his telephone number then invited us to stay at his Yacht Club. Peter told him we were heading for Nashville, Tennessee, via the Tombigbee, and he said he had charts he could let us have. It seemed we were being guided once again. As we rowed ashore, we passed the pretty green wooden yacht *Magnolia.* The owner hailed us, 'Come aboard.' He had overheard our conversation on the VHF radio and showed us his area chart. We shared a beer, and Paul suggested we tag along the next day so we wouldn't need to worry about a chart for Mobile Bay. Everything for our trip to Nashville was falling into place at last. It was a full moon, too, and so bright that night it felt like the wheel of fortune was turning in our favour.

As Paul had suggested, we were on cue the following day when our convoy of three boats set off at 7 am sharp. On the way, we enjoyed the lush green countryside bordering the banks. A fair breeze blew across the gulf, so we hoisted the sails and switched the engine off. The water of Mobile Bay is 10 miles wide by 35 miles long and links 16.000 miles of inland waterways. We could travel to Louisiana, Texas, and the Mexican border.

Under full sail, we kept pace with the sleek 40-foot yacht *Illusion* as we made for Fly Creek. We saved a few miles across the bay with Paul's local knowledge.

We tied up alongside a wooden jetty at Fairhope Yacht Club and headed for the bar to celebrate. We registered at the club and were treated like heroes. I prayed that our good fortune would follow us up to Nashville.

31. The Third Coast

'Be aware of alligators,' Jack at the yacht club warned us. 'If you're in the water and see one, swim calmly the other way and get out as soon as possible.'

'I'd probably break the 100-metre freestyle record,' I remarked.

Jack grinned, then continued: 'That's not all. You'll be meeting barges the size of horizontal skyscrapers. When approaching a tight bend, you must announce your presence on channel 16 so the captains can alert you they are coming. Then, you'll have to hold off until they pass. They'll *toot.* One *toot* will tell you the captain intends to pass you on their port side, and two to starboard. Two years ago, a tug with a bow 50-foot wide, with nine barges three abreast, struck down a motor yacht around a tight bend, pushing it under the full length of the tow. All that remained were fibreglass fragments of the vessel. As for the crew, they never recovered their bodies.'

Did I need to hear more?

'*Red Necks* are another breed to reckon with. They have 'shootouts' amongst themselves over fishing territories. And if they're in their skiffs and a boat makes too much wake, they'll pump lead into the superstructure to teach the crew a lesson. Watch out, those guys have taken "The Law" into their own hands.'

'*Capricorn's* wake wouldn't swamp a paper cup,' Peter chuckled. (He had carefully studied the rules of navigation on the Tombigbee.)

'One more thing,' Jack added, 'Don't expect to go ashore much. It's nearly all primeval forests, and watch out for moccasin snakes, racoons, coyotes, and other creatures.'

What Jack said didn't deter us from tackling the Tombigbee Waterway, which runs parallel to the Mississippi River 200 miles east of it. Seeing the Deep South by boat to Nashville would offer a different perspective of this vast country. I read that it would take two hundred and thirty-eight times the size of Switzerland to cover America.

In the music business, New York is known as the 'East Coast,' Los Angeles as the 'West Coast,' while Nashville is named 'Third Coast,' although it is just a river bank. Singer-songwriters have arrived in the city by helicopter, hot air balloon, parachute, horseback, and camel as publicity stunts. Would Peter and I be the first to have sailed to Nashville from the other side of the world? I reflected upon the word 'hope' - Isle of Hope, - Fairhope. The word kept recurring. It symbolised how Peter and I travelled, putting our trust in providence. We believed higher powers were guiding us on our musical treasure hunt. Although sailing to Savannah, Georgia, to be near Atlanta for our meeting with impresario Eric didn't lead us to where we thought it might, forensic photographer Rob was the catalyst for a change of direction when he said, 'Why not try to break into the big time there?' Then, meeting other yacht aficionados at English Cove led us safely across Mobile Bay to Fairhope Yacht Club.

Armed with charts from the Corps of Engineers, we bid our friends farewell and cast off. The weather wasn't ideal; rain and thunderstorms had been forecast. But it was time to press on since we had been waiting three weeks for the Mobile River level to drop. We motored across the bay past the industrial area.

Mobile was the first modern city in America to be laid out in a grid pattern with no walls. Built in 1702, it had been under the rule of the Spanish explorers, the French, the English, the Confederates, the Yankees, and then the USA. Leaving it to port, we soon enjoyed miles of uninhabited shoreline. Here and there, the odd fishing cabin on stilts (only accessible by boat) broke the spell. The vegetation was so dense that we could imagine ourselves on the Amazon River. Otters were first introduced in some of the river tributaries to help keep the swamp lands irrigated, but they became pests, so alligators were brought in to reduce their numbers. It begged the question, what would they think of next if alligators became a problem?

Our first fuel stop was at Lady Landing, between Mobile and Demopolis. On top of the 30-foot bank was a statue of the Virgin Mary, with trees overhanging the saint like a vaulted roof. After filling our tanks, we went ashore, using a skiff tied up to the fuel pontoon. How odd. Next, we walked up the hill and found a shop adjacent to a house. A woman with a masculine demeanour took our money for the fuel. She explained that the county organises a road leveller machine once a year to take the bumps and hollows out of the five-mile track leading to the nearest tarmac road. On one occasion, after the driver had finished his levelling, he shut off his machine to get a soft drink. When he returned, the battery had expired, and to get at the switch to jump-start it, he crawled underneath the vehicle, which then suddenly leapt into gear and careered over the bank, taking the steel stairs with it and pushing the pontoon fifteen feet out into the river. Now we understood why the skiff was there.

In the early evening, we anchored by the old river, now bypassed after a new cut was made to eliminate an awkward bend. There, we watched baby alligators swim past *Capricorn.* When night fell, the sky lit up with myriad fireflies shining like stars. Every tree in the forest looked as if it were adorned with bright Christmas lights. We whispered to each other for fear of breaking the magic. Not only did this unique and daring adventure offer us the great wilderness of the south, it also led us in the wake of history. In 1817, thirty-five exiled partisans of Napoleon Bonaparte came up the Tombigbee River to Demopolis. The United States Government granted them land if they cultivated grapes and olives. The crops failed, so cotton was introduced. The town's colonial architecture reflected the days when cotton was king.

From then on, the choice of beautiful places to anchor abounded because of the many cut-offs where the Corps of Engineers bypassed big loops in the river. We stopped for the night in an off-shoot. I remembered Jack warning us about moccasin snakes, which could drop onto our deck from overhanging branches. I wondered what we would do; we didn't have an Indian flute or a wicker basket!

Until then, we hadn't seen a barge but had been calling out on the VHF radio to warn vessels of our presence. One afternoon, somebody responded, yet we had no idea how far away from us the tug was as we couldn't see beyond the next bend. Then, it came into view, pushing its six loaded coal barges. We tucked ourselves close to the bank and tried to hold back. But *Capricorn* was being sucked out into the river by the tug's wake and the wind funnelling down the valley. For a moment, I thought: *The monster will open us up like a sardine can.* Finally, the barge passed, and we lived to see another day.

We anchored in Rattle Snake Creek in the late afternoon, hoping to have it all to ourselves and recover from the ordeal. But it wasn't long before a three-barge convoy came along. The captain drove his heavy load to the bank, feet away from us, as easily as if he were parking a car. Then, he took off in his tug, leaving his barges behind. Two other tugs pushing loads of coal followed shortly after and moored nearby. Peter made brownies that day. I wasn't sure if it was to calm his nerves. He had never baked before.

Ahead was a 300-foot long by 110-foot wide lock, which wasn't just impressive but terrifying, let alone getting inside its dungeon-like chamber where the sky was only a narrow slit a long way above us. One couldn't just step ashore and tie up to the dock overhead. There was a floating bollard let into the side of the lock, where we tied a rope. Then, we rose 80 feet up, one inch a second, as smoothly as a water lily floating on a pond. It took us sixteen minutes to reach the same level as the control tower. Americans do things in a big way.

Later, as we motored past what looked like the White Cliffs of Dover, I thought we might be lost, but we were well and truly near Gainesville, Alabama. Still, we started singing: *There'll Be Bluebirds Over The White Cliffs of Dover.* This brought me back to our bumpy night anchored in

Dover Harbour, where I wanted to call the coastguard to book me a hotel room in town.

It was muggy and rather windy when we motored into the next lock, making it difficult to tie up to a bollard with it blowing from the stern. How unnerving it felt with these high walls of concrete looming above us. Exiting the lock didn't come too soon. We stopped at a visitor's centre next, where we met Gloria, who worked there. She introduced us to Mike, the park ranger. She knew his wife Patti had spent some time in England and thought we would have a lot to say to each other. Mike was excited to meet us and suggested we spend the 4th of July together on the Kentucky Lakes, where they had a house. It would be a journey of a day or two for us, travelling there aboard *Capricorn,* but only a short drive away for him.

While we were there, Gloria offered to drive us to Aliceville during her break so we could do some shopping. On the way, we passed large cotton fields and lush countryside. Gloria mentioned that cotton had suffered after all the recent rain.

Aliceville was a shanty town. Peter and I looked so out of place that the supermarket owner, an Asian Indian, asked us who we were and how we came to shop at his store.

When we returned to *Capricorn,* the lock-keeper invited us to the control room and explained how he operated the lock. 'Sometimes, things go wrong,' he said. 'I once had a motor yacht coming downriver. The skipper missed the entrance, and he and his boat descended the overflow, which looked like a mini Niagara Falls. Thankfully, the man survived, although he suffered serious injuries.'

We were curious about the racoon in a cage we had seen at the bottom of the steps to the control room and asked the lock-keeper, 'Is it your pet?'

'No, I'm going to skin the animal, eat it and then make a furry Davy Crockett hat with its tail hanging from the back.'

My stomach turned, but I managed to smile with a frown.

We visited the Snag Boat Montgomery while we were there. Built in 1925 as a steam-driven rear-paddlewheel riverboat, the Montgomery was later converted to oil and decommissioned in 1980 after fifty-four years of service. It is now a museum.

The following day, thousands of flies had turned our top sides black. There was no explanation, but *Capricorn's* decks looked eerie. Thankfully, they flew away when we cast off. Then, we came across two young chaps in Henderson Lakes puzzling over their outboard with its cowl off. We approached them, and Peter asked if he could help. 'Our engine has given up, and we have left grandma, our wives, and four kids marooned on Sand Island, north of here. They must be panicking by now.'

'I could offer you a tow. It's on our way,' Peter said. We threw them a line and set off. After a few minutes, they pulled at the tow rope to bring their ski boat alongside *Capricorn* and jumped over the rail like two long-haired, tattooed pirates. The only thing missing was a cutlass, an eye patch and a squawking parrot. They startled us. I thought Peter was too trusting. I started to fret, expecting them to make demands. But my fears were unfounded because all they asked was how we got to the Henderson Lakes.

As we approached the island, the children waved and jumped up and down. Then, they all insisted we share their barbecue. They cooked steak and cornbread, served with salad and plenty of beer. Later, the two men asked if we would extend our kindness by towing them back four miles to their town. When we arrived, one of them invited us to stay at his house for the night, but we were eager to move on.

We entered the Kentucky Lakes a few days later. When Peter checked the chart, he saw *Newby Cemetery* in Duncan Bay. His curiosity was aroused as he bore the same family name. Besides, the cemetery was on our way. We read in our pilot book that before they flooded the valley, which is now part of the Kentucky Lakes, the authorities removed Civil War graves to higher ground.

It was a short uphill scramble to reach the place. I noticed Peter looked apprehensive when we walked through the arched iron gates with *Newby Civil War Cemetery* written across the top. After all the mishaps he had experienced in his yacht *Ellis* and now *Capricorn*, was he worried about tripping over a tombstone and then being laid to rest in the Newby cemetery? Needless to say, the two 'Newbys' were relieved to return to *Capricorn* later that day.

In the morning, the lake was serenely still. We motored across, and with the clouds reflecting in the water, we thought we were floating in the sky. I picked up my guitar and sat on deck, inspired to write a country song. Songwriting in Nashville is a craft that relies strongly on telling a story and finding a hook. I told myself I should be ready and came up with a chorus line: *If We Break Up, I Break Down.*

The song describes a woman who pretends she doesn't know her husband is cheating on her. Desperate to win him back, she changes her appearance and style. The story has no conclusion; it is left to the reader to guess if the woman succeeds.

As I continued composing, a police launch with a forward cabin and a blue light on top was motoring in the opposite direction. It was the first time we had seen any sign of authorities since arriving in America. Moments later, the officer did a U-turn and headed our way with his light now flashing. We looked at each other apprehensively and couldn't help feeling a sense of guilt, wondering what we had done to warrant being stopped. Had we committed some misdemeanour unknowingly? The sheriff brought his launch alongside, instructed us to keep our course and speed, and skilfully tied a rope around *Capricorn's* midship cleat. Portly and in his fifties, the sheriff took his sunglasses off and tucked them in his top pocket that displayed his badge. He began questioning us with one hand on his holstered revolver and the other on the launch's wheel.

'Where have you come from, and where are you headed? he asked abruptly.

'We have sailed from England,' Peter replied.

By the look on his face and the twitching of his fingers on his revolver, he must have thought Peter was pulling a fast one on him. Being so far from the sea, the sheriff wouldn't have recognised the English ensign. Peter told him briefly about our Atlantic crossing and coming up the Tombigbee from Mobile Bay. The sheriff's stern face mellowed. He lifted his star-studded trilby hat and said apologetically, 'Y'all, have a good day.' Then, he slipped his line and peeled away.

Mike kept his promise to celebrate the 4th of July with us on the lakes. We invited him and his wife Patti to watch the fireworks aboard *Capricorn.* Mike had served in the Army and fought in the Vietnam War. He had a lot to tell about the terrible loss of lives and his traumas. Later, he took us all for a night out in the next county where alcohol was permitted. There, we had a beer at a restaurant and ate catfish. Then, we played darts with a digital self-counting board. We hadn't seen one before.

The following day, Mike and Patti took us to a wildlife centre, where we saw vultures and a bald eagle. While there, a little black boy, with his grandmother, took my hand to show me around. He wouldn't let go, as if he always knew me. Strangely, I felt the same about him. I cried inside when I took him back to his grandma. It was also the first time we saw a herd of buffalo in a prairie setting. Until then, it had been in *Cowboys and Indians's Western* movies.

After leaving our friends, we reached the far end of the Kentucky Lakes. If we had gone through the lock, we would have joined the Mississippi and, ultimately, the Canadian Great Lakes. Instead, we turned to starboard through a narrow canal and joined the Barkley Lake, which runs parallel to the Kentucky Lakes. Here, the scenery changed with high stone bluffs to our port side. To starboard was the 'Land Between the Lakes,' with 170.000 acres of rolling fields and woodlands separating the Barkley and Tennessee Lakes. Its forests, ponds, and meadows of wildflowers with populations of whitetail, fallow deer, wild turkey, eagles and bobcats, including a large herd of buffalo, offered us a unique slice of the American Heartland.

On the next leg of our journey, we encountered a spectacular array of ducks in a field by the river bank. As we motored closer, I said to Peter, 'Those ducks don't seem to be moving.' Then, it dawned on us when we saw several men with hunting rifles behind bushes. The ducks were all decoys to attract flocks of real birds. Had we spoilt their day of shooting? We gave the hunters a friendly wave, hoping they wouldn't start pumping lead in our direction, and we only relaxed once this bizarre scene faded away behind us.

There wasn't a ripple when we entered the Cumberland River with the sun shining hot and bright. Thirty-eight centigrade heat wasn't unusual, and I felt uncomfortable with so little wind cooling the air. Later, we came across an open wooden boat with a small engine on the stern. We didn't see anyone on board but could hear the throbbing of an auxiliary diesel motor. There was an anchor line tied to the bow and something resembling a rubber hose disappearing over the side amidships. We wondered if the fisherman was lying at the bottom of the boat or if he had fallen overboard. Peter set *Capricorn's* engine into neutral, and we drifted towards the vessel to go and investigate. After we approached the craft, Peter climbed onto our top handrail and hung on to the rigging to see if anybody was lying in the bilges. At that moment, something like a leather bucket with a window and a pipe broke the surface, and a diver scrambled aboard and removed his apparatus.

'Gee, you gave me a start,' he said. 'I could hear your engine from way off. I thought it might be somebody muscling in on my territory. The last thing I expected was to see a yacht with a *Limey* flag. Where the hell have you come from?'

'We thought this was an abandoned craft,' Peter explained. 'We hadn't seen a boat or any commercial traffic for days. We're heading for Nashville.'

'Has this dam thing got wheels?' the diver quipped.

We laughed. Peter mentioned our journey and explained I was a singer-songwriter.

The tension eased. The man turned his compressor off, then explained, 'I'm diving for freshwater clams, and the pipe you see is my air supply.' 'We've had a few gunfights over territories. The clams are lucrative, but one has to know where they are.'

Peter mentioned his surprise at the numerous thunderstorms in the area.

'Many people get struck by lightning,' he commented. There were eleven cases last month. I don't want to worry you.'

We left him to his dangerous occupation, and with a friendly wave, we slipped *Capricorn* into gear and motored on.

It had been such a journey of contrasts, from the muddy Mobile Bay through rivers, lakes, and canals to reach our destination finally. Around the next bend was *Third Coast*, the Mecca for songwriters, drawn there to give the wheel of fortune a whirl. I thought of people who had warned me about my chances of success. They believed that even Jesus couldn't break into the music business in Nashville. A loin cloth and sandals evidently wouldn't cut it!

No matter what, I was ready to try my luck. After all, I had nothing to lose but much to gain. I didn't know what it would take to make a name for myself, even if it appeared as impossible as climbing the Jungfrau Mountain with flip-flops. Above all, I wondered how much Peter was prepared to compromise our lifestyle so that I could pursue my musical quest.

Our story cried out to be told. It was a journey driven by hope, faith, passion, desire, love and ambition. I wouldn't settle until I had pushed my dream as far as possible. Belgian-born actress Audrey Hepburn wrote: *'Nothing is impossible, the word itself says. I'm possible.'*

But for now, we needed to find the narrow gap blasted through the high granite bank leading to the flooded quarry of Rock Harbour Marina, which was only a short distance from downtown Nashville. I felt the tug of anticipation when the entrance came into view. Tears and stars filled my eyes. Peter looked churned.

I slowly motored in while my skipper stood by. Inside the Marina were multiple pontoons with canopies over them. Although it looked busy with motorboats, we couldn't see any sailing yacht. However, there was one short pontoon without a canopy. I let *Capricorn* drift gently to a standstill. Then, as we debated how to approach the dock and where to place fenders, we saw a man in a suit and tie walking down the pontoon to the vacant berth. He gestured for us to come alongside. I saw his gold cufflinks glinting in the sun and wondered if he was the marina manager. I threw him the bow line, which he made fast to a cleat, then trotted to our stern to take Peter's aft mooring rope. The man looked astounded. I could read on his face: 'How did these people get here, and where have they come from?'

Then, before we could say anything, he asked, 'Are you guys lost?'

Take Me Home, Capricorn

The Sequel

Monique enjoys Nashville's music scene while recording her album *Life's a Boat*. But will she achieve what she hopes for with Peter by her side?

ACKNOWLEDGMENTS

I want to express my heartfelt gratitude to my long-standing friend, Felicity Redman, for her unwavering support in helping me with my first book, *Stranger to Caution*, and my latest work, *Slow Boat to Nashville*. Her patience and insights have been invaluable to me.

I would also like to thank my friend Liz Page for her nurturing encouragement, critique, and suggestions. My appreciation extends to Alan Dodson for his support and acknowledgement and to Avril Davison for her guidance and discernment.

Additionally, I want to acknowledge the renowned novelist Wendy Perriam, whose creative writing classes at Morley College in London inspired me greatly. I am also grateful to writer SallyAnn Sheridan, who often reminded me that, being a French speaker, writing in English offers a unique nuance to the language.

Above all, I would like to thank my husband, Peter. His diverse skills have allowed us to experience the adventures I am fortunate to write about.

Slow Boat to Nashville

ISBN: SBN 978-1-7391967-1-4

ACKNOWLEDGEMENT

I want to thank my long-standing friend, Felicity Redman, for all her support in helping me with my first book, ***Stranger to Caution*** and the latest ***Slow Boat to Nashville***. Her patience and input have been invaluable. I want to thank my friend Liz Page for her nurturing encouragement, critique and suggestions—Alan Dodson for his support and appreciation, and Avril Davison for her help and discernment. I also want to mention renowned novelist Wendy Perriam, who greatly inspired me when I attended her creative writing classes at Morley College, London. I would also like to mention writer SallyAnn Sheridan, who often reminded me that being French-speaking and writing in English could offer a different nuance of the language. Finally, I would like to thank my husband, Peter. His multi-skills have enabled us to experience unique adventures I have been happy to write about.

Slow Boat to Nashville

ISBN: SBN 978-1-7391967-1-4

Printed in Great Britain
by Amazon

54770502R00215